MORE STUDIES
IN MURDER

MORE STUDIES IN MURDER

BY
EDMUND PEARSON

1936

HARRISON SMITH & ROBERT HAAS

NEW YORK

This book is dedicated to my dear Sister

MABEL CARLTON WHEELER

CONTENTS

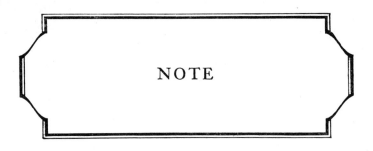

NOTE

THE first of my books on this subject, *Studies in Murder*, was planned in 1923, published in 1924. At that time, writing books and essays about actual cases of murder was not the industry it has now become. For example, there was perhaps one magazine devoted, in part, to this theme. Now, there are eight or nine, some of them firmly established. Two new ones began publication this year.

Such an increase in the number of readers and writers makes it difficult for an author to find subjects which shall not be too familiar. He is aware that there now exist enthusiasts to whom almost everything criminous has been revealed; they frequent the tree of knowledge, and carefully pluck its flowers of evil.

Yet it is possible for me to hope that amateurs of crime may find, in these pages, things not yet stale. To that end, there are included some personal observations at recent trials, together with accounts of crimes which made a mighty noise in their own day, but are now forgotten. I shall be surprised if the majority of these chapters do not describe cases which will be novel to all but the expert.

Of the other chapters, a few are frank experiments with familiar cases, although they are not widely known in America. The absurd adventures of the Druce family offer a fine example of the growth of a legend, and the pleasure of relating the story was too great to resist. To write the chapter on Elizabeth Canning, four or five of the major authorities were compared, and some additional facts were collected from a dozen other sources. In order to discuss that elusive creature, Jack the Ripper, without plunging into melodrama, it was necessary to turn over a ton of rubbish and, in addition, to read half a shelf-full of reliable books.

As to whether it is desirable to tell an old tale once more, I can only decide from my own experience. To me, there are stories which will bear another telling, if only they are readable. One such story, not told in this book, narrates the perpetually amazing case of Oscar Slater. Mystery attaches to the victim as well as to the perpetrator of the murder; there was the extraordinary miscarriage of justice, partly atoned for, twenty years later; and the fact that, after so much investigation, the name of the person who killed Miss Gilchrist is a secret. When this name is guessed at, it appears only under the mask of fictitious initials.

Numberless writers have told the story; the one masterly account, of course, being Mr. William Roughead's volume in the *Notable British Trials*. Yet a new résumé of the case, in Mr. Roughead's *Knaves' Looking-Glass*, has been read recently by many people and with fresh enjoyment.

What the vulgar never understand, but what the erudite know perfectly, is that many murders are trumpery affairs, worth a paragraph in a newspaper, and then oblivion. Perhaps only two or three times a year, throughout the whole round world, may be discovered an almost flawless gem, meriting the attention of Thomas De Quincey himself. It is with murders as with detective fic-

tion: many of the current detective novels are read once,
for the solution of their puzzles, but books like *The
Moonstone* are read and read again.

To mention the *Notable British Trials* recalls the fact
that writers, English and American, pursue their quarry
in that great poaching-ground, sometimes with a word of
credit, often in the grander manner of the literary pil-
ferer, whose brave soul despises all who say "thank you."
In this book, while I have, once or twice, leaned pretty
heavily upon friends and colleagues like Miss Tennyson
Jesse and Mr. Roughead, I have also usually consulted
other and contemporary narratives.

The chapters in this book are from articles, sometimes
changed or amended, which appeared in *Vanity Fair,
The New Yorker, Mystery,* and *Liberty.*

Ten years ago, the author of such a book occasionally
met the grave reproof of some commentator who was
pained because it dealt neither in psycho-analysis nor
psychology. Looking into the histories of the peculiar
people who are described herein, it has taxed my ability
to discover what they *did.* I leave it to writers of supernatural power—whether called clairvoyance, psycho-
analysis, graphology, or any other form of big-medicine
—to find out what these people thought.

                                    EDMUND PEARSON

*Scituate, Massachusetts
September, 1935.*

PART ONE
MORE STUDIES IN MURDER

THE CORPSE
ON THE
SPEAK-EASY FLOOR

L OOK at him!" shouted the lawyer for the defense. "Look at him, the slick bootlegger! There he sits now, with his paramour on one side of him and his fancy girl on the other!"

Naturally, all of us in the courtroom turned our heads and looked at him. And there, calm under this rather disturbing introduction, sat Mr. Amos Peters: small, neat, white-haired, chocolate-colored, and so like another agreeable middle-aged Negro whom I used to know—steward of a country club—that I expected to see him advance toward me with a well-cooked omelet, or a check to sign.

And on either side of him, blandly smiling, sat the plump, colored ladies who had just been characterized with that frankness permitted to no one on earth but lawyers for the defense. Instead of resembling sinful sirens, however, they looked far more like Aunt Jemima, propagandist for pancakes. The "fancy girl," in particular, was most inaptly thus described: she had an untamed appearance, as if recently captured from a Zulu kraal.

Here, in the Criminal Courts Building, next the Tombs, we had often seen Mr. Peters, on the witness stand, sometimes for hours. He was, so said the People of the State of

New York, by their assistant district attorney, a humble citizen of Harlem, engaged, it was true, in an illegal occupation: making and selling rye whisky. But did that prejudice anyone in court (except the lawyer for the defense) against him? Apparently not, judging by the delighted attention given by the twelve jurors when, under oath, he described how he made it. And instead of lingering there like a vampire, a blood-sucker, hoping to hear the doom of the two innocent prisoners at the bar—as the defense would have us believe—he was the chief witness for the outraged and offended People, and he was in court because he couldn't help it.

Not so, however, according to the silver-tongued orator for the accused. Mr. Peters was not only an acolyte at the altars of Bacchus and Priapus but he was under dark suspicion of having committed the murder of which "this boy" and "this little lady" were now accused. And so around the white, kinky hair of Amos Peters raged the contention in the case of the People versus Shakespeare and Burns.

The prisoners with such illustrious names might both have been about thirty. Although Shakespeare was indicted under that name, his real one seems to have been Dills. He was a commonplace, low-browed darky—you felt, on looking at him, that it might be safe to let him wash your windows, provided everything in the house of negotiable value was locked up. When you had heard his police and prison record, you would hire someone else. Sophy May Burns was an anxious, thin-faced, slender woman, with beautiful eyes. She had reason to look anxious: she was in some slight danger (really very slight, as she was a woman) of going to the electric chair.

Let's take Mr. Peters' story, get it out of the question-and-answer form, and learn the history of the crime.

"Yas, suh; Ah lives at 4567 East 136th Street, with mah wife, and Ah makes and sells whisky to anybody—anybody Ah knows—by the drink, or the bottle, or by the gallon. In mah apa'tment there; yas, suh."

His wife—*de facto* rather than *de jure*—was one of the ladies brusquely described by the defense attorney. Lawyers spent much time inquiring into the extra-matrimonial status of every witness produced by the opposing side, and fully established that while everyone was married to someone, no one, by any chance, was married to the person with whom he or she was then in residence. This irrelevant point was so labored that at last the judge dryly remarked: "Gentlemen, this is a trial for murder. It will keep the jury here two months if we explore every love affair in Harlem!"

Mr. Peters continues:

"Ah knows Sophy May Burns, the gal I sees yonder; yas, suh. Ah know her for three years, she was a friend of mah wife, and Ah have taken her and one of her gen'el-man friends home in mah car. . . . No, suh; Ah never went out with her mahself. Sophy May come to mah house most ev'ry evenin', sometimes. Ah remember the night of the eleventh of April; Ah guess Ah won't never forget it. About nine o'clock, Sophy May Burns comes in and says to mah wife: 'Grace, kin Ah tab you for a drink?'

"And Ah says: 'Sophy May, you don't have to tab no drink here. Ah'll *give* you a drink.'

"And Ah got a bottle and three glasses from the nex' room, and we all sat down, mah wife and Sophy May on the divan, and me by the table, and jes' set there, talkin' and drinkin' about five minutes. Then there was a buzz at the do'bell and Ah went and opened the do' and there was two fellahs, with guns in their hands, and they just scrouged me backwards right down the passage. One of 'em says: 'Stick 'em up!'

"And he kep' his gun shoved right into mah vest. It was a .45 automatic. . . . Do Ah see him now? Yas, suh; Ah sho' do. It was Shakespeare, sittin' ovah there beside Sophy May Burns. Only, his name was Henry Dills when Ah useter know him.

"Sophy May, she yelled: 'What's this? A stickup?'

"And she jumped up and turned round, face to the wall, and stuck up both her hands. Shakespeare, he says: 'Stick 'em up, Ah tells you! And that goes for you, too, Grace!'

"But mah wife jes' kep' sittin' there on the divan. And these two fellahs stood one on each side of me, with their guns, and Shakespeare says: 'Give us that money you got!'

"And Ah reached down into mah pants pocket and Ah took out all the money Ah got—forty dollahs—and Ah threw it down on the table and he grabbed it up, and says: 'You got mo' than that. Dig it up!'

"And Ah remembered ten dollahs mo' in mah watch pocket, and Ah threw it down on the table and Ah los' mah tempah ——"

"And," said the examining attorney, "you called him a vile name, did you not?"

"Yas, suh."

"You'd better tell the jury what it was."

Mr. Peters did so. I have been present at one other Negro murder trial, a court martial, and the same epithet was in evidence. And, as in this case, Death quickly stalked upon the scene. You will have to take my word for it that the phrase was completely insulting. Not Mr. Hemingway, not even Mr. D. H. Lawrence has introduced it in literature.

"What happened then?" said the lawyer.

"This Shakespeare, he brought the barrel of his gun right round, with a swingin' lick, and whanged me right ovah the eye—see, here is the scar it made—and when he did that the gun goes off and hits this other fellah, standin' right beside me, ker-plunk in the middle of his forehead, and he fall right down on the floor—blam!

"Shakespeare, he run to Sophy May, and grab her by the wrist, and says: 'Here, you, you come along outer here!'

"And they both run downstairs together, and Ah leaned out the window, and Ah see them goin' ovah to Lenox Avenue together."

After this, Mr. Peters went back and surveyed his apartment. He had lost fifty dollars, and received a violent blow on his eyebrow. Blood was running down his face. And lying on the floor, between the living-room and kitchen, in a pool of blood (afterward estimated at a quart and a half) was the dead body of a total stranger, in a black overcoat.

The Peterses began to tidy up. They wiped the blood from the countenance of the proprietor. They wisely conveyed the stock of whisky, by way of the fire-escape, into the home of a kindly neighbor. Then they went out for the police.

The worst of it was that corroding suspicions were forming in their minds as to the conduct of Sophy May Burns. They wondered if she were really their friend. There was something in her departure, with Shakespeare, which raised the question if she was a stranger to him, and

ignorant of his schemes. Or had she come ahead to see if
the coast was clear?

As for the murdered man, never was the victim of a
shooting so anonymous, so insignificant. There he was,
merely a black man in a black overcoat, with a bullet
rattling around in his head. The bullet got in, but the
thickness of the skull kept it from getting out, so the
medical examiner was able to produce it—a big, battered
slug—in court. Harlem was diffident about admitting acquaintance with the *corpus delicti*, and finally a man had
to come from Washington to say that he recognized it
and that its name was— What was that name? No one
could remember, and the lawyers more than once were
on the point of calling him Mr. Whoozis, or Whatyoumaycallit.

He was just a playboy who, with a friend and two
guns, had gone in there to rob the proprietor. No idea of
becoming a corpse had entered his mind—nor did he or
his friend desire to kill anyone. As Mr. Darrow gently
says of the men who slaughtered twenty printers in the
building of the Los Angeles *Times*, murder was not in
their hearts.

The situation, however, was curious. The harsh law of
New York and other States is that a killing done while in
the commission of a felony is murder in the first degree—
and no lesser degree. It doesn't matter who is killed: the
victim of the robbery, or a bystander, or even your own
pal. You may say:

"Honest, Judge, I didn't go for to kill this guy! I was
only goin' to about *half* kill him, d'yer see, so I could get
away with his roll. Me hand slipped!"

But the judge is not allowed to reply:

"I understand, my boy. Be more careful next time.
Better use a sandbag."

So Shakespeare and Burns, when they could be found, were liable for murder in the first degree.

The part of Sophy May Burns in the plot, by the way, is still mysterious. Her presence at the shooting and her departure with the gunman are not disputed.

It took the police more than a year to find the pair. But as Shakespeare was a lad who varied the commission of felonies by the commission of misdemeanors, he did not remain forever obscure. When they were at last discovered, it seemed that from that chance meeting on the April evening had blossomed romance. At all events, they were negligently clad, and reclining together on a bed. Other people were in the room, it is true, but everything indicated what may be called "a certain intimacy."

The only question was the identity of Shakespeare with the fellow whose hand held the pistol which shot the man in the black overcoat. Mr. Peters looked him over at the police station and was not quite sure. He asked for ten minutes to think it over, walked around the block, came back, and said that he was now positive, and would swear to the identification.

Of course, this was not wholly satisfactory, and the defense made the most of it. It might have been, as experts suggested, that Mr. Peters in those ten minutes was not resolving doubts, but screwing his courage to the sticking-place for the unpleasantness which he knew must follow.

One privilege of assisting justice in America, by appearing as witness for the State in a murder trial, is hearing yourself described, inferentially or directly, as a liar, an informer, a sneak, a yellow dog, an adulterer, a murderer, and anything else which suggests itself to the invention of counsel for the defense.

Neither Shakespeare nor Burns cared to go on the

witness-stand, and describe the events of that night. But at the last minute, when matters looked far darker than their own complexions, there came relief from a strange quarter. Into the court tumbled a bunch of white men: fresh-faced, honest-looking farmers from northern Vermont; a contrast to the Harlemites who had been flitting before the eyes of the jury.

These men swore up and down, right and left, that Shakespeare, on that night of April 11 eighteen months before, instead of holding up a Harlem speak-easy had been engaged in the perfectly lawful business of collecting garbage for his uncle's pigs way up north, almost at the Canadian line.

All of these men, or nearly all, seemed perfectly honest. And all of them, as it was pretty clearly shown, were probably right as to the day and month, but mistaken as to the *year*. If they were right, it was odd that Shakespeare himself, at the time of his arrest, asserted that never during the year of the crime had he been farther from New York than Jersey City.

Perhaps it was this dubious, last-moment alibi which saved the prisoners. Or it may have been Mr. Peters' doubtful identification. Possibly it was the fact that no verdict in the *second* degree was permitted. The Peters story of the holdup sounded, to everyone who heard it, truthful from beginning to end. The jury, however, were unwilling to start "this boy" and "this little lady" on the way to the chair. They deliberated two hours, and acquitted both prisoners. And for the death of Mr. Whatyoumaycallit, there will be no vengeance but the Lord's.

Shakespeare remained in prison. Another trifling charge—the possession of burglar's tools, or something like that—temporarily clouded his reputation.

But Sophy May Burns rapturously joined her waiting

friends. They quickly sped uptown. A considerable thirst can be accumulated during a six months' stay in the Tombs, and if, that evening, she inquired of the neighbors on 136th Street:

"Kin Ah tab you for a drink?" it is to be hoped they all replied:

"Sophy May, you don't need to tab no one for a drink. We'll *give* you a drink."

SARAH JANE ROBINSON

AROUND a supper table sat a woman and two girls. Darkness had fallen; the shades were drawn, and the three were talking together. They spoke in hushed tones, since they were discussing painful subjects. It was a household in which hushed voices were not uncommon, because with appalling frequency, it was visited by death.

The woman was bright-eyed, sharp and alert in her manner, quite in command of herself and of any situation in which she might be placed. The two girls listened to her with respect—more than that, with a little terror. One girl was her daughter, and as she very well knew, her mother was one of those awe-inspiring people who dream dreams and see visions. To her came the spirits of the dead, with fearful warnings of fate, and of the uncertainty of human life. There could be no doubt of this: time and again, this lady's dire predictions of death had come true.

This supper table was spread in a humble little apartment on a back street of Cambridge, Massachusetts. It was but a short distance to the buildings of Harvard College, where William James was, at about this same time, investigating the mysterious Mrs. Piper, the medium. A great many people in New England, and elsewhere, were convinced that they were receiving com-

24

munications from "the spirit world"; they spoke of "messages," "spiritual influences" and so on.

The older woman at the supper table—her name was Mrs. Robinson—was discussing an absent member of the family and her usually silky voice grew bitter.

"Half-baked—that's what he is! Half-baked and no good to anybody. He doesn't earn any money at all, and what he does get, he spends in carfares. He doesn't care a snap for me—after all I've done for him and his! Now he's taken to straying off to his own folks; I know he's going to leave me, and go and live with them . . . Lizzie, you ought to be nicer to your uncle; talk to him, and make him more contented, so he'd stay with us."

"Oh, Ma," said the girl, "he's all right. He'll stay with us. . . . Of course he feels sad and lonely since Aunt Annie died."

"He's no good," pursued her mother viciously, "no good at all. . . . I wish some one would give him a dose of something and put him out of the way."

She paused suddenly, turned pale and shuddered. Then she glanced quickly over her shoulder. Her daughter nudged the other girl, under the table.

"Look, Belle!" she whispered.

Mrs. Robinson swayed in her chair until both girls thought she might swoon and fall to the floor. They hurried to her side, one of them with a glass of water. But she recovered herself somewhat, and waved them away.

"What is the matter, Mother," Lizzie asked. "Has Father come to you again?"

"Yes," said her mother faintly, "I think your father tapped me on the shoulder."

The girl gasped in terror.

"Oh, Mother! It was Father, and he has come for Uncle!"

"That is it!" said Mrs. Robinson, staring intently before her, with her hand to her forehead. "That is it! I shouldn't wonder but something would happen to your uncle, soon!"

Uncle's name was a high-sounding one: Prince Arthur Freeman, but no name could be less appropriate. Instead of being either a prince or a free man, he was bound in chains, in the chains of poverty, in the chains of his own feebleness. Anybody could order him about, and none so easily as that masterful woman, his sister-in-law, Mrs. Robinson.

Freeman had a curious job: he was a pickler of iron at some works in South Boston. Every day he went from his sister-in-law's house in Cambridge to the iron works, where he spent long hours plunging iron bars in a bath of sulphuric acid and hot water, in order to remove the scale from the iron.

One morning, shortly after Mrs. Robinson had received the ghostly warning, Mr. Freeman ate breakfast and set out to work. He was, however, taken sick on the way, with violent nausea, and severe pain. At the workshop he was unable to do anything, and after feebly hanging round for some hours, he was permitted to go home. Mrs. Robinson was all ready for him; she had a bed prepared, and a doctor was soon in the house. To friends and relatives, she announced that Prince Arthur would never leave his bed again. The spirits never deceived her.

As much as they told her about life and death, however, there were some worldly matters which she had to investigate for herself. There was, for instance, insurance. Spirits could not be expected to attend to that. And on the first night of her brother-in-law's illness, Mrs. Robinson sent her daughter, Lizzie, together with Lizzie's friend, Miss Belle Clough, in to Boston, "to see if Prince Arthur's insurance was all right."

The two girls went to the officers of the Governor Dudley Colony of the United Order of Pilgrim Fathers. This was a fraternal, benefit association, of which Prince Arthur was a member, and in which his life was insured. The girls learned that the policy was in order, and with that message they returned to Cambridge.

Mrs. Robinson was busy taking care of the sick man —whose symptoms were painful and distressing—but she made two more inquiries about the insurance during the next few days, and on Friday night received a call from one of the officers of the Colony, a Mrs. Stanwood. This lady told her again that the insurance was "all right." The next day, Prince Arthur Freeman died. He was by no means an old man, hardly middle-aged, and he had been sick only five days.

In a few weeks the money, $2,000, was paid to Mrs. Robinson. Prince Arthur's insurance had been assigned to her only a few weeks before his illness. She needed the money, as she explained, not for herself, but for Mr. Freeman's little son, now an orphan.

The use which she made of the money was to pay off her debts, to buy herself some furniture, and clothes, and to take a trip to the West. Then, with some more of it, she insured the life of her daughter, Lizzie. It does not appear that the little orphan got much, if any, of it.

After this, Mrs. Robinson began, as never before, to be visited by dreams and visions; to feel unseen fingers tapping her on the shoulders, and to receive fearful warnings of doom. In the following January, her daughter Lizzie fell sick.

I hope that the poor girl did not discuss with her mother the question whether "Father had come for her" or not, but she could have had little doubt that hers was the same strange and fatal illness which seemed to be the bane of the Robinsons. She was sick about a week, her mother grimly telling people that she had received a warning from "the other world" that Lizzie would not get well.

Lizzie did not get well. Mrs. Robinson soon collected the insurance on Lizzie's life. In the summer, Tommy Freeman, the seven-year-old son of Prince Arthur, became ill. And now the spirits of Lizzie and of Lizzie's Aunt Annie (the child's mother) returned from the grave to tell Mrs. Robinson that they had come for little Tommy.

Curious people will wonder how long this sort of thing might have continued. Tommy died July 1, 1886—it was probably only coincidence that four deaths in Mrs. Robinson's family occurred on the first day of various months. About five weeks after Tommy's death, Mrs. Robinson began to receive ghostly warnings about her son, William. And, again her gift of prophecy was clear: William had a week of the same agonies that had marked the illness of his sister, his uncle, his cousin, and others of this household. Then he died, early in August. He left at least one brother, Charley. But before the spirits got around to Charley, other things happened.

Probably it was this same summer that Mrs. Robinson had a conversation with a family friend named Chandler —a man rather less soft-boiled than some of her other intimates. He told about the conversation at a later date.

"She told me," said Mr. Chandler, "that when she dreamed one of her family was going to be sick, that one always was sick. And the sick person always died."

"I said to her," he continued, " 'Mrs. Robinson, you better not have one of those dreams about me!' "

He was asked if she had said anything about dead people coming back with messages.

"Yes," was the reply, "she told me about these dead folks, and I says, 'Mrs. Robinson, what have you done to all these people that they are coming back to you?' "

"What did she say to that?" pursued his questioner.

"Nothing. She went over and lay on the lounge. I guess she fainted."

If Mrs. Robinson really fainted, it was an unusual exhibition of weakness. She was not of the fainting kind; few ever saw her off her guard. But the death of her son William was the fifth in the Robinson family in eighteen months, and a little too much for the peace and composure of the United Order of Pilgrim Fathers. They were getting weary of paying off so many insurance policies, all to Sarah Jane Robinson. Someone suggested that it would be a proper thing to consult the police. They did so, and two days later, Mrs. Robinson, cool, defiant and protesting her innocence in the name of everything that is holy, was lodged in jail.

She said it was an outrage. That it was all spite. That "her enemies" had "trumped up" this ridiculous charge against her. That she was a church-going, God-fearing, hard-working woman, who had been sadly afflicted. That the Hand of Heaven had rested heavily upon her, and carried away many of her "loved ones." That she had tenderly nursed them all. But that they had died, nevertheless, and now, as a crowning insult, the police were charging her with the murder of her dear son.

And while some people quickly believed the accusation made against her—without really knowing much about it, many others refused to credit a word. They said, as they always do say, that "a woman couldn't do such a thing," and that was all they needed to know.

Meanwhile, the name of Sarah Jane Robinson became famous throughout New England, and all the country heard of the strange woman of Somerville (for she had moved to that Boston suburb) who had had so many deaths in her family and who received messages from beyond the grave. There were a few people—acquaintances, business associates, and others—who really knew something about Mrs. Robinson. Among these folk, the police and law officers of Middlesex County began to make inquiries.

In a short time, they drew back in horror. To newspaper readers, and to the public in general, they might have said, in the phrase of a later day:

"You ain't heard nothing yet!"

Some time before the Civil War there crossed the ocean and came to Boston two sisters, named Sarah Jane and Annie Tennent. They were about fifteen and nine years old, respectively, so they traveled in care of the ship's captain. They came from a small town (said to be "Newton Hamilton") in Ireland, to join a brother in America.

In the years that followed, they lived in various parts of Boston, or in towns nearby, where Sarah Jane was employed as a milliner, while Annie was a domestic servant. Both seem to have been good-looking girls; each found more than one man who wanted to marry her. Annie married a man named McCormick, and after his death she became the wife of Prince Arthur Freeman. By this marriage she had two children, a girl and the little boy, Tommy.

Sarah Jane, the elder of the sisters, married Moses Robinson, by whom she had eight children. The sisters were of the Protestant religion, so it is not surprising that the husbands of both were, in all probability, native New Englanders.

In 1881, five years before her arrest, Mrs. Robinson's landlord, a man named Oliver Sleeper, had suddenly died. He had lived in the house with her. Evidently the history of his illness and death attracted the notice of the authorities who were now looking into her career. His body was exhumed and found to contain a fatal dose of arsenic.

It is not known to me what quarrel existed between Mrs. Robinson and Mr. Sleeper, or whether it was anything more than the hostile relations between landlord and tenant. The habitual poisoner does not always kill in order to receive a direct reward in money; sometimes it is to remove a hated person; sometimes merely to get rid of a person who is a cause of expense to the murderer. There was probably no insurance on the life of little Tommy Freeman. His death, however, relieved his aunt of the cost of caring for him.

A year after the death of Mr. Sleeper, Mrs. Robinson's husband, Moses, died. She had a law-suit to get his insurance. His body was now exhumed, and it contained arsenic.

During the three years which followed this death nothing happened to attract the especial notice of the law. There were a number of incidents in the life of Mrs. Robinson which may have been dark and suspicious. At any rate, they were never investigated. At the time of the supper, when "Father came for uncle," there were, as far as I can discover, only three living out of the eight Robinson children. These were Lizzie and William (both of whom, within the year, were to descend into the grave, through the tortures of arsenic), and there was Charley, who escaped. The causes of the deaths of the other five are unknown to me. Perhaps they were natural.

Then there was the little baby, daughter of Prince Arthur and Annie Freeman, who died, while in Mrs.

Robinson's house a few weeks before her father's death. Perhaps she died of natural causes. The law presumed that she did. The child, like her brother, had a claim to her father's insurance money.

The bodies of other relatives of Mrs. Robinson were now examined: of Prince Arthur, her brother-in-law; of Lizzie, her daughter; and of little Tommy, her nephew, as well as that of William, her son. All contained arsenic.

It will be wondered how so many tragedies escaped attention at the time; how the doctors were deceived into certifying deaths from various natural causes. The answer is that although arsenic is easily traceable, once suspicion is aroused, its symptoms resemble those of one or two ordinary diseases. The doctors, in conversation with members of the family, had called the illnesses of these people "stomach trouble." Today, they might ascribe such symptoms to "gastro-enteritis." They would not, in an ordinary household, suspect that a cold-blooded poisoner was at work. Especially would they be unlikely to distrust a pleasant-appearing, good-looking woman, who was apparently devoutly religious and was also, to all outward signs, the loving nurse of these cruelly suffering people.

Whether it is wickeder to murder a grown person than a child, is not easy to determine, but the hard-hearted treachery with which the death of Annie Freeman was brought about is almost unsurpassed. This woman, it will be remembered, was the younger sister of Mrs. Robinson and the wife of the poor mechanic, Prince Arthur Freeman. She was the mother of two young children, and, with her husband, lived in South Boston.

In February, 1885, Mrs. Robinson was working in Boston at the store of R. H. White & Co. News came to her that her sister had pneumonia. Instantly, she moved over to her sister's house, and assumed entire charge. Annie Freeman, under care of a nurse, was recovering from her illness. Mrs. Robinson promptly discharged the nurse and took her place. In a day or two the sickness changed, the signs of pneumonia gave way to violent nausea, torturing thirst, and the other symptoms which marked every sickness over which this woman presided.

Mrs. Robinson made the usual predictions, as soon as she arrived: that her sister would not recover. Everyone had thought she was recovering, but Mrs. Robinson knew better. Her spirits had given warning. This was not all: she promptly began a campaign to force the widower, Prince Arthur, to move with his children, over to Cambridge, and live in her house, as soon as his wife should be dead. She told him, and told others, that he was only "half-baked," and needed her care. She was talking about this even on the day of her sister's funeral. She feared that her brother-in-law might "stray" off to his own people, and come under some influence other than her own.

This spider did not rest when she had spun her web for her victims: she saw to it that they were driven into its meshes.

It should be remembered that her sister's death profited her nothing. In bringing that about, she merely removed an heir. The next and necessary steps had then to be taken: Freeman induced to come to her house in Cambridge, and badgered into assigning his insurance, not to his children, but to his sister-in-law.

All this was accomplished, and Prince Arthur Freeman, when he put his name to the assignment of insurance, was making out his own death warrant.

From the death of the mother, Annie Freeman, in February, '85, to the death of Tommy, was less than a year and a half. The whole family were wiped out in that time.

The legal authorities found the case of Mrs. Robinson a tough nut to crack. On the face of it, everything seemed simple. The woman finally stood indicted for seven murders. All these people had died from the same poison. All of them had died, either in her house, or under her care. She stood to profit from most of these deaths. And she had shown guilty knowledge of the deaths, beforehand.

On the other hand, no arsenic was traced to her possession, and she was never seen to administer any. Many poisoners probably escape punishment because of such a defect in the case against them. None of Mrs. Robinson's murders, until the last, had been generally suspected of being other than a death from natural causes; time and again she hoodwinked the doctors.

There was this fact to protect her: she was a murderess by system; the perpetrator of a series of murders. And such a thing is often hard to prove. By a provision of the law, meant to protect the innocent, it sometimes happens that a person guilty of a number of murders has a better chance to escape than somebody who has only committed one murder. This is true unless one of the murders can be proved without reference to the others—a thing not always possible.

Mrs. Robinson, for instance, was first tried for the murder of her son, William. The state was not allowed to refer to any of the other murders. After a six-day trial, the jury were out nearly twenty-four hours, but were unable to agree.

The authorities did not think it right to set free a woman who, it was morally certain, had murdered more than half a dozen people. So they put her on trial for the murder of Freeman, and argued that they should be allowed to tell the jury about the previous murder of his wife, as a part of the same scheme.

This the Court permitted, telling the jury that the evidence as to the death of Annie Freeman was introduced, not to prove that if Mrs. Robinson were wicked enough to have killed her sister, she would therefore have killed her sister's husband, but to show that she was acting from the same motive in both murders. The two killings had the same object.

It may be that the jury found this legal distinction a little hard to follow, but it is probable that they thought it was commonsense to let them know all about Mrs. Robinson. The ordinary man has a good deal of contempt for the fine-spun theories of the law, and it may be that this contempt is not as unreasonable as lawyers like to believe.

Many interesting things came out at this second trial. Mrs. Robinson's motives became clear; she was sometimes in pressing need of money and had practised fraud in order to get it. Thus, she had mortgaged her household furniture to several different persons at the same time, and done this under false names.

A man named Desmond testified that Mrs. Robinson had applied to him for a loan on her furniture. She said that she would soon have plenty of money and be able to pay the loan.

"Where is it coming from?" he asked.

"Oh, I am going to get it; it will be all right," was the reply.

"How much will it be?"

"Oh, it will be several thousands: two, three or four thousand; not less than two thousand."

This was a little before the death of Freeman, whose life, it will be recalled, was insured for $2,000.

Mr. Desmond more than once had heard Mrs. Robinson refer to her expenses, resulting from so many deaths in her family.

"It is very singular," said he, "that you are having so many deaths in your family; can it be explained?"

She replied:

"Yes, I think I shall lose them all!"

"Why, what appears to be the matter with them?"

Her answer was:

"I think they are in a general decline."

The mother of Prince Arthur Freeman testified that less than a week before his death he came over to see her, and told her that he shouldn't have come, because he had got work, only that Mrs. Robinson said he ought to go and call on his mother, as he might never see her again!

After his death, Mrs. Robinson told the elder woman that she had sent Prince Arthur Freeman on that dutiful call for the reason he stated. Old Mrs. Freeman was asked:

"Did Mrs. Robinson tell you why she thought he would never get well?"

"She said she had had a vision."

Altogether, at least six people, both men and women repeated under oath, the remarks they had heard Mrs. Robinson make about her dreams and visions, about her "spiritual visitors" and ghostly advisers.

When the prisoner herself went on the witness stand, she calmly disputed everything. None of these supernatural things had ever happened to her. According to her statement, all these witnesses were liars.

Although she had testified for hours, she was given another chance at the close of the case, to address the jury. She said:

"I am advised by counsel not to say anything. I am satisfied with the way they have conducted this case, and the kindness they have shown to me. I decline to say much I would like to say, but I must say this much: we never will meet again: but will meet in a higher court before the Judge of all the earth, and there I will not be charged with this terrible crime, for I never administered poison, nor know of anyone administering it to Prince Arthur Freeman or anyone; therefore, I am innocent of this terrible crime of murder."

Mrs. Robinson was sentenced to death, but agitation in her behalf resulted in a commutation of the sentence to life imprisonment. People who were demanding equal rights for women saw nothing incongruous in asking a special favor for Mrs. Robinson on the sole ground that she was a woman.

For nearly twenty years (until her death in 1906), she maintained, in prison, "an air of placid innocence." She used the flowers, sent to her by her admirers, to decorate the photographs of her victims with which she ornamented her cell.

Of her, Dr. Charles F. Folsom, assistant professor of mental diseases in Harvard Medical School, wrote:

"Her mental condition, to all appearances, remained sound and unchanged."

She had never been insane, and quite properly refused any such defense. She was cool, shrewd and calculating; she well knew what she was about. Mrs. Robinson was of that type, by no means very rare, which is quite lacking in pity or compassion. The wrongs and suffering of others were of no more importance to her than is the death of a mosquito to the rest of us. She knew her own needs and desires, and to compass them could sweep from her path, in the cruelest fashion, either a little child, or the child's mother and father. The delusion that murderers suffer from remorse may have originated when, for dramatic effect, Shakespeare showed Richard III haunted by the ghosts of his victims, and told us that Macbeth had bad dreams, and Lady Macbeth walked of nights.

Mrs. Robinson, the real and not the fanciful murderess, slept at ease.

The ghosts which had visited her were of her own special kind. As soon as the light of commonsense was turned on her, they fled away and left her revealed: quiet now, and sleek.

But, nevertheless, a tigress, who had long fattened on human blood.

THE DEATH
OF
BELLA WRIGHT

THERE was a murder case in England which not only needed a Sherlock Holmes but seemed as if it had been devised in solemn conclave by Conan Doyle, Holmes, and Watson themselves. It could be entitled The Mystery of the Green Bicycle; or, The Curious Incident of the Dead Raven.

Unfortunately, there was no great hawk-faced detective from Baker Street in it. Only, at the beginning, a local constable named Hall. Perhaps that is why one of the men best informed on this case says that it has "considerable claims to be regarded as the most fascinating murder mystery of the century."

Bella Wright was twenty-one and lived with her father and mother in a tiny place called Stoughton. This is within a mile or two of the city of Leicester, and in that city she was employed in a rubber factory.

She was a girl with good looks and good character, and was engaged to be married to a stoker in the navy.

The country round about Leicester is full of little villages connected by old Roman roads or by lanes with high hedges. To the north is the famous hunting center of Melton Mowbray.

The lanes are charmingly picturesque and lonely, but were made for a less motorized age. They are sometimes full of surprises and excitement for the pedestrian or the cyclist. At a curve he may suddenly be confronted by a flock of sheep just as an enormous motor bus, brushing the hedge on either side, comes up behind him.

Miss Wright was accustomed to go to and from her work on a bicycle, and sometimes, in the long daylight hours of the English summer evenings, to cycle from one hamlet to another to do errands or to call on her friends. Her uncle, a man named Measures, lived in the village of Gaulby, three miles from her home.

She was on the late shift at the factory, and one Friday evening in July rode home from her work at eleven o'clock, going to bed soon after. Next day seems to have been a holiday, so she thoroughly made up her sleep, not getting up again till four o'clock Saturday afternoon. Then, after writing a few letters, she rode with them to the post office at Evington. Again she came home, but finally, at 6:30 P.M., set out on her cycle in the opposite direction, away from Leicester. Her mother had seen her start for Evington, and never after that saw her alive.

At nine twenty that evening (still daylight) a farmer named Cowell was driving cattle along the old Roman road called the Gartree Road or *Via Devana*. At a point about two miles from Gaulby, where the way is very lonely and the hedges, at that season, more than eight feet high, Cowell found Bella Wright lying dead in the road. Her head was covered with blood, and her cycle lay askew, with its front wheel pointing toward Stoughton— that is, toward home.

The farmer supposed that she had been killed by a fall or similar mischance. He placed her on the grass at the side of the road. Her body was still warm. Close to the spot where it was found—and this may be important—

there was an opening in the hedge: a field gate which led into the grassy meadow beyond.

Constable Hall and a doctor came later, after it was dark. The doctor's hasty examination led to nothing more than a general impression that Miss Wright, being thrown from her bicycle, had fractured her skull on a stone. Cowell's statement as to his discovery of the body seems to have been accepted as quite satisfactory. This was due, I suppose, to his good reputation, since the only witnesses he could call to prove his story were his cows.

Miss Wright's body rested that night in a cottage near-by. Early next morning Constable Hall decided to make further investigation. He carefully examined the road; and seventeen feet from the bloodstain which marked the spot where the girl's head had lain in the dust he found a bullet, caliber .45, partly embedded in the road as if it had been stepped on or run over.

He made another exceedingly curious discovery: the gate which led into the field was painted white, and on the top bar were marks of claws—marks in blood. There were tracks of these claws, also in blood—twelve such sets of tracks, six going and six returning—leading from the body to the gate. In the field the constable came across a large bird with black plumage—dead. This bird was found to be gorged with blood. Indeed, that surfeit of blood was supposed to have killed it.

In England everybody is keen about birds and their habits. As soon as the Leicestershire police said that this bird was a raven, other folk flew to the defense of ravens. They said that (a) there were no ravens around Leicester; and (b) if there were, they had never been known to drink blood.

(The bird of which the Book of Job says "Her young ones also suck up blood" is not the raven but the eagle.)

This creature, said the bird experts, must be a rook or a carrion crow.

Whatever bird it was, there are two schools of thought about it, and all the authorities, Messrs. H. R. Wakefield, Edward Marjoribanks, and others, have discussed it. There are the severely practical ones, who think that the raven (or rook) had no connection with the death of Bella Wright; and there are the romantics, who believe there was a very close connection.

At all events, how did the bird obtain so much blood from the poor dead or dying girl as to cause its own death? Was that really the cause of its death? How did it chance to be in that vicinity at the moment? Since the body is supposed to have been found within a few minutes of death, how was there time for all this gruesome feasting and tracking back and forth from road to gate?

Let's return now to Constable Hall and the bullet. He and the doctor made another examination of the body. After the blood had been washed from the girl's face, they found a small bullet wound one inch below the left eye, and another slightly larger, the mark of the exit of the bullet, in her hair. Thus it seemed that this heavy bullet had passed through the girl's head, yet had gone no farther than seventeen feet from her!

At all events, this was murder; and it was the duty of the police to inquire where she had been, and with whom, between six thirty and nine twenty of that summer evening—daylight all the time.

At seven thirty she had ridden up to the cottage of her uncle, Mr. Measures, in Gaulby. Calling on Measures at the time was his son-in-law, a man named Evans. So both of them were important witnesses to her arrival and departure. With her, when she came, was another cyclist, a young man. Bella Wright went in, leaving the young man outside. She remarked that he was "a perfect stranger," and added:

"Perhaps if I wait a while he will be gone."

Yet she did not ask her uncle to drive him away, as if he were objectionable. And when, an hour or more later, they came out again, the young man was still there—having either returned or waited. This time, he greeted her, so said Measures and Evans, with the remark:

"Bella, you *have* been a long time. I thought you had gone the other way."

Evans had some friendly conversation with the stranger about his bicycle. And finally, the girl and the young man pedaled away together—at, say, eight forty. Forty minutes later, or thereabouts, Cowell, the farmer, was finding Bella's dead body in the Gartree Road.

Now, as the reader has noticed, there are some contradictions in this. If the man was "a perfect stranger," how had he progressed so far as to call her Bella? This has been answered by the statement that what he really said was "Hello!" And that certainly goes more reasonably with the rest of his remark.

How is this for an explanation of the incident? That he was a stranger, as she said, who had joined her as she rode along; and that, while his company was perfectly tolerable to her, she had offered a little tribute to strict propriety when she said to her uncle that if she waited around a bit he would go away. Girls do not, to-day—if they ever did—scream and say, "Sir, I have never met you!" when a presentable stranger starts conversation, while riding along a country road. They may welcome it, or they may simply bear it, not wishing to make a fuss, and knowing that, in most cases, the man will soon go away without becoming an annoyance.

Measures and Evans had had a good look at this man

and his cycle, and so in a few days the police were offering a reward for a man of thirty-five, about five feet seven to nine inches in height, hair turning gray, and with rather a high-pitched voice. They gave a description of his clothes and various other particulars.

The notable thing was that he rode *a green bicycle*.

And for the next few months each man in Leicestershire unfortunate enough to own a green bicycle wished to heaven that he had never bought it. After he had satisfied the police as to where he had been on that July evening, he had to encounter the jeering remarks of his friends as to his diversions and his murderous disposition.

But the man really sought—the last man alive with Miss Wright—was not so easily discovered. Scotland Yard had a try at it, but could do nothing with the murder, the missing green bicycle, or the dead raven.

Half a year went by, and Bella Wright had long been lying in the churchyard, past which she rode that evening. Then, one day in February, something happened: a most peculiar chance, which, for a time, probably revived faith in the ancient falsehood, "Murder will out."

A canal boat was passing through Leicester, carrying a load of coal to the rubber works where the dead girl had been employed. A boatman named Whitehouse was idly watching his tow rope when he saw it slacken down into the water and then tighten. As it became taut it brought up part of a bicycle, which hung in plain sight for a moment—long enough to change the whole current of a man's life—then slipped back into the water. Whitehouse had not forgotten all those police advertisements and the reward: he came back next day and dragged the canal. He hauled up the bicycle frame again, and, as he hoped, it was green.

The police were soon busy—dragging the canal for

other interesting objects and examining the one the boatman had found. From the canal they fished other parts of
the machine; also a revolver holster with twelve ball-
and seven blank-cartridges in it.

The green bicycle was of a special model, made in
Birmingham, and from it the name and number-plate and
other identifying marks had carefully been removed. But,
in an obscure place, was found the number 103,648—and
this was the number of a bicycle sold years before to a
Mr. Ronald Vivian Light.

This gentleman was found teaching mathematics at a
school in Cheltenham. He was a good-looking, rather
earnest man; a little prematurely old in appearance, possibly as a result of his experiences in the war. He was a
Rugby School boy; a civil engineer, who had served four
years in France, part of the time with an officer's commission. Shell-shocked and slightly deaf since the great
German attack in 1918, he had been discharged in 1919.
For about a year thereafter (the year 1919, in the summer of which Miss Wright was killed) he had been out
of work and living in Leicester with his mother. His present position dated only from January, 1920, the month
before the discovery of the green bicycle.

Invited by a police inspector to explain how the fragments of his bicycle happened to be at the bottom of the
canal, Mr. Light proceeded to tell a pack of lies. He said
he had never owned a green bicycle; he had never seen
Bella Wright; he had never been in the village of Gaulby
—certainly not on that crucial evening last July.

Naturally, there was nothing to do but arrest him—
especially as Bella's uncle, Mr. Measures, and Evans also,
positively identified him as the mysterious man who rode
away with her so shortly before the murder. And two
little girls, Muriel Nunney, aged fourteen, and Valeria

Caven, twelve, believed they recognized him as a man who had followed and frightened them, about five thirty on the day of the murder, and in the same vicinity. They remembered this many months after the event. Some of the cartridges, by the way, found in the holster suspiciously near the sunken bicycle, had bullets like the one found in the road. But of course Mr. Light denied the holster as firmly as he did all the other relics.

Now, here was a beautiful case of circumstantial evidence. The net was drawn tight around the poor young man, who would, of course, be convicted—as in the detective novels.

About three months after his arrest, Ronald Light was placed on trial. The Attorney-General stated the case against the prisoner in all its deadly detail. He began to prove by his witnesses that the bicycle belonged to Light; that he was with the girl shortly before her death; that he had concealed evidence, and lied about it, over and over again.

In the middle of this testimony, the prisoner's counsel quietly interrupted. This was Sir Edward Marshall Hall —the famous defender of accused persons, for whom everybody sent, in time of great trouble. Sir Edward courteously intimated that the learned Attorney-General was going to unnecessary pains. He need not prove that the bicycle belonged to the prisoner; they admitted it. He need not prove that his client rode up to Mr. Measures' house that evening, with Bella Wright; they admitted that. Most of the Crown witnesses would not be cross-examined by the defense; only one or two points did they deny.

The Attorney-General and the police were probably somewhat disgusted. Here was the defense conceding three-quarters of the case at the outset. What about the other quarter?

Sir Edward denied, and his client would deny, that his client had used the name "Bella." He had said "Hello." And Sir Edward took in hand, very kindly and gently, the two little girls, who said they had met Ronald Light near the scene of the murder, and who described him going about the lanes seeking to molest unprotected damsels.

When he got through with Miss Muriel and Miss Valeria, they no longer looked like two little angels of justice, but rather more like two busy little brats who, feeding for months on sensational newspapers and pictures, had suddenly begun to remember something which *might* have happened to them on some day or other—but which they obligingly fixed for a *certain* day, after the police had suggested the date.

At the end of the trial the judge advised the jury not to trouble themselves at all with the testimony of Miss Muriel and Miss Valeria.

When he began to present his case, Sir Edward played his ace. He called the prisoner to the witness stand. Ronald Light was serious, calm, and dignified. He was what we call "a shell-shocked veteran," who had, moreover, become partially deaf as the result of an exploding shell. There was no attempt to emphasize Light's wartime services, except in so far as his shattered nerves might explain some of his conduct.

Light now testified that he had never had a revolver or pistol since he had been sent home from France on a stretcher. On the evening of the murder he left home at about five forty-five for a bicycle ride, expecting to return at eight o'clock. He rode through Gaulby, a district he did not know very well, and at six forty-five he was near a place called Little Stretton. He did not see the two small girls anywhere. As it was still early, he turned about to go home by the long route, and this led him again toward Gaulby.

He met a girl, who was a stranger to him, standing at the roadside examining her bicycle. She asked if he had a wrench. He had not, but he looked at the front wheel, which seemed merely to wabble a little. There was nothing he could do for it. They rode on together, chatting as they went. She said that she was going to see some friends in Gaulby, and added:

"I shall only be ten minutes or a quarter of an hour."

Light then testified:

"I took that as a sort of suggestion that I should wait and we should ride back together. I waited for ten minutes or more, then walked my machine up the hill to the church. Here I got on the bicycle to ride back to Leicester, when I found the rear tire flat. I pumped it up, and sat down on a gate; but the tire went down again and I had to mend the puncture. By this time it was eight fifteen, and I knew I was late anyhow. I thought I would ride back and see if this girl had come out. She came out the gate as I rode along, and I said, 'Hello, you've been a long time. I thought you'd gone the other way.' I talked with Evans, and all that he says is correct, except that I did not say 'Bella.' "

He further testified that they rode together for only about ten minutes; that he had still more trouble with his tire; and that the girl left him at a crossroads. He kept on the upper or more direct road; she took the lower, the Gartree Road. He had to walk nearly all the way home and did not arrive till nearly ten. On the following Tuesday he heard of the death. He read the description of

Bella Wright and of his own bicycle and came to the conclusion that he was the man wanted.

He was utterly terrified. Both for his own sake and for his mother's, who was an invalid, he wanted to escape the horror of an investigation, perhaps a trial. Foolishly, as he now admitted, he refrained from going to the police at once, and drifted into a policy of silence, then of concealment, and finally of falsehood. He never went out on the green bicycle again, but hid it and at last broke it up and threw it (together with the holster) into the canal. He now frankly admitted all the lies told when the police came to him.

"I see now, of course," he said to the judge, "that I did the wrong thing."

He must have been astounded again when the evidence rose against him from the canal. It is recorded that he had looked at this water from his cell, while he was awaiting trial, and exclaimed:

"Damn and blast that canal!"

Ronald Light's story, as he now told it, could not be contradicted or disproved in any detail. Five hours of cross-examination failed to trip him once.

His lawyer, who was himself an expert on firearms, sharply questioned the Crown witnesses who testified on technical points: about the wound, and about the bullet. Sir Edward maintained that such a heavy bullet, fired, as they thought, from a distance of seven feet, would have blown out the back of the skull. It was absurd that it should not have traveled farther. The only explanation would be that she was shot as she lay on the ground, and even this was not wholly satisfactory.

That it was the same caliber as bullets found in Light's holster meant nothing: bullets like this one had recently been made in England by the thousand million. Sir Edward suggested that the bullet found in the road might not be the fatal one at all, and that she might have been killed by an accidental shot fired from the neighboring field. It could be a rifle bullet.

No one had appeared who could testify that Light and the girl were together on the Gartree Road; he was never placed at or even very near the scene of the crime.

The Crown had shown no motive. It was not a lovers' quarrel; the two were strangers. There had been no sexual assault. Why should Light have shot her?

The defense, of course, slid over the fact that certain kinds of murders, particularly of women and children, are committed for no apparent motive whatever.

The judge, in his charge, seemed rather to lean to the side of the defense. The jury argued the case for three hours, standing nine to three in favor of the prisoner. Then the three were won over, and they reported Ronald Light "not guilty." The verdict was cheered.

But who did kill Bella Wright? Probably we shall never know. Probably, also, we shall never know whether we ourselves, if innocent, but in a predicament like that of the rider of the green bicycle, would behave any better.

Now to come back to our raven. A gentleman named Trueman Humphries went down to the Gartree Road, took pictures, and looked about. At the end he wrote, for the *Strand*, an entertaining bit of fiction. He imagines a scientific detective challenged to solve the mystery of the green bicycle. This detective organizes, in the neighborhood of Gaulby and Little Stretton, a shooting match. A prize is offered and all the boys and men in the region are drawn in.

There are various targets: disappearing images of deer, running rabbits, or the like. All of them are sprung upon the contestants suddenly and as a complete surprise. Before one of these sportsmen—a young lad—as he lies on the ground, firing, there rises what seems to be a dark hedge cut in the middle by a white gate. And on this gate sits a raven!

The boy tumbles over in a faint. When he comes to, he is ready to make his confession. He was in the field near the Gartree Road that July evening. He had sighted a bird of some kind on the white gate. He lay behind a sheep trough two or three hundred yards away (there is really such a trough) and fired. He killed the raven—but the bullet also killed the girl who rode by the gate at that moment.

Far-fetched? Very likely. But it's not unworthy of the great Sherlock!

THE
SLEEPY HOLLOW
MASSACRE

TARRYTOWN and Sleepy Hollow still brood in a mild atmosphere of romance. Sixty years ago this was more noticeable; the ghosts of Washington Irving and his gentle characters were local deities. When a hobgoblin came into Irving's stories, the kindly author made it clear that it was only somebody playing a sort of Hallowe'en joke; the weaknesses of mankind were treated in the most distant and amiable manner, as in the allusion to Katrina Van Tassel, her "provokingly short petticoat," and her pretty foot and ankle. This was rather strong stuff for the children, but everybody knew it was only dear old Mr. Irving, being roguish. There was not an atom of harm in him.

When, on New Year's Day, 1870, the glades and dells of Sleepy Hollow rang to the echoes of a horrifying triple murder, accompanied by rumors of other dark sins, the newspapers of New York were aroused and the episode was described as "The Tarrytown Horror" and "The Sleepy Hollow Massacre."

About three miles from Tarrytown, in the center of the Ichabod Crane country, lived Isaac Van Wart Buckhout, a brawny farmer nearly fifty years old. Named for one of the three heroes who captured Major Andre, Mr. Buckhout was a farmer only by brevet; his wife had enough money to enable him to spend his time partly with rod and gun in pursuit of game, and partly in snooping about trying to unearth scandals relating to his wife and various men in the vicinity. Whatever spare moments were left, he employed in drinking, so that while he was never quite drunk, he was able to claim that he "kept his tick full all the time."

His neighbors were the Weekses, the Millers and the Rendalls, all of whom lived on or near the road to Pleasantville. Mr. Buckhout was *persona non grata* with the Weeks family because he had succumbed to another of his failings, and made some kind of attack upon one of their daughters, a school-girl, aged fourteen. He found it wise to flee the neighborhood for a season, but had at last adjusted the matter by a payment of money.

Another neighbor was Alfred Rendall. Born in England, he had lived in Sleepy Hollow for the past four years. His business was that of a wine merchant on Pine Street, New York. He was a few years older than Buckhout; was described as "florid and stately" in appearance; and he dwelt, at peace with the world, with his wife, two daughters and his son, Charles. The last was a man of twenty-five, and, like his father, of good repute.

On Christmas, Mr. and Mrs. Buckhout dined at the Rendalls', and afterwards had a round of cards. *Vingt-et-un* was proposed, and when Mrs. Rendall declined to play, because of scruples about cards on Christmas, the four who sat down to the game were Miss Lizzie Rendall, Mr. Buckhout, Charlie Rendall and Mrs. Buckhout.

The game went against Mr. Buckhout, and like the sportsman he always was, in little things and great, he became cross and peevish.

Before he left the house, however, he invited the Rendalls to call upon him on New Year's Day, and taste his cheer. During the following week, he renewed the invitation, sending two or three messages to Mr. Rendall, to be sure not to fail him. On the morning of January 1st, he took down his shotgun; went outside and fired both barrels; cleaned and reloaded the gun, and then took it, not to its usual place, but to a bedroom back of the sitting-room. He also loaded a revolver and put it in his pocket. An early morning caller, who observed these preparations, thought he was getting ready for a hunting trip.

The Rendalls, father and son, came over at eleven in the morning. On account of the illness of one daughter, neither Mrs. Rendall nor her daughters came. Exactly what sort of reception genial burgher Buckhout had planned for the ladies is not known, but with his fowling-piece and revolver he had at least eight shots in his locker; and perhaps he could have met the situation.

The callers were invited into the sitting-room and made comfortable; Mr. Rendall on a chair in the center of the room; his son on a sofa. Mr. Buckhout withdrew to fetch the cider, his wife being engaged in the kitchen with the New Year's goose. When the host returned, he carried a pitcher and two goblets. The latter he filled and bade his guests drink hearty. He poured out no cider for himself.

Whether this was because the cider was insidiously doctored is not disclosed. If it was, Mr. Buckhout scorned to wait on such subtleties. He went out again, to the bedroom, this time, and came back with the shotgun. Standing in the doorway, he fired and instantly killed Mr. Rendall. Swinging the gun around, he emptied the second barrel at Charles. Part of the charge hit him in the left side of the head, some of the shot breaking the glass goblet which the young man had raised to his lips. Bits of the glass were embedded in his forehead and eye.

Buckhout hurried toward the kitchen, meeting his wife who was coming to inquire about the shooting. With the empty shotgun, trying first the butt, until he broke the stock, and then, with the barrels, he beat out his wife's brains. He then rushed outdoors.

Charles Rendall, meanwhile, blinded in one eye, his face covered with blood, and his mind confused as to what had happened, got up and went to his father. He spoke to him, and shook him, but got no reply. He then staggered outdoors, passing the body of Mrs. Buckhout, which lay on the kitchen floor. Once outside the door of the house, he fell senseless. He recovered consciousness only after three days, when he inquired of the people around him why Buckhout had shot him. He seemed not to be aware that his father had been killed.

Charles Rendall lived to testify at the trial. So, merely owing to Buckhout's haste, it was a double, not a triple, murder.

The contriver of this slaughter, as soon as he was sure his wife was dead, ran down the road with the revolver in his hand. He met a boy, who, having heard the shots, asked if he had been killing a hawk. Mr. Buckhout smiled but made no reply. He burst into the house of Ira Miller, shouting:

"I've killed Charlie Rendall! Arrest me, arrest me! Don't let them lynch me!"

After the neighbors had viewed the carnage at the residence of Buckhout, his request was complied with, and he was taken to jail.

He had long been murmuring his suspicions to this one and that. Consequently, the murders were followed by an outburst of scandalous gossip. Buckhout had pretended to believe his wife unfaithful, and had suspected his own brother, as well as two or three other men. One of these had boarded for a while with the Buckhouts; he had been recommended to them by the Rendalls, and some folk thought that it was for this reason that the Rendalls were offered up for sacrifice. At all events, the friends of Mr. Buckhout were prompt to poison the sources of public opinion, and began their attempt to save the slayer by the familiar method of blackening the characters of his victims.

According to the stories which flew about Tarrytown, the "frailty" of his murdered wife, who was born Anna Louise Coop (or Koop) had always been a matter of common knowledge. Her influences at home were deplorable, and a "too close tie" between her father and herself had kept the ladies of the neighborhood from calling. Her conduct with youths as well as with elderly men had been scandalous, and Mr. Buckhout's friends were horrified when he married her. Thus was laid the foundation for the usual defense; the dead people described as sinners and their assassination as an act of conspicuous public virtue.

In case there might be some one on the jury not simple enough to credit this, the second line of defense was that the murderer was a maniac who had no idea what he was doing. Having fallen from a horse at the age of thirteen, he had never been "bright mentally." Perhaps some of the jury might believe both yarns.

Mrs. Buckhout and her father were, in fact, decent people; the old gentleman generous in his financial aid to his worthless son-in-law. Buckhout was an irritable loafer, with a bad temper still further frayed by too much drink. He was loose-mouthed, and accustomed to fling insinuations in every direction. His own standards of morality, which permitted him to take advantage of a school-girl, did not qualify him as a censor of other people's behavior, nor suggest that he was entitled to execute his judgments with a shotgun. No one had ever asserted that he was insane until he needed some pretext by which to save his neck.

Buckhout's case was dragged out for two years. He was tried three times, always at White Plains. What little sympathy he may have aroused, subsided, and the general opinion in Westchester was that for him to evade punishment so long was a scandal. He appeared in Court wearing a full beard, perhaps from a desire to look patriarchal and Old Testamenty.

Except for a few clumsy attempts to sham insanity when he was first arrested, he seems to have acted normally at all the hearings. Nothing was adduced to show that either his wife or the Rendalls had given him any cause for grievance (except beating him at *vingt-et-un*) so the only possible defense was insanity. Few of his acquaintances believed in this; they thought he was "just naturally a mean cuss."

In all three trials there was the usual conflict of expert evidence. Two or three doctors, and experts from asylums, testified that he was sane; an equal number swore that he was—or had been—mad. The first jury disagreed, standing eight to four for conviction.

At the second trial, there was another disagreement, eleven of the jury voting for "Guilty." It was explained by an odd incident, which has been described by Henry L. Clinton, the New York attorney, who prosecuted at each trial.

As the second jury stayed out from Thursday night until Sunday without reaching a verdict, Mr. Clinton, after the jury had been dismissed, inquired into the antecedents and behavior of the obstinate man.

It turned out that he had been on the jury by mistake; accepted because he happened to bear the same name as one of the talesmen. Mr. Clinton, with legal caution, refrains from giving their real names; let us call them both Percy Hunt. The one whose name was actually on the jury-list was from Chappaqua; the other from White Plains. In selecting the jury, the clerk had called "Percy Hunt." The man from Chappaqua was absent, but nobody knew this when a voice chirped up:

"Here!"

Everyone in Court was ignorant of the fact that they were dealing with the wrong person.

It was Percy Hunt of White Plains, an apparently harmless codger, who had come mooning into Court, through sheer curiosity. In a moment, he was being examined for the jury. The lawyers for the prosecution decided, from the answers he gave, that he was a nonentity, who would vote as the others voted. In order not to waste a challenge, they made the mistake of accepting him.

During the week of trial, nobody had a chance to discover his deadly powers. But as soon as the jury had gone out, and a ballot had been taken, his talent for destruction was disclosed. Eleven jurors voted "Guilty." The false Percy Hunt refused to vote. The others argued with him. They argued for three nights and two days. They told him he had to vote. He merely answered:

"Why?"

He then added:

"I never wanted to have anything to do with this here case, anyway."

They pointed out that now he was on the jury he must vote. Said he:

"Look here, this whole thing was really between Buck-

hout and his wife. It's none of my darn business. I can't
help it if he did kill her and that other fellow. I ain't goin'
to interfere. Besides, it's all I can do to keep my own wife
in order."

At night he would tell them he was tired and was going
to sleep; if he chanced to dream anything about the case,
he would tell them in the morning. Nothing nearer to a
vote than this was ever extorted from him. Of course, he
was playing Buckhout's game, but apparently there was
no malice or corruption in him—he was merely a goofus.

At the third trial, as at the second, the defense alienists
failed to convince anybody. And, this time, no village
idiot had succeeded in getting on the jury. Buckhout was
convicted of murder in the first degree. And after a few
more pleas and petitions; writs and stays; respites and
postponements; delays and debates, he was actually
hanged.

```
┌─────────────────────────────────┐
│                                 │
│          THE DAYS              │
│             OF                 │
│          FLORADORA             │
│                                 │
└─────────────────────────────────┘
```

I. THE WICKED HANSOM

IT WAS sad that hansom-cabs should fall under a
blight. A curse descended upon them thirty-two years
ago, come the fourth of next June. Although they were
jolly, teetery-looking carriages, and more innocent than
your limousines, pious folk thought of them, for many
years, as chariots of sin.

The notorious hansom which disgraced all its tribe in
New York was driven by Frederick Michaels, and the
black hour came upon him on a fair June morning in
1904. The time was as early as half-past seven—when
the wicked have usually gone to bed, and the virtuous
are abroad. Michaels and his horse belonged with the
good and the pure, and so they were looking for business
in Columbus Circle, while the dew was still on the grass
in Central Park.

A man and a girl hailed the cab. They got in; the
hansom turned, I suppose, through 59th Street, and
started down Fifth Avenue.

The only noise it made was the familiar cloppety-clop
of the horse's hooves on the asphalt. But if Michaels had
been endowed with second-sight—no, with second-hear-
ing—he would have detected the Fates, or other sinister

creatures, muttering the soon-to-be notorious names of:
"Miss-Nan-Patterson-and-Caesar-Young . . . Miss-Nan-
Patterson-and-Caesar-Young."

And, as an accompanying chorus of doom, like the
unpleasant old busybodies in a Greek tragedy, the grum-
bling voices of half a dozen New York clergymen, who
were very shortly to be repeating the names of the man
and the girl, and adding: "The-wages-of-sin-is-certainly-
death . . . the-wages-of-sin-is-certainly-death."

Ann Elizabeth Patterson, a fatally beautiful lady of
twenty-two, was a native of the city of Washington.
Newspapers said that three men had already died—absolutely perished and crossed the dark river—for love of
her. From her sixteenth to her twentieth year she had
been the wife of a railroad official named Martin, but she
secured a divorce in 1903.

Her real celebrity, up to the moment she entered this
hansom, lay in the fact that she was a "Floradora girl."
As it is said to be a scientific fact that when "the original
Floradora double sextette"—i.e., twelve persons—held a
reunion in Pittsburgh, it took five hotels to accommodate
them, we must inquire into Nan Patterson's exact status
in that vast chorus. Good authorities say that she belonged to the second sextette, organized by Edna Wallace
Hopper in 1901.

On a westbound train, before her divorce, Nan Patterson met Frank T. Young, called "Caesar." Mr. Young,
an Englishman, had come to America, years earlier, to
compete in track and field athletics for the Manhattan
Athletic Club. He married; fell upon hard times; took up
book-making at Morris Park track, where he prospered
greatly—sometimes as a result of the excellent advice of
his wife, who was a good judge of horses. He was said to
possess $750,000. In his pocket, as he sat in the cab, were

$1,820 and two tickets on the *S.S. Germanic*, sailing for Europe that morning at 10 o'clock.

The second ticket was not for Miss Patterson, but for Mrs. Young, then waiting on, or near, the ship. She was patiently and tolerantly hoping that her husband's promise to sail with her indicated the end of his affair with "that Patterson woman."

Early in the morning, Miss Patterson had been called by telephone at the St. Paul Hotel in 60th Street, where she lived with her sister and brother-in-law, the J. Morgan Smiths. Caesar Young bade her meet him at the 59th Street station of the 6th Avenue "El." This she did, and she is the only witness to most of the events which followed, for the cabman remained more aloof than the gods upon Olympus.

It was, by her account, a bibulous ride. Caesar had already been drinking when she met him. They had a drink together before taking the cab. On the way down the Avenue, Caesar discussed his old hat, and the universal opinion that he needed a new one. At Knox's, in Madison Square, he alighted and bought a new hat. In Bleecker Street—they were on their way toward the pier —he demanded another drink. They had this, and when they were once more in the cab, Caesar was melancholy, affectionate, and despairing, by turns.

"Are you going to leave me? Or are you going to follow me to Europe?"

The girl replied:

"I am not going to Europe."

She went on: "When he grabbed hold of me, and kissed me roughly, I pulled away from him . . . there was a flash, and he was dead."

She added: "I never saw the pistol."

This happened in West Broadway, near Franklin

Street. Michaels was at last made aware that something was going on. He drew up to the curb; a policeman came, and found Miss Patterson kissing her companion's face, as his head lay in her lap. Caesar never spoke, but died five minutes after reaching the hospital.

Whose was the pistol? Where did it come from? Which hand pulled the trigger? No jury which tried Miss Patterson for murder ever found an answer to these questions.

The defense steadily maintained that "Caesar" Young, in profound melancholy at this separation from his sweetheart, or from a recent loss of $30,000 on the track, or from drink, or from all three causes, held the pistol under his coat and shot himself.

The prosecution's theory was that Nan Patterson had been urged to the slaughter by J. Morgan Smith, who feared that she was losing a wealthy friend. The evidence, by which they sought to bolster up this doubtful idea, failed them altogether. (How would it profit her to kill him?) The ownership of the pistol was not satisfactorily traced to anybody. But for eleven months, the sob-sisters and the Sunday newspapers continued to discuss the beautiful defendant, her affairs, and her venerable father, while the country at large had a good time deploring the wickedness of New York.

Rural communities righteously thanked God that as they had no Floradora girls and no hansom-cabs, therefore they had no wayward husbands and no violent deaths.

The first trial was stopped by the illness of a juror. At the second trial the jury disagreed—6 to 6. At the third trial there was another disagreement: 7 to 5 for acquittal, and the prisoner was discharged.

Miss Patterson's subsequent career upon the stage, in Pennsylvania, was brief and unsuccessful. Her later life, as a happily married woman on the Pacific coast, has, it is said, brought her the esteem of her neighbors. It is a pleasure to record this, since, if I may venture an opinion, she deserved an acquittal. The government's theory that she plotted to commit the crime, seems all but destroyed by the fact that the meeting, that morning, was not the result of her arrangement.

We know the fate of some of the participants in that early morning drive down the Avenue. The horse, in the natural course of things, would be dead. But where are the cabman and the hansom itself? Properly stuffed and mounted they could well form an important exhibit in the Museum of the City of New York. As one of the most famous vehicles in our history, the cab deserves a place beside Boss Tweed's fire-engine, with the Tammany Tiger on it.

II. MURDER IN
GREENWICH VILLAGE

WHEN Dr. Buchanan lived in Greenwich Village
it was a simple place. People in Maine and Oregon
had not yet heard of it as the abode of queer artists, or as
a region full of cabarets called the *Fried Cat* or the
Howling Owl. There were—it was in the 1890's—some
genuine painters and sculptors at work in their studios on
West 10th Street. And Greenwich Avenue, Sixth Avenue
and West 11th Street—Dr. Buchanan's haunts—were full
of ordinary shops, drug-stores, barrooms and restaurants—
much as they are to-day, except that everything was
smaller and chummier.

Dr. Buchanan, the young physician from Nova Scotia,
ate, drank and loafed in the saloons and pharmacies. He
had been in the Village long enough for people to call
him "Doc." He was an unimpressive little man, with a
scraggly mustache and golden pince-nez. On Sundays
and state occasions he emphasized his insignificance by
wearing what he called a "Prince Albert" coat, and a tall
hat. He was versed in the etiquette and ritual of the 1890's
and knew how to conduct himself as pall-bearer at a
swagger funeral, or as guest of honor in an unusually
respectable bawdy-house.

Unluckily for the Doctor, the spirit of Greenwich
Village descended upon him long before its proper time.
He was bedeviled by the itch for self-expression. He
talked too much, wrote too much and married too much.
To the chemists behind the screen in the drug-store; to
the men at his favorite eating-place; to the other drinkers
at the saloon, he laid bare the troubles of his hearth and

65

home. His chosen restaurant has vanished; its proprietor was named Macomber.

To Mr. Macomber, and others, Dr. Buchanan one day announced that he had divorced "Mrs. B." Everyone was surprised; Mrs. Buchanan was young and pretty. But the Doctor sadly observed that the divorce had been granted upon "statutory grounds." Briefly, she had departed with another man, leaving behind her little adopted daughter.

The injured husband had his plans, however. To his cronies he had more than once murmured:

"There's an old dame over in Newark who is stuck on me."

And within a few days of his divorce, the Doctor led a sort of embassy to Newark. His associates were the restaurateur, Macomber, and a large, gloomily mustached person, with a heavy "haw, haw," manner, who was known as Captain Doria, late of Her Britannic Majesty's forces.

He conducted these gentlemen to the home of Mrs. Anna Sutherland, a lady about twenty years the Doctor's senior. She explained in a slightly kittenish manner that she wished them to witness her will.

A bottle of Maryland rye was produced, to facilitate the legal procedure, and there, in Mrs. Sutherland's parlor, amidst macramé tidies, and wall decorations such as the prints "Wide Awake" and "Fast Asleep," and the large steel engraving of the signing of the Emancipation Proclamation, she read the document which devised all her real estate to her husband, if she should be married at the time of her death, and all her residuary estate to her beloved physician and friend, Dr. Robert W. Buchanan.

The will was signed, Macomber and Doria witnessing the signature; the bottle of rye was drained; and the three gentlemen departed, with many courtly bows, and much waving of their glossy toppers, as Mrs. Sutherland flirted her lace handkerchief at them through the purple portières.

The little Doctor did not tell his two aids and supporters, but Mrs. Sutherland was a woman of property, worth about $50,000. She was proprietress of two or three of "the most exclusive" bordellos in Newark. (I adopt the phrase, as to their exclusiveness, from a reporter of that period.)

Two days after the signing of the will, the Doctor slipped over to Newark again and became the lady's husband. He did not admit this to any of his Greenwich Village friends, even when Mrs. Sutherland moved into the Doctor's house in West 11th Street. He described her status as that of "housekeeper." Some knowledge of the source of her income had come to Mr. Macomber and Captain Doria, and the Doctor preferred to have them suspect that he was guilty of moral turpitude, rather than that he had actually bestowed the grand old name of Buchanan upon a woman whose feet went down to death and whose steps took hold on hell. (*Proverbs, Chapter V, 5th verse.*)

But the marriage did not prosper. Night after night the Doctor came into his favorite Sixth Avenue saloon, called for a "rye high" or "a bottle of Slits" and confided to Mike the bartender, that his sorrows were great. The old lady had a sharp tongue. Worse still, in the presence of the Doctor's little daughter, her speech was rather coarse. It was regrettable. Happiness did not reign at 267 West 11th Street.

"She says now she's going to commit suicide," he told the men at Macomber's. "Says she'll swallow poison. I told her 'Help yourself. You know where the stuff's kept.'"

The Doctor's most casual chatter became a part of Village gossip, and was finally embalmed in legal records. Long afterwards, the justices of the highest court in the State of New York shook their gray heads sadly over the fact that Dr. Buchanan had said, one evening:

"I wish I could dump the old girl."

He made even more unfortunate remarks. New York, during the year or two of Dr. Buchanan's second marriage, was bitterly divided as to the guilt of Carlyle Harris. This young medical student, so the evidence indicated, had killed his secret wife, a school-girl of nineteen, by the administration of morphine. Many persons ignored the evidence, and founded their faith in Harris's innocence on the two ancient arguments that he was "such a nice-looking young fellow" and that he was "good to his mother."

At all events, the physicians who had tried to save the girl's life had deduced the presence of morphine by various symptoms, one of which was the contraction of the pupils of her eyes. To his assembled companions, one night, Dr. Buchanan remarked tersely:

"Carlyle Harris was a damn fool. If he had known enough to mix atropine with his morphine, the contraction of the pupils would have been counteracted, and nobody would have suspected morphine."

Mr. Macomber remembered this saying and treasured it up in his heart.

At last it was rumored that "the old girl" was ill, and likely to "step out." Dr. Buchanan called in other—and reputable—physicians, but on one occasion, in the presence of a nurse, he was seen giving his wife two spoonfuls of medicine, and the sick woman was observed to reach instantly for an orange, and suck it vigorously, as if to remove some bitter and disagreeable taste.

The Doctor had no troubles as to the death certificate. The reputable physicians ascribed the decease to some natural cause, and the old girl's funeral ceremonies were performed with that solemnity on the way to the grave, and that hilarity on the return which are far from unusual. That is, on the way back from Greenwood Cemetery, the Doctor joined some of his friends in their carriage, and stopped at three saloons on the Brooklyn and three on the Manhattan side of the Bridge. One, or two, of his favorite "rye highs" at each of them, and the Doctor was twittering like a linnet.

A few days later, he departed for Nova Scotia, the home of his earliest romance. He arrived glorified—wearing lavender spats, a light fawn overcoat with pearl buttons the size of poker-chips, and a pale-gray top hat the shade of the first, faint streaks of dawn. In three weeks or less, he had remarried his first wife and returned to New York.

Now, it is usually considered a rather fine thing (see the motion pictures) for divorced people to remarry, but, for some reason, Dr. Buchanan tried to keep this, his third marriage, a secret, as he had unsuccessfully tried with his second marriage. But he had too many things to conceal, and the Furies were after him.

They took varied forms: some of them were reporters, especially from *The World*. It is a little difficult to discover in *The World* of that date the holy spirit of the crusader, which the intellectuals of our time confidingly believe animated its entire career. Its reporters, however, were certainly relentless sleuths. Flatly, and in print, they accused the Doctor of poisoning his second wife.

The other avenger was an old reprobate named Smith. He had lived for many years in the shadow of the greatness of Mrs. Sutherland of Newark; he claimed that he had started her in her wicked but lucrative business; and certainly he had looked upon himself as her heir apparent. Now, he was in New York newspaper offices, and in the antechambers of the district attorney, peeping and muttering.

The Carlyle Harris case had filled New York with tales of exhumations and autopsies, of analyses and investigations. All of these words made Dr. Buchanan jump. He hired a man to watch that grave in Greenwood, and to give him prompt warning if the old girl were not allowed to rest in it, undisturbed.

One day the warning came, but Dr. Buchanan made no use of it. He should have fled, instanter, to the innermost jungles of far Brazil. He stayed to face the music—and he nearly won.

His trial was a long-drawn and withering campaign of experts, in which lawyers, doctors, chemists and toxicologists sniffed the battle smoke and dashed, shouting, into the fray. For weeks and weeks, Dr. Buchanan sat alone and neglected; nobody even mentioned his name, while chemists arrayed their test tubes and retorts, their pipettes and their bottles of bacteria; created diabolical stinks and triumphantly disproved each other's contentions.

The assistant district attorney, Mr. Wellman, was there, gathering the experience which led to the writing of that popular textbook, "The Art of Cross Examination." Professor Dr. Witthaus, and all the other chemical experts of the day gave testimony. The prisoner had, among his counsel, the great Charles W. Brooke, whose indignation could scorch like a hot gust from Vesuvius. He also had the aid of William J. O'Sullivan, who had been a doctor before he became a lawyer, and could therefore tie into double bowknots not only the opposing attorneys, but other medical men as well.

In the end, everything was in a fog highly gratifying to the legal mind, and all was set for an acquittal or a disagreement. And then the jurors were allowed to see a letter from Buchanan to Macomber. It had no reference to murder, but it betrayed a state of mind as to the sins of the flesh which is said to have shocked the jury beyond measure. This was a fatal blow to the Doctor, for in the 1890's the Puritan's voice was still loud in the land, and many folk were ready to believe that unchastity is twin brother to murder.

To-day, such a letter might have been a trump card for the defense. It would have been so, assuredly, before a jury of literary critics and dramatists, to whom illicit love is a kind of guarantee of spotlessness, so far as all other misconduct is concerned. But Dr. Buchanan's jury stayed out a day and a night, and found him guilty.

Two years later, after every possible and one or two impossible devices had been tried in his behalf, the Doctor seated himself in the electric chair. He was courteous to everyone; still rather precise and mincing in carriage; and probably the most dapper little man who ever occupied that undesirable seat.

III. MR. ELWELL

YOU might have seen the murder yourself. Never has a first-class mystery been so open to the passer-by. If you had been walking along West 70th Street, New York, on that June morning, you could have looked in the window and seen the murderer at work.

As this would have made the lives of thousands of newspapermen duller and drabber, it is lucky that you, like everyone else, were at breakfast, reading about Harding's nomination at Chicago. And so there was preserved, unspoiled, the great detective-story murder of our times.

It had all the elements. The "murdered millionaire" alone in his house. The crowd of "suspects." The spirit of Anna Katharine Green brooded over the place. It happened in the heart of detective-story land. Anthony Abbott, detective novelist, lives in the same block; Miss Carolyn Wells but a few streets away. And some of the most remarkable adventures of Philo Vance took place just around the corner.

We know all about Mr. Elwell: his past life and scandals, and what he had been doing the night before. We have a time-table of his telephone calls, and of his death. We know everything—except who killed him, and why.

And, as in all unsolved murders, we have a lot of wise-acres, folk with the "inside dope," who nod their heads, look owlish, and say:

"The police know perfectly well who did it."

Joseph B. Elwell was gifted with an extraordinary memory. It may have passed unremarked in his native

town in New Jersey; it did not advance him perceptibly
as a salesman in Brooklyn. But when he took up card
playing, and especially bridge, he ceased to be an unknown salesman of hardware at $60 a month, and became
a king of the game: "Elwell on Bridge." He was also a
cool and ruthless gambler, who found other games even
more profitable than bridge.

His rise to magnificence began with his marriage in
1904. His career lasted for sixteen years, and there were
in it two great steps upward. As a teacher of bridge, as
an expert whose fame was world-wide, and as the osten-
sible author of handbooks to the game (his wife wrote
the books), he became fairly rich. But the fact that he
was a born gambler made him a daring winner at bac-
carat, and a successful plunger on Wall Street.

When he added a Kentucky racing stable to his pos-
sessions, he not only had three or four sources of income,
but he became a celebrity in the sporting worlds of
Europe and South America. Besides his house in New
York, he also had houses at Palm Beach and Saratoga.

His wife did much to advance his career, but they now
lived apart. If you believe only one-half of the stories
about Mr. Elwell's ways with women, it is still easy to
credit the suggestion that there were jealous husbands,
indignant fathers and brothers, and vengeful ladies who
may have wished him ill.

If I were a conscientious yellow journalist, nothing
should make me raise any doubt about the card catalogue
of ladies' names, addresses and telephone numbers, which
was found in his house. That this was a "love index," is a
revered legend of the tabloids. As a minor historian, I
am inclined to favor Detective Inspector Carey's belief
that this may have been only a list of bridge-pupils.

Mr. Elwell, on June 10, 1920, dined at the Ritz. With

him were Mr. and Mrs. Walter Lewisohn, and Miss Viola
Kraus, the sister of Mrs. Lewisohn. Strict sobriety prevailed: there were neither cocktails nor champagne.
Their merriment, such as it was, arose chiefly from the
fact that by a court decision of that day, Miss Kraus had
ceased to be Mrs. Victor von Schlegell, and that the
ex-husband himself, and his newly affianced sweetheart,
Miss Emily Anderson, were at the next table.

After dinner, Mr. Elwell's party went on to the New
Amsterdam roof to the *Midnight Frolic*. The piquant
situation continued: Mr. von Schlegell and Miss Anderson had, by chance, followed them.

The great authority on bridge was in good trim; he
danced twice and seemed as merry as a grig—a forty-
five-year-old grig.

Around two in the morning, they all departed for their
respective homes. There are tales of Elwell's adventures
en route, that he got into a fight; that he went somewhere, picked up a woman, and took her along.

The only evidence is that of the driver of the taxi, and,
according to him, Mr. Elwell was alone, and the only
incident was that his passenger stopped the cab long
enough to buy a *Morning Telegraph*. This has about it
the depressing ring of truth.

By 2:45 A.M., Elwell was in the bedroom of his house
at 244 West 70th Street, and was attired in pajamas. He
did not have a restful night, and his sleep, if any, must
have been fitful. The telephone was busy. Miss Kraus
was said to have called him up to apologize for some small
misunderstanding. At 4:30, worried about his horses,
Elwell called up his stables at Far Rockaway. He got no
answer. Around 6 o'clock, he tried to get a number in
Garden City, but the chroniclers do not tell us the result.

Soon afterwards there began, in West 70th Street, the

familiar sounds of the beginning of a new day: the milk wagon of the Sheffield Farms Company and the United States Mail. The milkman at about 6:30, and the postman, an hour later, left milk and letters in the vestibule.

There were no resident servants in Mr. Elwell's house. The only one due in the morning was Mrs. Larsen, the housekeeper. She came, after 8 o'clock, and as she entered, glanced into the small room at the right of the front door.

There sat an elderly man whom she did not recognize. Her employer had luxuriant brown hair and very regular teeth. But this person was as bald as a coot, and his mouth was toothless. He was in pajamas; a letter which he had been reading had dropped to the floor; and there was a bullet hole in his forehead. He was unconscious, was breathing heavily, and was plainly *in articulo mortis.*

He died an hour or two later, at the hospital. Mrs. Larsen had learned that this bald and mumbling gentleman was really Mr. Elwell: neither she nor anyone had ever seen him without his false teeth, nor without a brown wig. He had a hiding place in which he kept forty wigs, guarded as the secret of his life.

Up to a point, it was easy to see how the murder took place. Mr. Elwell had come downstairs, in pajamas and barefoot, after the arrival of the mail at 7:30. He picked up his letters from the vestibule and went into the little reception room to read them. He had time to open one envelope. Then someone shot him with a .45 automatic pistol.

The bullet, after passing through his head, struck the wall, recoiled, and landed on the table beside the dying man. The empty shell lay on the floor. The shot had been fired from the distance of a few feet. Judging from its upward course, it was either fired from the hip, or held by someone crouching on the floor. That the weapon was heavy is conclusive, to some people, that the murderer was not a woman.

Of that fact, there is still better evidence. Mr. Elwell's untidy appearance showed that no woman was there by his permission. That no uninvited lady came, bent on vengeance, is indicated by the hour. Neither the betrayed maiden nor the cast-off mistress is enthusiastic enough to go on the warpath at 7 A.M.

All the members of the party of the night before were questioned and investigated and reinvestigated. The police were satisfied that they were not at the West 70th Street house. Everyone—except the wise bird who knows more than the police—is still satisfied of this.

There is a feeble theory that Mr. Elwell killed himself, and that Mrs. Larsen, the housekeeper, as the pious daughter of a Church which denies full burial rites to a suicide, spirited the weapon away to make things look like a murder.

Why he should kill himself is not explained, except for the reason which impelled the Little Cossack, in Mrs. Laura Richards's rhyme:

> If my lovely teeth be crockery
> And my hair of Tyrian dye,
> Then life is a bitter mockery
> And no more of it will I.

Did the police, I wonder, shake up the rival teachers of bridge; the exponents of different systems? There, if you like, is bitterness for you!

One hesitates to enrage the romantics, who love a murder for revenge; a "sex-murder." But Inspector Carey, who was on the case, viewed it by the light of common sense. He believes that a casual thief, who followed the postman in order to steal letters, found the inner door ajar, and got into the house. Surprised by the master, he shot his way out.

Such a suggestion would have wounded the yellow journalists to the soul. A woman "high in society" or a "Wall Street magnate" was their preferred dish. So they dug around in Mr. Elwell's circle of acquaintances and found the names of the Countess Sonia Szinswaska and the Princess Dalla Patra Hassan el Kammel, who was said to be a niece of the Khedive. Of course, neither of them had any more to do with the crime than the gentleman who had just been nominated for the Vice-Presidency, Governor Calvin Coolidge of Massachusetts.

In fact, I question whether there was such a person as the Princess Dalla Patra Hassan el Kammel: she sounds to me like an advertisement for cigarettes.

IV. WILLIE'S LEGS

THERE was a man who had a duck—a white duck. He lived in Woodside, that not over-fashionable suburb of New York, on Long Island. One summer evening—it was around the Fourth of July in 1897—the duck came tottering home in a condition which amazed her owner, and made him rub his eyes. Could this be the sunset glow, or had it something to do with the approach of Independence Day? For the ordinarily white and stainless breast of Julia, his well-behaved duck, was crimson, incarnadined, red, with blood.

The man examined her closely: there was no mistake. All through the summer night he pondered, until a thought came to him. In the morning, when he liberated Julia to her diversions, he followed her on tiptoe. In a few moments she was quacking merrily as she entered a small pool, and a mystery had been solved—a mystery which had been giving the great Mr. William Randolph Hearst chronic insomnia. For "The Murder House" had been discovered; Mr. Hearst's men and the New York police came piling over to Woodside, and everyone achieved fame—everyone except Julia and her owner.

For a week there had been assembling, at the Morgue in New York, the fragments of a man. On a Saturday, two boys in swimming at the foot of East 11th Street found a bundle which contained shoulders, arms and chest. There was no head, and the chest had been partly flayed. On Sunday, other boys, exploring Ogden's Woods near East 176th Street, found another bundle—wrapped like the first in red and gold oilcloth—containing the lower part of a torso.

And a few days later, sailors on the U.S.S. *Vermont*, at the Brooklyn Navy Yard, recovered the legs which belonged with this body. But since the head remained elusive, the reporters of New York got no sleep. Who was this dismembered person? The people must know, and in the meantime the people's curiosity must continually be flogged.

Late one night a reporter was drinking a glass of beer in a Third Avenue saloon. He overheard a conversation between two men whom he recognized as "rubbers" in the Murray Hill Turkish Baths. Said one of them:

"Willie hasn't been to work to-day."

"No," said the other, "and not since Friday."

The astute reporter was soon at the Baths, inquiring for Willie.

"Oh," said the superintendent, "Willie Guldensuppe? Yes; he works here. I don't understand where he is."

The reporter mentioned the "headless mystery."

"It would be easy to identify Willie," remarked one of the *masseurs*, "he had the head of a woman tattooed on his chest."

"And a scar on one of his forefingers," said another.

"Where does he live?" pursued the reporter.

The boss consulted his address book.

"At 439 Ninth Avenue."

"With a lady named Nack," added the helpful one.

In the morning the *masseurs* were at the Morgue, engaged in the mournful business of identifying Willie. And in a day or two more Mrs. Augusta Nack was undergoing a long questioning at police headquarters. A shopkeeper from Astoria had recognized her as the purchaser of six yards of red and gold oilcloth.

Mrs. Nack was calm and dignified. At the end of the interview, the police captain tried an old gag of the kind which used to be thought infallible. He led her out the back door of his office, and let her almost stumble over the severed legs which had been fished out of the East River.

"Are those Willie's legs?" he yelled.

But he didn't know Mrs. Nack. She had no lorgnettes with her, but there were lorgnettes in her manner and in her voice, as she surveyed the fragments and then turned to the captain. She would show him she was both lady and logician. First, the lady.

"How should I know? I have never seen Willie's bare legs."

Next the logician:

"And moreover, since he is alive, they *can't* be his legs."

Unluckily, she had taken a partner in crime, whose heroism was not of this cast. He was a barber and he couldn't keep his silly mouth shut. Born in Posen, and called Martin Torzewski, he had shortened this to Martin Thorn. To his fellow barbers at Conrad Vogel's place, on Sixth Avenue, he had loudly announced that he intended to kill Guldensuppe—with a revolver, with a poison dagger, and by six or seven other methods. After he *had* killed Guldensuppe, like the thirsty woman in the sleeping car, he still must dwell on the subject. So he talked to a barber named Gotha—invited him to tea, to discuss the assassination in minutest detail—and Gotha told the police.

All of this butchery was for the love of a lady—for big, beefy, forty-year-old Augusta Nack, a German midwife. She practised, without license, the profession of helping people into this world. And at least once, and equally without license, he practised the profession of helping them out of it. For years, she had beamed upon the gentlemen and they found her not to be resisted.

Herman Nack she had married in their native Germany. They came to New York, where he set up on Tenth Avenue as a dealer in Bologna sausages. Business interfered with his pleasure, which was drinking beer, and one day he readily sold out his shop, for the price of several kegs, and applied himself to his heart's desire.

By the summer of 1897, Mr. Nack had faded into the background, and was driving a wagon somewhere. His regret at the death of his rival, Guldensuppe, was so sincere that the police could not suspect him of any part in the slaughter. His only wish had been that Guldensuppe should go on living with 'Gusta. It served him right.

But Willie Guldensuppe, the triumphant adulterer, was in turn supplanted by Martin Thorn. To the end, Mrs. Nack persisted that she had not really cared for Thorn—at any rate, not greatly.

"I never loved him," said she, "only since the time when he choked me."

This display of tenderness softened her heart. Besides, Thorn had money, while Willie the rubber got only $10 a week, and commenced to borrow from Mrs. Nack. There was trouble in the *ménage à trois* on Ninth Avenue.

Martin threatened Willie with a revolver. Willie uttered a loud "Ho, ho!" of Teutonic merriment; took the gun away from the barber, and proceeded to beat him up. He knocked him down—right in Mrs. Nack's parlor—picked him up again, gave him two black eyes, a bloody nose and a lame jaw. Then he knocked him down twice more, kicked him in the ribs, and finally—his imagination failing—threw him downstairs.

It was a mistake. Thorn was offended. He began to assemble his weapons, and talk of revenge. There must have been in Thorn a strain of the Dyaks of North

Borneo, for he announced again and again, that he would have Willie's head.

The horrified judge, who listened to this recital in court, when Augusta turned State's evidence, interrupted hastily.

"Said he would have *what*?" he asked.

"His head," repeated the placid lady, with a respectful bow.

The last straw, with Mrs. Nack, was that she caught Willie philandering. So she joined forces with Thorn, and they took a little villa at Woodside. Willie was persuaded to go out there to inspect the property, where, so said Augusta, she was going to start a baby farm. Augusta waited in the side-yard, while Willie went puffing through the house.

In a closet, upstairs, waited Martin Thorn, with a gun and a dagger and a bottle of poison—and maybe a noose and a blackjack and a Malayan creese.

He shot Willie and he stabbed him and he cut off his head with a razor. Mrs. Nack went over to Astoria to buy red oilcloth. Thorn put in a long, hard day, wrapping up bits of Willie in bundles, and the two of them made several trips to distribute these bundles. The head—the only part of Willie which Thorn really wanted—he encased in plaster of Paris and sunk in the river. The other parts all returned to plague him.

Thorn was defended by Big Bill Howe, who used to wear a yachting cap and diamonds. Mr. Howe blustered and said that his client would be acquitted. Instead, Thorn was executed.

Mrs. Nack was defended by Emanuel ("Manny") Friend, who was quieter about it and more successful. He said his client should not be electrocuted. And she was not. She got nine years for manslaughter.

I must not forget Julia, the duck. You see Thorn had done most of his dissection in the bathtub. Then he left the tap running for a day or two. Something like 40,000 gallons of water flowed down the pipes. And the blood of Willie Guldensuppe. Thorn believed this was all going into the sewers. But there were no sewers in that region, and a pool was formed near the cottage. And to this pool came Julia.

But, as usual, Mr. William Randolph Hearst got all the glory.

NINETEEN DANDELIONS

THERE was a tennis party, and Major Armstrong was skipping about the court, playing in a set of doubles. He was correctly and spotlessly dressed in flannels, and was as fussy and polite as usual.

Suddenly a figure of gloom appeared at the sidelines, and Mrs. Armstrong's voice boomed out:

"Come, Herbert! It's six o'clock—how can you expect the servants to be punctual, if the master is late for dinner?"

Now, the little Major, in obeying his wife, was a perfect lamb. So he tucked his racquet under his arm, apologized to his astonished partner and opponents, and trotted away behind Mrs. Armstrong—who was a good six inches taller than himself.

Of course, the match was ruined for the three remaining players. They stood staring for a moment, until they were reminded that others were waiting for the court. Then they moved resentfully off, and sat down with the spectators—who were smiling and whispering. The only ones who were much astonished were those who did not know the Armstrongs very well.

Almost everybody in the town of Hay did know the Armstrongs. The Major was pretty well liked, and he was even courted by some who thought it wise to keep on good terms with him. Mrs. Armstrong was respected, and, moreover, was probably admired by ladies who approved of her system of keeping a husband under strict discipline.

She gazed forbiddingly from behind steel-rimmed spectacles. She was a martyr to frail health—nothing much the matter with her. Her ideas of etiquette were firm; she even let young Mr. Martin, the lawyer, feel her disapproval for coming to one of her tea parties in flannel trousers and a sports coat. Martin was Major Armstrong's brother lawyer, and for that reason, if for no other, had been treated by the older man with courtesy.

But to Mrs. Armstrong, her husband's military rank, his university education, and his position as Clerk of Courts, were matters of importance. You did not attend Mrs. Armstrong's tea parties in tennis clothes any more than you would try to get into Buckingham Palace in shirt sleeves.

Tennis seemed to get small consideration from Mrs. Armstrong. It had no claims on her good manners. On another occasion she broke up the Major's game by reminding him that this was his "bath night."

You could not fail to notice Major Armstrong. When you talked with him, you were constantly aware of his blue eyes. Very blue they were; light-blue; some one said they were the color of forget-me-nots. And they shone, as with a light, while he looked straight at you, and talked—at great length—about himself and his affairs. It is not true that all murderers have blue eyes, but it is true that they have been a noticeable feature in a number of men whose careers were full of danger to people about them.

The Major was small and very dapper. He weighed ninety-eight pounds. He was neatly made, and carried

himself so well—perhaps as a result of military training—
that he did not seem little until he stood near some one of
ordinary height.

His dress and adornment expressed his personality, for
it was of a kind only to be described as natty. He wore a
boutonnière; his straw-colored mustache was waxed at
the ends; his collars and cravats were a joy to the haber-
dasher. His glasses—behind which glittered those eyes of
heaven's blue—were of the *pince-nez* variety, and I think
they were secured by a slender gold chain and a gold
hook which encircled his right ear.

He was concerned with tiny details and fond of dicker-
ing over trifling matters of business, and playing with
mechanical gadgets. Yet this little henpecked man, with
his gold eye-glasses and his nice manners, became a terror
in the community. People were afraid to eat or drink in
his presence, and two of his neighbors—a man and wife—
lay awake at night, fairly trembling at the thought of the
blue-eyed Major.

Most of us think of murder as something far distant. It
happens among gunmen or gangsters, generally among
people a long way off. Certainly, not among our neighbors; not on our own street. If we know anything about
life in a small town, it is hard to imagine that someone
whom the neighbors respect is, as a matter of fact, as
dangerous as a rattlesnake. That while he is talking to
you, he may be deciding that you will be the next on his
list. That if he offers you a cup of tea or if he invites you
to dinner you will accept at your peril.

"No," we say, "that does not happen in our town."

And that is what the people of the town of Hay would
have said until they found out about Major Armstrong.
Hay is a little place, on the border of England and Wales,
and it had no more respectable citizen than the Major.

He was Master of Arts of Cambridge University, and
held the King's commission in the Great War. He had
not dropped his military title, but insisted on being addressed as Major. His law firm had borne the quaint name
of Cheese and Armstrong, but now Mr. Cheese was dead.
The Major had only one rival for the legal business of the
whole region. This was Mr. Martin.

Armstrong may have looked back upon the years of
the war with longing. Living with Mrs. Armstrong was a
little like being married to the president of the W. C.
T. U., the general director of the Anti-Tobacco Society,
and the author of an encyclopedia of etiquette, all at once.

She was a rigid teetotaler; therefore her husband must
not drink wine nor spirits. When they dined out, and the
servant prepared to fill Armstrong's glass, the Major
would be given no chance to decline for himself. From
the other end of the table, Mrs. Armstrong's stentorian
voice would be heard:

"No wine for the Major!"

Mrs. Armstrong played the piano with acid correctness, and she disapproved of tobacco. The Major actually smuggled his pipe into his pocket, or tossed his cigar
over a hedge—like a schoolboy caught by the master—if
he met his wife coming along the street. In his own home,
there was one room only in which she permitted him to
indulge in the foul practice of smoking.

The Major must have been one of those men who read
with amusement the resolutely gloomy novels which so
many literary men have written about the horrors of war;
the dreadful life of camp and trench. A career under
military regulations must have seemed lightsome and free
as compared with the way he was kept goose-stepping at
home.

His house was a pleasant villa called "Mayfield," and

here he had a number of enemies. They were dandelions. He had a fine lawn—what Mr. Kipling called a mint-sauce lawn—and he had also a garden. The lawn was infested with dandelions, and the Major hated them. He used to come out and glare at the weeds, marring his closely mown turf. Then he would sigh heavily, go downtown, and order five more gallons of weed-killer. Sometimes, for variety, he would buy half a pound of arsenic. He even bought arsenic in the winter, which was a curious time to prepare for dandelions. Still, it is always well to be ready for the changing seasons. Probably he murmured—"If Winter comes, can Spring be far behind?"

He had a little squirt-gun, a delightfully delicate thing, with a tiny nozzle. This was for punishing dandelions. You see, if your lawn is like a putting-green, to dig up a dandelion makes a nasty hole. But if you fill a squirt-gun with powdered arsenic, and then tiptoe gently up to the dandelion, when it is off its guard, insert the nozzle near the root, and then—quick—press the plunger, why the dandelion begins to peak and pine, and pretty soon it passes away altogether. Without harming the grass.

The Major had great fun with his dandelion destroyer.

About this time—it was in July, 1920—Mrs. Armstrong made a new will. She had some property, which had been willed, in part to her children, and in part to her husband. Now, another will was made—all in the Major's hand-writing, and rather irregularly witnessed. The whole property now was to go to her husband.

In August, the dandelions began to get bold and mischievous once more, and the Major resolutely went out and got three cans of poisoned weed-killer. He would show 'em!

In the same month, Mrs. Armstrong's health declined.

She had obscure complaints, and it was said she was not altogether right in her mind. Rheumatism, it is true, she had had for years. But these new troubles were serious, and, from now on, the poor lady is entitled to sympathy. Even the hardest-hearted tennis player or wine drinker must admit that. She was frightfully sick, and in the midst of it all was certified as insane, and carried off to a private asylum. Her doctors and her sister agreed that this was wise. Nobody could be more attentive—no one could, to all appearances, be a more dutiful husband than the little Major.

At the asylum, she seemed slowly to get better, mentally and physically. By January she had made such a recovery as to be able to come home. It was just before her return that the Major bought, in midwinter, the half pound of arsenic. Still thinking of his lawn, and the accursed dandelions!

Mrs. Armstrong's improvement, so marked while she was away, did not continue when she was back at "Mayfield." Soon she was ill again, and a nurse was called in. The delusions returned; she heard people walking about the house. She could take or retain no food, and spent most of the time in bed, slowly getting feebler.

The Major was solicitous, often coming home from his office in the middle of the day, and sometimes relieving the nurse on watch. This was not the dandelion season; he had no present foes in the garden or on the lawn, and the squirt-gun, presumably, was put away.

At last, late in February, after weeks of distressing sickness, Mrs. Armstrong died. Dr. Hinckes, the local physician, and a good one, certified that she had a complication of diseases. She was buried in the churchyard. Only a few friends came to the funeral; they noticed that the widower seemed calm. In fact, while the coffin was being brought down, he was chatting with one of the other mourners, about fishing rights.

Next Sunday his grief was more apparent. At the church they held a kind of memorial service for the late parishioner, and Major Armstrong, himself, read the lesson, "with great eloquence and feeling."

Winter vanished, and the warmer days arrived. Dandelions began to threaten the lawn at "Mayfield" and the Major planned his spring offensive. He had been away for a few weeks, for rest and change of scene, and during these holidays renewed his war-time acquaintance with the mysterious lady known only as "Mrs. ——". After he got back to Hay, he gave little dinner parties, mostly for gentlemen. Wine was no longer forbidden. From one of these dinners, a guest—the local inspector of taxes—went home rather ill, and had a bad night.

It is a curious thing about the poisoner: one success almost always makes him try again. The crime for which a poisoner is arrested is usually not his first, nor even his second. The employment of poison gives a sense of power; a feeling which seems to make the poisoner say to himself:

"Nobody knows what a weapon I have. People, if they recognized my power, would respect me more—and fear me more."

Poison is, therefore, frequently the weapon of quiet, furtive people; of small, inoffensive-appearing persons; of meek-looking women; of men who are a little effeminate, a bit sly in manner.

The Major's next experiment may have been upon Mr. Davies, from the neighboring city of Hereford. He had a small business controversy with Major Armstrong, and came to Hay to discuss it. The Major invited him to his house to tea. How the business was settled I do not know, but Mr. Davies no sooner got home than he had a very bad pain. He called the doctors, and they operated for appendicitis. When the certificate came to be signed, it appeared that Mr. Davies had had acute appendicitis, resulting in peritonitis, which, in turn, resulted in death.

Summer was a-coming in. "Mrs. ——" appeared on the scene again. She made a brief visit to "Mayfield," and seems to have been considering a proposal of marriage. The Major showed her his garden and lawn, and perhaps told her of his triumphs over the dandelions. It was her great good luck that she took some time to consider whether she wished to become the bride of this man.

The legal business meanwhile was improving, with nobody but the friendly Mr. Martin to dispute it, or to appear on the opposite side in litigation. Mr. Martin, who was a wounded veteran of the war, had persuaded a young lady to marry him. He brought his bride to the town of Hay, where they set up housekeeping. In the late summer, they received a package by mail; a present of some chocolates. There was no name enclosed, and they mildly wondered who sent them.

There are still people who receive these strange gifts, from nobody in particular, and who go right ahead and eat them. Others let them stay around till someone else tastes them. The Martins did not care for chocolates, but put them in a dish and brought them out at a dinner party. Someone took a bite, and this someone was beastly sick. Afterwards—when many other things had happened —the remaining chocolates were found and examined. On the under side of a number of them there was a small hole, as though a tiny nozzle had been inserted. And in these chocolates there was a little bit of arsenic.

Mr. Martin and the Major were representing the parties to a business deal—a sale of land. The Major's client did not complete the contract and Martin had to press him, and, after a year's delay, to threaten to declare the contract broken and demand return of the deposits. The Major was agitated and kept pleading for more time. In October, after postponements, Martin's client finally refused to go on with the sale, and insisted that the deposits be returned.

Major Armstrong's remedy for this was tea. There is something about tea conducive to friendliness, and it seemed to him that these troubles would clear up, if he could only get the other lawyer looking at him across a tea table. He began to urge Mr. Martin to come and have a cup of tea. You must remember that at this time nobody had examined the chocolates, and that the deaths and illnesses which had occurred were attributed to various diseases.

After repeated invitations, Mr. Martin did go, late one afternoon, to "Mayfield," where his soft-spoken little host received him with smiling courtesy. The two lawyers' offices were directly opposite each other, on the business street of the town, but the Major had gone home first—to see that everything was prepared and pleasant.

There was tea, and there was bread and butter, and there was bread with currants in it, and there were buttered scones. The two men did not discuss legal business at all, except in a general way, and the question of the land contract did not come up. But very soon after the tea was poured, the Major—for a man so fussy and so well-mannered—did a strange thing. He reached across and picked up a buttered scone, which he put on Mr. Martin's plate with the remark:

"Please excuse fingers."

Mr. Martin ate the scone; then he had some currant bread, smoked a cigarette, talked a while and went home.

He found himself with poor appetite for dinner, although he ate a little. In the evening he tried to do some work, dictating to a secretary, but had to give it up. He became, first, very uncomfortable, and then for twenty-four hours, violently sick. The same doctor who had attended Mrs. Armstrong was his physician.

Martin remembered the urgent invitations to tea; he recalled the scene, and, during the week that followed, as he slowly returned to health, resolved to deny himself the pleasure of any further teas with the Major. He had a father-in-law who was a chemist, and this gentleman thought that he recognized something about the symptoms of his son-in-law's illness. He insisted upon an analysis. When this revealed the presence of arsenic, both of them, as well as the doctor, thought it time to communicate with the government.

The officials did not hurry; they agreed that things were suspicious, but nothing more than suspicious. The doctor began to remember peculiar circumstances of Mrs. Armstrong's last illness. And all of them warned Mr. Martin not to accept any more treats at "Mayfield."

It was good advice, even if not needed. But it was hard advice to follow. Major Armstrong began to talk about tea once more. He called on his brother lawyer, as soon as he returned to work; commiserated him upon his illness, and playfully recalled that he had warned him against lack of exercise. In the Major's opinion, Mr. Martin was taking too little exercise. He ought to walk more, and use his motor car less.

"And it may seem a curious thing to say," added Major Armstrong, "but I fear you will have another attack just like that one!"

Mr. Martin looked at him, and almost turned green. He hoped not.

"And now, old man," pursued the affable Major, "we must have another talk about that sale. My clients have a proposal to make. Come to tea to-morrow."

Mr. Martin was sorry. He had an engagement. No, positively. He could not come.

"Oh very well," returned Armstrong.

But next day he was back again—this time by telephone. "Come in to tea, won't you?"

"Sorry," said the terrified Martin, "not taking any tea to-day."

Next day the business really did require a settlement, and Martin realized that he must talk with his neighbor.

"Will you come over to tea, this afternoon?" telephoned the Major.

"No," was the reply. "I can't come to tea. But I will look in afterwards—around six o'clock."

But this wouldn't do. There was something about this contract that could be settled only over the teacups.

"Well, never mind," the Major replied, "come to tea tomorrow."

Then, it occurred to Armstrong that taking your tea in your office is a good English custom. Perhaps Martin didn't like to go so far as "Mayfield." The Major set up a tea-caddy, cups and spoons in his office, had his housekeeper send down some scones, and instructed one of his clerks to order some bread and cake from the restaurant near-by.

"I tell you what," said he, "we'll have tea in my office. Come over about half-past four."

Mr. Martin could only stammer. He had run out of excuses. He and his wife were thoroughly agitated now; they saw the Major's gleaming blue eyes everywhere. They actually took turns in keeping awake all night; one of them on guard while the other slept. Evidently they expected the Major to come climbing up the wistaria vine, armed with an arsenic bottle.

That afternoon the telephone rang again.

"Where are you?" came the Major's voice. "The tea is spoiling; been waiting half an hour."

"Oh, I've had my tea," said the wretched man, "had it here in my office."

After this, Martin—while the police investigated—was reduced to bringing tea into his own office, and hastily gulping it down at three o'clock, in order to fight off the invitations.

I have wondered why he didn't accept some day; go over, and give Major Armstrong every opportunity to prepare the dishes; take them from his hands, then turn on him, and say:

"Oh, Major, I couldn't think of taking these. Look, this cup of tea, so nice and hot! And this lovely buttered bun! I want *you* to have these!"

And back the little viper right into a corner with the stuff.

But this might have given the show away, and ruined Scotland Yard's investigations. The Major, so far, had the whip hand and he knew it. Martin was frightened. When the tea invitations ceased at last, and Armstrong began to ask Mr. and Mrs. Martin to dinner, the younger lawyer was desperate.

All this time Scotland Yard was working on the case, and telling Martin to hold out a little longer. It was a serious thing to arrest such an important and respectable person as the Major, and to accuse him of the extraordinary offense of trying to murder a fellow-lawyer with a poisoned scone. It would not do to make a mistake.

Finally, a detective inspector came down from London, and, to the utter amazement of everyone—except the

Martins, and one or two others—arrested the Major for attempted murder.

At the same time—a dark winter night—strange men appeared in the town, and strange lights were seen in the churchyard. England's famous pathologist, Sir Bernard Spilsbury, and his aides were exhuming the body of Mrs. Armstrong.

As soon as the coffin was opened, all the doctors knew, by the extraordinary manner in which the body was preserved, that this was probably a death by arsenic. And the autopsy revealed the largest amount of that poison ever found in such circumstances.

It was for murder, the murder of his wife, that the Major was tried. He was defended by one of the great criminal lawyers of the day, Sir Henry Curtis Bennett, who did his best to show that Mrs. Armstrong—utterly helpless at the time—might have arisen from bed, and taken the poison herself.

Mr. Martin's story of the tea party was admitted as evidence, and the judge (Lord Darling) took a vigorous part in cross-examining the prisoner. In the United States, it is probable that the Major's lawyers would have succeeded in excluding Martin's evidence, and the prisoner would have escaped. The theory of Mrs. Armstrong's suicide might have seemed stronger if her husband had not been revealed as a systematic poisoner.

Major Armstrong sat bolt upright in court, calm, and attentive; staring, with his pale blue eyes, straight ahead. While he was on the witness stand, he and the judge had a long verbal duel, conducted with icy politeness. The Major described how he had made up twenty little packets of arsenic, each containing a deadly dose for a dandelion.

It was also, the judge pointed out, a deadly dose for a human being, was it not?

And he had used nineteen of these packets on nineteen dandelions. As the Major described the process, in his precise voice, you could almost see the graves of the nineteen dandelions.

And there was one little packet left over (as the judge observed) and it was found in his pocket, when he was arrested, in December.

The jury—most of them farmers—were capable of noting that in December the dandelion season is practically over.

A year or two later, that graceful writer, Mr. Filson Young, visited the town of Hay, and sat on the lawn at "Mayfield." The dandelions, he says, were thicker than ever.

They had triumphed. The Major was far away. He was not even lying in that churchyard whither he had sent one, or two, or how many others? For the concluding words of the dread sentence of the law in England are:

". . . and that you be there hanged by the neck until you be dead; that your body be buried within the precincts of the prison in which you shall last be confined; and may the Lord have mercy on your soul."

And the chaplain, standing behind the judge, replies:

"Amen!"

MRS. COSTELLO
CLEANS THE BOILER

MRS. NELLIE AYERS, an aged peddler of candy, is known to many of her customers in Peabody, Massachusetts, as "the fudge woman." One morning in February, '33, intent on business, she called at the home of the Costellos. After a little sales talk, while patting the baby on the head, she entered into covenant with Mrs. Costello for a pound of fudge.

That lady went upstairs for her purse, but immediately began to utter shrill screams.

"She screamed something terrible," said the fudge woman in a later description.

The only other adult person on the ground floor of the house was a temporary helper, a Polish woman whose name ought to mean something, since she was called Mrs. Simbolist. She did not hear the screams, possibly because she was busy with the favorite occupation in the Costello household: cleaning the kitchen boiler. And she was wiping her streaming eyes, as a result of trying to shine the copper with some curious hellbroth furnished by her employer. She had never used this stuff before.

Mrs. Costello rushed downstairs again, exclaiming:

"Bill's dead!"

"And who," inquired the fudge woman, "may Bill be?"

"He's my husband," cried the other, "an' he's up there, lyin' on the floor, dead."

"All of this," replied the peddler of sweets, with some hauteur, "is beside the question. Here's your fudge. Where's my money?"

"Oh, I couldn't," moaned the young widow, "I couldn't think of fudge, now. With Bill up there dead—an' all!"

"Madam," said the majestic saleswoman, "a bargain is a bargain. That's my last word to you."

And she stalked across the street into a neighbor's house, where she explained her ideas of commercial honor.

"In my day," said she, "people kept their promises."

She repeated this loud and long, and at last to reporters, so that her complaints reached the press, and her grievance became known throughout New England.

For the fudge woman, like many another innocent bystander, had stumbled upon tremendous events; she had smelled the smoke of the fire that is never quenched. Bill's death had been sudden, its cause obscure, and into his house came neighbors and physicians, then detectives and pathologists.

Bill, officially known as Captain Costello of the Peabody Fire Department, had returned early that morning from a night spent with a company of friends in the ancient rites of watching over the body of a deceased associate.

He had been in good health and spirits, quite the life of the wake. Partaking of ham sandwiches, pie, and coffee at midnight, he left at 2 A.M., promising to return in five hours. Even this short rest had not interested him, for—according to Mrs. Costello—as soon as he got home he embarked upon the great family recreation of cleaning the boiler. Or, rather, of mixing the pestilential brew which—again according to Mrs. Costello—was their familiar and favorite lotion for that purpose. The brightness of their boiler was the chief concern of the household; they rubbed it by day and muttered about it in their sleep. Once more, our informant is Mrs. Costello.

Despite scandalous rumors, despite hundreds of newspaper articles, there was no immediate arrest. But the autopsy revealed that Captain Costello had cyanide of potassium in him. A detective learned that the night before the Captain's death, Mrs. Costello had bought this substance, together with oxalic acid. Her mind, of course, was bent upon imparting a still greater radiance to the pride of the family, the kitchen boiler. Tales of neighborhood scandals caused this detective to call upon the widow and ask if she had had any poison in the house.

"Absolutely not," said she; "devil a bit."

But he pursued the subject.

"How about cyanide of potassium?"

"Oh, if you call that stuff poison!" she replied.

That is exactly what the Commonwealth of Massachusetts, in its prim, old-fashioned manner, does call potassium cyanide, and so for many pleasant days in the following July and August, a jury in Salem listened to Mrs. Costello's explanations. The lid was taken off the section of Peabody where the Costellos live, and the reek of neighborhood gossip went up, as thick and poisonous as the fumes from the cauldron when Mrs. Simbolist tried to clean the boiler.

The trial was conducted with a dignity, and at the same time a kind of antique simplicity that (as I like to think) would be found in few other places in America. In front of the solid and forbidding old Court House there daily gathered a crowd, mainly of women and

children, to watch the defendant arrive and alight from
the Sheriff's motor-car. This group was kept within
bounds, so that the street, and most of the sidewalks,
were quite clear for traffic and passers-by.

Shortly before ten o'clock, the jury appeared, walking
slowly, two by two. At the head of the column, and at
its foot, went a tipstaff, in blue, and with brass buttons.
Each of these officers carried a wand, about seven feet
long, gilded at the end. The jury came from the Haw-
thorne Inn, where they had apparently spent a peaceful
night. The hour after breakfast, between nine and ten,
was usually passed in Dr. Phippen's garden, and on
some days each juror wore a boutonnière. The day I saw
them these decorations were absent, but the tipstaves
each solemnly carried, in addition to his wand, a big
bouquet of flowers. Whether these were for judge or
prisoner, or merely to decorate the jury-room, I did not
discover.

After the jury had gone inside, there drew into the
street the Sheriff's car, with two or three officers, and
the defendant. Jessie Costello had become a personage,
discussed from Eastport to Westport, a lady with a reputation for beauty and a talent for invective. To see her
skip out of the limousine, and run smiling into the Court
House, people waited for hours in the hot sun. To get
one of the seats allotted to spectators, other people stood
in line all night.

In the Court Room, people did not perch on window-
sills, nor stand in the aisles. Thirty spectators were allowed to occupy seats, and no more than thirty were
admitted. Reporters were restricted to their section.
Judge and jury, lawyers and witnesses and officers had
room to move and think and deliberate. The walls of the
room, and the green-shaded windows, were tall and

cool. The national flag and the beautiful gold and white
emblem of the Commonwealth were on either side of the
bench. The Judge was austere and self-possessed: a typical judge of a State which does not require its justices
to curry favor with the electorate, nor canvass for votes.
Over his head was a full-length painting of Chief Justice Shaw, who delivered the famous charge in the trial
of Professor Webster. And, on a black-board near the
witness-stand, a diagram, in chalk, of Bill Costello's
stomach.

Among the women Massachusetts has tried for murder,
one must go far back—probably to Bathsheba Spooner
of Revolutionary days—to match Mrs. Costello in charm.
Perhaps for the first time in her life, she was dressed in
good taste; in black, with a big white jabot. Her figure
was a trifle dumpy, and her slightly rolling gait could
have been a waddle if she had not tripped in and out the
court so merrily. Her clear white complexion might have
seemed—after months in jail—too pallid, had she not cor-
rected this, very skilfully, with her only cosmetic, a little
rouge. Her dark eyes, under heavy unplucked eyebrows,
were her best feature. For a few days, many of the reporters were highly appreciative of these fascinating eyes,
until, one morning, they saw them narrow like a snake's
and her whole countenance harden with anger at a
camera-man, as she spat at him the single—and inappropriate—word:

"Bitch!"

But let not those who have never been hounded by
press photographers chide Mrs. Costello. She made no
pretense of agreeing that "No Nice Girl Swears," and
the charge of using "vulgar, profane, and blasphemous
language" urged against her by witnesses for the prosecution is the only one she did not deny.

"Never in the presence of the children" was all that she said.

Mrs. Costello, as the trial progressed, emerged as the only truth-teller in court. The people who perjured themselves, in great matters or small, included some of her own witnesses and friends, as well as witnesses for the State. For instance, the pharmacist who sold her the cyanide warned her that it was deadly stuff, and she replied that she knew all about it. But in her testimony she declared that she never knew it was harmful until Bill died.

His fellow-firemen and his friends at the wake bore witness to Bill's sound health and spirits, but his widow assured the jury that he was mentally decayed and physically feeble—quite in the mood to seek death (although a pious Catholic) by gulping down a big hooker of boiler polish.

"They'll have to go like hell to find any poison in Bill with all that embalming fluid in him."

This remark, as the autopsy drew near, was attributed to Mrs. Costello. But the lady denied it, and a male relative gallantly assumed the blame for this cynicism.

Medical testimony suggested that the poison was administered in a capsule, probably under pretense that it was some simple medicine, appropriately taken the morning after a wake. Mrs. Costello denied all knowledge of capsules. She didn't even know what they looked like. And then a neighbor, Mrs. Bisson, most unwillingly testified that she had seen Mrs. Costello buy and fill capsules in an earlier instance of private doctoring.

A curious incident in the trial was the appearance of the manager of a local moving-picture theatre to testify that the film being shown just before the tragedy was "Payment Deferred." It was suggested by the defense that this might have given Costello the idea of self-destruction by cyanide. But the theme of that play is murder, and the expression in the eyes of Charles Laughton as he watched his nephew die of cyanide would hardly attract anyone to this form of death.

The contention of the State was that Mrs. Costello had a waning regard for her husband, an excessive interest in his insurance money, as shown when she went to the fire station to collar his policies before his body was in the coffin, and, most of all, an undue passion for a neighbor: young Patrolman McMahon of the Peabody police.

This officer was called in hundreds of headlines the "Kiss-and-Tell Cop." Kiss was but a schoolgirl's feeble euphemism for what happened, but tell he certainly did. Before the grand jury he perjured himself like a gentleman, and everyone seemed to approve. Then, either the influence of religion caused him to fear hellfire or the power of the law made him dread being included in the indictment. For upon the witness stand he recited a tale which put the record of the trial on the *Index Librorum Prohibitorum*, and sounded more like a fourteenth-century Florentine frenzy than the annals of Essex County, Massachusetts.

Reporters stopped writing about the Salem witches—who were tried right around the corner—and began references to Hester Prynne and the big, big Scarlet Letter.

It was a pickup, on the street, while McMahon was directing the Peabody traffic. Up drove the fatal Jessie in her car, with a very glad eye and the invitation:

"How would you like to be in here?"

After that, it was all up with Officer McMahon. While Captain Costello was on duty at the fire station, there were stolen rides to convenient parking places along the Newburyport Turnpike, as well as many trysts in the

Costello home. When his wife went to a hospital, poor McMahon was seized, like the Sabine women, and carried off to dwell with the Costellos. Even when he sought respite in an appendicitis operation, and retired to the hospital, there was no leave of absence. The determined Jessie visited him every evening, and strained the rules of the hospital by the length of her calls. Her family physician, one Dr. Pomeroy, a rather curious figure in the case, found her hiding one night behind the door of McMahon's room, and curtly bade her cease her foolishness and come out.

More angered by the recital of the love affair than by the charge of murder, Mrs. Costello rushed to the witness stand to deny it all, lock, stock, and barrel, and call Eddie McMahon seven kinds of a copper-riveted liar. Why, she barely knew the fellow; her friendship with him, like that of Bunthorne with the vegetables, was merely a passion à la Plato.

McMahon, by the way, was soon out of the Police Department, but it was one of the charming oddities of the case that he was offered and accepted a job with Lydia Pinkham, the woman's friend.

Nobody suggested any reason why McMahon should invent the story he told on the witness-stand, but the man in the street denounced him as a yellow dog. The same eminent man in the street listened to Mrs. Costello's tarradiddles and admired her for them.

"Of course, she had to say that!"

Truth is not highly esteemed in our courts of law; perjury, from most of the witnesses, seems to be expected as a matter of course.

The jury brought in an acquittal. Many people were astonished, but they cynically attributed the verdict to the fact that twelve male jurors sat for weeks in close

proximity to the prisoner, and as helpless as twelve rabbits under the influence of those glittering ophidian eyes.
This may be unjust. Perhaps they relied on the ancient
belief that "a woman couldn't do such a thing" and that
when the woman was, moreover, the mother of young
children, the charge must be preposterous. Or, perhaps,
the State tried to prove too much: it certainly allowed
one of its medical witnesses to introduce a complicated
argument on a pathological subject. It was as interesting, and as involved, as a chapter in one of Mr. Austin
Freeman's detective novels—but, unfortunately, was irrelevant to the point at issue.

Broadway had a brief glimpse of Mrs. Costello, but
offered her no theatrical engagement. Her partnership
with Mrs. McPherson, the evangelist of Angelus Temple,
was likewise brief.

To us home-lovers, who admire the New England
housewife and her traditional love of cleanliness, the
really important thing was to have Jessie at home once
more. The kitchen boiler had been neglected for months,
and nothing seemed so appropriate as to let Mrs. Costello
and her lawyers give it a good polish. Especially with that
widely used and reliable preparation, cyanide of potassium.

MISS HOLLAND'S
ELOPEMENT

THE police were discouraged. For five weeks of a late and cold spring they had been digging around an ancient farmhouse. The waters of the moat which gave the house its name—Moat Farm—were icy and black, and one man had almost been drowned in the flooded trench.

A moat suggests a dank and dismal place, from whose depths one might fish up old weapons or rotting bones. The searchers worked all day; their torches flared at night; they lived in discomfort, and after a while were derided by neighbors who came to watch. The lonely farm was in the English county of Essex; it was a gloomy spot, now under dark suspicion of crime.

The men found bones—the bones of animals—and someone discovered a battered skull which might have been there for a century or longer.

Then, at last, one of the diggers struck something hard. He scraped away the earth and saw a woman's shoe. It was a small shoe—size two and a half—and in it were the bones of the little foot it had been designed to cover. The shoe was made with care and lined with lamb's wool. Inside was stamped the word *Mold*.

The others came, and began—with great care—to clear away the hideous black slime.

Meanwhile Scotland Yard detectives had been looking into the history of the Moat Farm and its owners.

.   .   .   .   .

Miss Camille Holland had never had a husband.

And Mr. Herbert Dougal had never had enough money.

Now, Miss Camille Holland had enough money—easily enough for two, since she owned what would be equal today to seventy or eighty thousand dollars. And Mr. Herbert Dougal was rather distinguished-looking and extremely accomplished in the arts of courtship.

The conclusion is plain. What Miss Holland and Mr. Dougal ought to do is much easier to say than it is to give the answer to the simplest equation in algebra. First, as to Miss Holland—Miss Camille Cecile Holland—her peculiarities and her lonely life. She was easy game for a humorist—if you are that sort of humorist. W. S. Gilbert liked to describe her kind. He thought it amusing to make fun of old maids. He nearly always introduced the type; the woman who could

> *Easily pass for forty-three*
> *In the dusk, with a light behind her.*

Miss Holland, this gentle little sentimental spinster, was actually about fifty-six. But, as one of her landladies observed, when she had completed her preparations for the day, had applied powder and a little rouge (lipsticks were then the mark of the scarlet woman), when she had carefully dressed her gold-tinted hair and put on all her extraordinary upholstery—why, then she looked years younger.

It would have horrified Miss Holland, but most of the details of her toilet are known. There was the landlady who often helped her get dressed. And there is the modern novelist, Miss Tennyson Jesse, whose essays about real crimes are written with insight and a scholarly attention to details. Miss Jesse has recorded her astonishment at the array of clothing. Six ladies of today, even old ladies, she says, could be attired in what Miss Holland thought it necessary to wear.

Men always hasten to express their unfamiliarity with the topic. But I think it will be credited when I say that much of this list is mysterious to me. Miss Holland thought she was secure from drafts and chills when she went forth wearing a pair of "natural" woolen combinations, a pair of white linen combinations, steel-framed corsets, two pink woolen underbodices, black cashmere stockings, a pair of bloomers, and two petticoats.

Was there a dress over all this? I suppose so. (Neither of my authorities mentions it.) In addition, there was a "hair pad," a tortoise-shell comb, an elastic belt, and a bustle. Even the bustle was evidence of Miss Holland's chilly disposition, for, according to the landlady (Mrs. Henrietta Wisken was her name), it was "an unusual bustle—of a warm material."

Miss Holland got her shoes from a London maker. They were especially designed for her small and well formed feet; were size two and a half, lined with curly lamb's wool, and stamped inside with the name, the painfully prophetic name, of the maker. It was *Mold*.

We have got Miss Holland dressed. Let's see who she was. She belonged to that perilous class described once by Sherlock Holmes: the drifting and friendless woman. Her money had come, by inheritance, from an aunt. She herself had a niece and a nephew or two, but seldom saw them. They were self-respecting people who did not wish to bother their well-to-do relative nor seem too eager about her health. She had always been mildly attractive;

some gentleman was usually paying her little attentions. But that was all. There was a tender memory in her heart: a young naval officer, of whom she had been fond, was drowned, and Miss Holland still wore a ring taken from his dead hand.

She had a banker, who rarely saw anything of her except her signature. She took trips now and then, but only a few people knew her at all, or what she looked like. These exceptions were the other boarders at her boarding house in Bayswater.

In 1898 these gossips were in raptures over a bit of news. Miss Camille had a beau! Actually, my dear! The housemaid had seen him, and the landlady, Mrs. Pollock, had seen him too. Miss Camille gave him tea in the drawing-room. And they had been out on walks together.

What *was* he like? Well, he was tall and well set up: military-looking. Evidently a retired officer; Miss Holland called him "the captain." He had a brown pointed beard and was quite distinguished. A traveler, plainly, and a man of the world. Fancy that, my dear! And Miss Camille! Did you ever?

Old Miss Nibbets, who was eighty-two, chuckled over her cup of arrowroot that evening and said to Mrs. Budge that *she* was not going to give up hope if a thing like this could happen to Miss Holland.

I do not certainly know that Miss Nibbets and Mrs. Budge were their names, but think it possible. Into the romantic adventure of Captain Dougal and Miss Holland, in addition to Mrs. Wisken and Mr. Mold, there entered a Mr. Coote and a Mr. Turtle, as well as an ancient person called Old Pilgrim. So it seems that anything might happen in the Bayswater boarding house.

Mr. Dougal's first name was Samuel, but, always with an eye to what was dashing, he signed himself "S. Herbert

Dougal." He spoke with a slight Irish brogue—realizing, probably, that a good-looking Irishman starts with an advantage in almost any lady's affections. The brogue, however, was as much assumed as the title of captain, for he was a true cockney, born within sound of Bow bells. He was modest to give himself no higher rank than captain, for he had actually been a sergeant with twenty-one years' service. And the popular belief is that a veteran sergeant knows enough of the art military, and the best methods of roaring commands at trembling privates, to win any war single-handed. The wonder is that Dougal did not call himself a field marshal.

Ex-Sergeant Dougal had served both at home and in Halifax, and his military record was perfect. Never an absence without leave, not an unpolished or unbuttoned button to tarnish his discharge papers. He had been in enjoyment of a pension.

But (he sighed to Miss Holland, as they walked together the leafy walks of Hyde Park) there was a shadow on his life. A dark shadow, which kept him from proposing marriage. A wife—an estranged, ungrateful, and pestiferous wife. His respect for the law—and he drew himself up as one whose respect for it passed all belief—his respect for the laws of his country prevented him from suggesting a marriage ceremony which would lead them into bigamy.

And twittering little Miss Holland was left, after these walks, to struggle with the temptation to agree to the naughty proposal that he did make.

She was fed up with the boarding house, with old Miss Nibbets and the rest. An elopement with this handsome devil—it *would* be exciting!

Just as Dougal had been modest in awarding himself no higher honorary rank than captain, so he had been reticent about a number of his accomplishments. His discharge from the army (signed by a colonel whose name—believe it or not—was Mainguy) stated that the sergeant had the qualifications of "a very good clerk." This, of course, includes skill with a pen, and Mr. Dougal thought well of his ability with that dangerous weapon. He could, for instance, when he had time, make other people's signature—almost as well as they could do it themselves.

Employed in a military hospital in Dublin after his army days were over, he came across some checks signed by the major general in command—no less a person than Lord Frankfort of Montmorency. There were also some signed by the eminent Lord Wolseley, commander in chief. Now checks apparently signed but repudiated by these generals got abroad, and one, for thirty-five pounds, was cashed in London. A jury decided that Dougal was responsible, and he was sentenced for a year, and also lost his pension.

It was at least the third time that he had been before a court since he had returned to civil life. The other two juries, however, had been impressed by his good record in the army as well as by his eloquence, and they had let him go.

Naturally, Mr. Dougal did not mention these adventures to Miss Holland as they ate their muffins and tea in Mrs. Pollock's drawing-room. His was a nature far above thoughts of money, so he said, after he had tried (and failed) to get Miss Holland to reinvest all her securities in his name.

Nor did he say anything to her about his love affairs—other than this one unfortunate circumstance of the impossible wife. This is not surprising. There would not have been time to do the subject justice—not unless they had walked round and round Hyde Park until they dropped from exhaustion. The tale needed three volumes —like "My Life and Loves," by Mr. Frank Harris.

To give it in the briefest form, it included a wife who had died very suddenly in Halifax. Dougal attributed the death to oysters. By some curious military custom, he was permitted to bury her next day. He went back to England and returned with a new wife, who died in two months. Oysters again. And again a prompt burial.

Then, about to leave the army, he persuaded a young Nova Scotian to return to England with him without the formality of a marriage. She left him after about a year, and went back to Halifax with a baby. In England there were other unsanctified associations with various widows and maidens; a third marriage, in Ireland, to Miss Sarah White (the "shadow" of whom he told Miss Holland) and an illicit acquaintance with one Miss Booty. This lady's name seems to have suggested something to him, for she haled him into court, charging him with stealing her property. He replied with a countercharge that Miss Booty had robbed him of an incubator. The case came to nothing.

These were a few of his adventures up to the time he made the acquaintance—nobody knows how—of Miss Holland. No one knows all his exploits; the most resolute investigators have never attempted to catalogue all his children, born in and out of wedlock. If he did not let them be any expense to him, they certainly did not contribute to his support. In spite of his twirling cane and his swanky appearance, he was flat broke when he met the little old maid of Bayswater.

How he wheedled this cautious and mature virgin into such an adventure is a deep mystery. No slightest indelicacy had ever stained her career. She was religious, even

rather pious, and had lived hedged about by rigid propriety. Yet here she was—vanishing into strange regions
with this cockney Casanova.

First, like many elopers, they went to a place near
Brighton. They took a house—and Miss Holland paid the
rent. The ex-sergeant, however, wished to be a landlord, and negotiated the purchase of Coldhams Farms in
Essex. It was Dougal himself who gave it its new name
of the Moat Farm. There certainly was a moat, and one
had to cross it by a bridge.

Over £1500 of Miss Holland's money was paid for
the property, and Mr. Dougal had himself named as
owner. This deed, however, was torn up by Miss Holland, and a new one was executed in her own name. She
was giving away her heart and hand, but did not intend
to endow her lover with all her worldly goods.

While the farm was being made ready for its new
owners, Miss Holland took her household furniture out
of storage—piano, pictures, linen, and plate. For three
months before moving to their home, the pair, calling
themselves Mr. and Mrs. Dougal, lived in the neighboring
town of Saffron Walden. Here they lodged with and
conferred fame upon Mrs. Wisken.

This kind-hearted woman liked her tenants and thought
them to be what they appeared to be, affectionate married
people of complete respectability. She talked with them
both, and learned much, but by no means everything,
about them. Mr. Dougal was polite to Mrs. Wisken's
canary, and Mrs. Wisken, in turn, was very fond of Miss
Holland's little dog, Jacko.

You probably could have knocked Mrs. Wisken over
with a feather, as she would have said, had you told her
that her association with the Dougals was to lead her into
some very gruesome experiences: cause her to spend days

in attendance upon courts; blazon her name in all the newspapers of the land; get her examined and cross-examined by bewigged barristers; and plunge the Wiskens into a celebrity which should endure from generation unto generation.

One day in April, Dougal and Miss Holland, in a carriage driven by the laborer Old Pilgrim, left Saffron Walden and entered into possession of the Moat Farm. Their life there lasted three weeks. They had three different servants in that short time; the second was named Lydia Faithful, but even she stayed only a week. The third was Florence Havies, who had no sooner arrived than she found that "the master's" attentions were far too urgent to be agreeable. In fact, when he tried to break into her room at night, she took refuge with Miss Holland, and for the few remaining days that she stayed she refused to be alone on the place with Dougal.

On May 19 Miss Holland and Dougal drove away; to "go into the town and do a little shopping," said Miss Holland. Nobody ever saw her again. Dougal returned a few hours later, and—to the alarm of the servant—he returned alone.

"Where is the mistress?" said she.

"Oh, she's gone to London."

"What? Gone to London and left me here alone?"

"Yes, but never mind. She's coming back and I'm going to meet her."

Florence, who was a young girl, had stayed on only at Miss Holland's request, and she now felt herself deserted. She spent the night locked in her own room, sitting, fully dressed, by the window, ready to get out that way if anything happened. Dougal was in and out of the house most of the night, absenting himself for long periods and

returning to report that "Mrs. Dougal had not returned"
by this or that train. He pretended that he had been driving to the station. In fact, he had other and more urgent
business, nearer the house. The girl was too much terrified
to care what he was doing as long as he stayed away
from her.

In the morning her mother—to whom she had written
the day before—came and took Florence away. Mrs.
Havies told Dougal exactly what she thought of his conduct, demanded and received a month's wages for her
daughter and railway fares for both, and departed from
Moat Farm.

There now began one of the most curious events in the
history of these two people: Dougal's four years' residence at the farm. It was, in a way, a haunted place.
There were Miss Holland's piano and music, pictures,
linen, clothes, watch, and jewelry. The few persons who
made any inquiry were told that "Mrs. Dougal" was traveling, or that she was yachting. The real Mrs. Dougal
(Sarah White) arrived promptly on the day after Miss
Holland's disappearance. Her husband had told her that
he had been "managing an estate for an old lady" who
was now "away."

He continued to manage the estate rather profitably for
himself. In a few days Miss Holland's London banker
received a letter in which Miss C. C. Holland requested
a new check book. It was sent to her at the Moat Farm.
There followed a check made out to Dougal for thirty
pounds. The banker wrote to Miss Holland:

*Your signature appears to differ from that with which
we are acquainted. I shall be obliged if you will kindly
confirm the same by signing it afresh in your usual manner.*

He was reassured by a letter:

Dear Sir: Cheque to Mr. Dougal quite correct. Owing to a sprained hand there may be a discrepancy in some of my cheques lately signed.

Yours truly,

Camille C. Holland.

The banker's mind was now at rest. So, apparently, was Miss Holland's. Orders arrived from her selling four hundred shares of George Newnes, Ltd., forty-three shares of Great Laxey Mines, and £500 worth of United Alkali Co. Later in the same year Miss Holland withdrew over £600 from her London bank, and Mr. Dougal deposited the same amount to his own credit at another bank. This happened until Mr. Dougal had a bank account of nearly £3,000. When there was a delay in the conveyance of the Moat Farm, Miss Holland (who still remained on her mysterious yachting trip) sued for her rights and got a favorable settlement. Out of gratitude to her manager, she made over the farm to Mr. S. Herbert Dougal.

That gentleman was now living a life only attainable by the great lover who is also skilful with a pen. One of his first cares was to get Old Pilgrim to fill in an unsightly ditch near the house. It was completely filled and covered with many loads of earth.

Dougal became a sort of local magnate, an all-round, hearty, genial fellow, frequenting the public houses, and always ready and eager to stand treat; full of jests and boisterous conversation. He was something of a sportsman, fond of shooting. Hitherto he had been a cyclist, but now he bought a motor-car, which, as the first in that region, amazed and interested everyone.

He described his place in a letter as "a jolly English

home." Mrs. Dougal came and went, but finally found the place a trifle too jolly and departed with one of the laborers. There was a succession of servants, some of whom rejected, while some accepted, the attentions which "the master" had tried to force upon Florence Havies. How far the stories about Dougal's conduct during these four years are to be accepted as fact, and where they become legend and gossip, it is hard to say. There is no doubt that the master of Moat Farm got into serious legal complications with one or two of his maidservants.

Today if someone walking in the country happens upon a gentleman giving a girl a bicycle lesson, the girl wearing no clothes whatsoever, the intruder realizes that he has happened upon a colony of Nudists—and withdraws, pleased that this generation is one of so much purity. In the early 1900's we had not attained this state of idyllic innocence; there still existed people with evil minds. They thought that these goings-on within the precincts of Moat Farm were simply "not nice."

Mr. Dougal could not keep out of the courts. He sued his wife for divorce (apparently there were no oysters at hand) and he resisted a court order for the support of a child born to one of the servants. In 1902, when Miss Holland's yachting expedition had lasted for three years, there began to be unpleasant rumors. Why were her clothes still at Moat Farm? Where was she, anyhow? The local police and the Scotland Yarders began to consult and confer and to call upon Dougal. He received them genially and invited them to look about. They did so, and departed with the best of feeling all round.

Then a check for twenty-eight pounds, signed "Camille C. Holland," was shown to her nephew, who said that it was certainly not in his aunt's writing.

Mr. Dougal, after all his wanderings and his many

triumphs, was destined to begin the downward journey in a conspicuous place. While in London, partly for business and partly for pleasure, he called at the Bank of England to change some notes. They were notes for which the police were looking, and Dougal was arrested for forgery. On his way through the streets with a detective, he tried to bolt. Unluckily he chose a blind alley and was soon recaptured. When the police searched him they found in his pockets £564, seven rings, five watches, pins, brooches, a pawn ticket, two pairs of eyeglasses, and six moonstones, together with other things, like pens, knives, pipe and pouch, which a man usually carries. One of the rings was that belonging to Miss Holland's dead sweetheart.

Now for weeks the newspapers discussed "The Mystery of Moat Farm." The digging began. People began to see Miss Holland everywhere, and many innocent old ladies were annoyed. Wizards, clairvoyants, and dowsers told how to find the body. Dougal, from his cell threatened the Essex constable with a suit for damages: he did not like to have his grounds excavated and despoiled.

At last they found what remained of poor Miss Holland—hardly more than a skeleton, but clad in the garments which were recognized by the horrified Mrs. Wisken. Mr. Mold, the bootmaker, had no doubts of his handiwork. There lay the real owner of Moat Farm, where she had lain ever since that evening when Dougal had taken her out to drive, shot her, and buried her in the ditch.

Dougal denied everything, and carried on a lively correspondence with many ladies. Some of these were merely sympathetic friends; others had just cause to reproach him, but none of them seems to have done so. His top note was reached in a letter just before his trial:

I dare say the girls have received their notices to attend next Monday . . . have they not?

He referred to the trial. Then he continued:

There will be several from about there, and it would be a good idea to club together and hire a trap and drive all the way. It is a delightful drive through undulating country, and . . . would be a veritable treat for them all.

This sounds like a Sunday School picnic rather than a plan to attend a murder trial. When it is further realized that the accused man is laying out the programme and that the participants, or many of them, were the mothers or prospective mothers of his children, most of us will give up seeking for adjectives to describe Mr. S. Herbert Dougal.

The defense was that the body was not that of Miss Holland, or, if it was, perhaps she committed suicide and thoughtfully buried herself in the moat.

When Dougal had to make his final appeal to the king, he admitted the killing and said that it was accidental. But when at last he stood upon the trap, an officious chaplain twice called upon him to confess.

"Dougal, are you guilty or not guilty?"

The executioner waited for an instant, and in that instant Dougal turned his head to the chaplain and said: "Guilty!"

LEGENDS OF LIZZIE

IT OCCURRED to me, a few years ago, that one day I might write a book which should have nothing in it about Miss Lizzie Borden.

For a long time I nursed the daring idea, but had finally to realize that that day is still in the future.

If pushed into a corner on this subject, it is possible to urge two kinds of defense. One is that Miss Lizzie, of all the curious gallery of folk whose adventures I have investigated, seems to have the widest attraction.

After ten or twelve years, people continue to send me news of her, in song or story. From the eminent person who admitted that, if he chose, he could correct my grave blunders about her, to the English criminologist who loves to write about her exploits in what he quaintly terms the city of "River Fall", her devotees are many and various. They are all inclined to apply to her the hackneyed lines used in praise of Cleopatra: "Time does not wither . . ." etc. And so I venture to pass some of their stories along.

Moreover, one or two unrestrained admirers have assured me that except for my account of the case of Miss Borden, I would have done well never to set finger to typewriter key. To quote their flattery, verbatim, they said:

"That chapter of yours about that girl—what's her name?—Mary Borden—is the only thing you ever wrote that's worth a damn!"

This applause naturally encouraged me once more to set up my pulpit in Second Street, Fall River. Something else gave me the final impulse to relate some of the stories, mythical and true, which I have heard since Miss Borden's death, eight years ago.

This impulse came from the performance in New York of the play "Nine Pine Street", in which Miss Lillian Gish, (as "Effie Holden" of New Bedford, Massachusetts) depicted, with astonishing power, the great days in the life of Lizzie Borden.

The play received mild praise in most of the newspapers, and attracted audiences for about three weeks. Except for certain alterations, natural to the theatre, the story of the play followed many of the actual events of New England's extraordinary murder. The most painful variation from history was not that the dramatists gave Effie a suitor, (a young clergyman), nor that they caused Mr. Holden to marry his second wife *after* his daughters were grown-up. The really shocking thing was that the play adopted the dreadful heresy of allowing Effie to commit the first murder with a flat-iron, and the second with a loaded walking-stick, instead of using, for both murders, the canonical hatchet.

The two central acts, which were concerned with the murders, and the other events of that hot, August noonday, could (except for the *faux-pas* of the flat-iron) hardly have been improved. I cannot forget the picture as the Holden sisters, still in mourning for their mother's death, turned from their father, and their new and repulsive step-mother, and slowly ascended the stairs, their arms around each other. Their action implied that henceforth their father's house was, for them, possessed by the enemy: the scheming woman who had compassed their mother's death.

Everybody who saw the play will remember Miss Lillian Gish at the moment of the second murder. She had committed the first murder—in the manner of Greek tragedy—off-stage, and she now approached the parricide. Her father was dozing on the couch, as in the real tragedy of Fall River. The actress's sweet and gentle face, as she crept toward him with the heavy cane, became as venomous and implacable as that of the great murderous queen in the "Agamemnon", and the scene was suddenly filled with terror. The curtain descended before the creeping woman had raised her weapon.

It is, of course, the business of playwrights and actresses to present credible human beings. Miss Gish did this with Effie Holden. But the original of Effie Holden would be as incredible on the stage as she was everywhere. She had no such provocation as the dramatists were forced to give their fictitious heroine.

The actual Lizzie Borden of history was a plump and complacent person wearing rimless eye-glasses, a lady who liked to put on an apron and mess about with new recipes in the kitchen, who put up bird houses all around her garden, and like to go out with little-girl neighbors* and feed the squirrels, who loved sweet poems and novels—I think that the best-sellers of the nineties were exactly her meat: "Alice of Old Vincennes" and "When Knighthood Was in Flower"—who delighted to visit the Corcoran Art Gallery in Washington, who served as secretary of the Christian Endeavor Society, taught a Sunday-school class, belonged to a Fruit and Flower

* As, for instance, the one who became the distinguished author of "February Hill."

Mission and the Women's Christian Temperance Union, and presented one of her friends with a painting on porcelain entitled "Love's Dream."

Yet a majority of her townsfolk, as far as I can discover, believe that this gentle lady chopped her stepmother's head to bits with a hatchet; *waited for an hour and a half*, welcomed her father into the house, and then repeated the operation with him. And did all this, one summer's morn, on an empty stomach—except for half a cup of coffee and a few nibbles out of one side of a cookie.

The legal history of the Borden case began a long time ago: almost the same month that the sporting men in Boston were getting ready to travel down to New Orleans, all prepared to see John L. Sullivan beat Corbett—as, of course, he would. Its legal history has hardly ended, even now. Mr. Borden's only other heir, his second wife, died ninety minutes before he did, so, without the slightest trouble, his daughters, Miss Lizzie and Miss Emma, each inherited about one hundred and seventy-five thousand dollars.

That was supposed to be the object of the hatchet work. The sisters both died eight years ago, and distributed their estates, by will. There has been continued litigation over Miss Lizzie's will. The Animal Rescue League, and other charities, together with two or three private individuals, got their shares, but some details rumbled in the courts until lately and the executor had his bad moments, as long as he survived.

As for the history of the murders, what discoveries may not occur when the genial family now occupying the old "murder house" decide to pull it down, as, a few years ago, they pulled down the barn! At that time, some reporters happened along, and out of the crumbling rafters dragged a sort of hammer. By their literary skill, the reporters converted this into "the missing hatchet," and entertained their readers for weeks. The treasury of Bristol County was actually wheedled out of two hundred dollars to have this impossible weapon examined for bloodstains.

The legends about Miss Lizzie and her exploit are nearly as fascinating as the facts. Some have long vanished from memory and belief. It needed the excitement which instantly followed the murders to make anyone credit the stories of "wild-eyed" men and ruffians, who were to be seen a fortnight after the crime, haunting the environs of Fall River in broad daylight and flourishing hatchets, still dripping with hot blood. The tale of the "maniacal laugh" heard in the house that morning, and supposed to come from some frenzied unknown, is now recognized as a perversion of a much more interesting fact: Miss Lizzie really did stand at the head of the stairs, in sight of the body of her first victim, and utter a short laugh as her second victim, her father, entered the house of doom.

Nearly all experts and authorities upon the case who have emerged in recent years are now aware that it was the fanciful suggestion of amateur Sherlocks, and not a matter of history, that Miss Borden stripped herself quite naked before committing the murders—having foreseen that the police would examine her clothes for bloodstains.

One school of these writers, people who prefer never to discuss any event relating to New England without taking a crack at the Pilgrim Fathers and the Salem "witch-burners," have rejected this story of an early conversion to nudism, but only on the ground that Miss Lizzie, as an inhibited Puritan, beset by all the strict conventionalities, would have been too "prudish" to adopt such a sensible working costume. I can tell these gentlemen that they are right; the maidens of Massachusetts are *not* accustomed to undress before committing homicide. In fact, so rigid are their notions of propriety that a good many of them do not slaughter their parents at all, even when fully clothed.

One of the choicest bits of folklore goes back to a date prior to the murders. Miss Lizzie was then a bouncing schoolgirl, with a face rather heavy, not at all prepossessing; a little menacing, in fact. It is curious that at the age of thirty-two, when she was tried for murder, she had nearly lost this unpleasant appearance of her youth. At this earlier period, she had a school friend living in Hartford, and to her home she went upon a visit. The two girls, Lizzie and Blanche, shared the same room. Lizzie had not changed her first name to Lizbeth, as she did later, in the Fall River telephone book.

One morning, Miss Lizzie came down alone to breakfast, and the meal began without waiting for the daughter of the house. After a little, one of the family mildly inquired:

"I wonder where Blanche can be?"

At this, Miss Lizzie looked up from her stewed prunes, and in the manner of one glad to enlighten, replied:

"Oh, I forgot to tell you. Blanche died during the night."

These Hartfordians seem to have been an impassive and taciturn group, but this news did jog them a little out of the regular morning routine. Some of the more excitable members of the family actually went upstairs to investigate. Miss Lizzie was right; there was Blanche, and, sure enough, she was dead.

They talked it over a little among themselves, as

people will, and agreed that it was odd. The doctor came, glanced at the girl, and said:

"Oh, heart failure, I suppose."

Then the family, not wishing their guest's holidays to suffer, invited Miss Lizzie to stay for the funeral. Said she:

"Aren't you going to read the will?"

They froze a trifle and someone said:

"Why,—no. Is that the custom in Fall River?"

"It certainly is," briskly replied the guest.

"It isn't, here. We read the will *after* the funeral."

"Oh, all right," said Miss Lizzie, pettishly; "I'll stay."

So, the day after the burial rites, the testament of Miss Blanche was produced. It only caused more trouble, because Miss Borden flatly accused the family of suppressing the true will. She said that she and Blanche had each made a will in the other's favor, and that she was named in Blanche's will as sole beneficiary. The family thought that this conduct was "most unfeeling," and they persisted that, as far as they were concerned, there had been absolutely no hocus-pocus.

Their little guest from Fall River departed in a huff, and "it was not until years afterwards" (so runs the tale), when she was being tried for murder, that they recalled the incident. Then they did wish that old Dr. Dibble had been a little less casual in determining the cause of the death of Blanche.

There is another version of this engaging yarn. The scene was Fall River. The victim now, was an invalid named Bessie—daughter of a neighbor. Miss Lizzie was in the habit of calling to "sit" with the girl. At last, however, after one of these sittings, Bessie was found dead, with marks of strangulation on her throat. When things belonging to her were found in Miss Lizzie's possession, uncharitable suspicions were entertained.

At a dinner in Fall River where this macabre tale was told, someone asked why no action was taken. The reply was:

"Oh, they knew that Bessie had an incurable disease anyhow, and, naturally, no one wanted to incriminate Lizzie."

It should be said, by the way, that for preposterous stories about the Borden murders, there is no place like Fall River. The belief is still nourished there that three days before the murders, Miss Borden wrote to some friends in Fairhaven that she had a fine, new axe, and that she was having a lovely time whetting it. This story, shortly after the murders, was investigated, and exploded. I have seen District Attorney Knowlton's letter in which he says that no such message was written or received.

It is in Fall River that the story is repeated that when the neighbors arrived and beheld the body of Mr. Borden, weltering in his blood, someone sent for a sheet to cover the dreadful form. No one up to that moment had remembered Mrs. Borden, or considered that she also might be slain. So far, the tale is in keeping with known facts. But when the servant was ordered to go after the sheet, the legendary story begins. According to this, Miss Lizzie, hearing the order for *one* sheet, piped up:

"Better make it two!"

A laborious theory has reached me from a person in high place, who is related by marriage to the Bordens. He graciously acquainted me with what is called "the family view" of the crime. It is that not Miss Lizzie but her sister, Miss Emma Borden, was the guilty one.

Miss Emma, ten years her sister's senior, was in Fairhaven on the day of the murders. The new theory rests on the belief that there was a conspiracy between the sisters, both of whom wished to keep the stepmother from inheriting their father's property. Up to this point, it is all probable.

But the further idea was that Miss Lizzie stayed at home, since *she* could clear herself of suspicion. It is not explained why they were sure of this—for she utterly failed to clear herself of suspicion. And Miss Emma, pretending to be in Fairhaven, really slipped away early on that August morning, with the hatchet in her little reticule. She came unseen to Fall River, walked to the family home, undiscovered, though she traversed a street of lynx-eyed neighbors, killed the victims, unobserved by the servant, and went back to Fairhaven, still undetected and invisible.

This theory depends on the notion that the police did not investigate Miss Emma's alibi and satisfy themselves that she had not left Fairhaven. Such a notion is untenable. The police work on this case was, at any rate, painstaking.

A certain peculiarity of what is flatteringly called the human mind, is always to be discovered in the history of any notorious crime. The very people who loftily discard every conclusion which has been weighed, tested and established in open Court, are the ones who willingly swallow any bit of rumor or gossip, so long as it rests on hearsay and backstairs tattle. They almost seem to announce:

"Give me a big, gaudy lie and I'll believe it; but as for proven facts, I simply despise 'em!'"

Why anyone should reject the claims of the sister who had every opportunity, and nominate as murderess the one for whom it would have been fantastically difficult, is hard to see. But it is also true that many persons who credulously repeat all sorts of rumors seem to be unaware that one damning fact rests not on gossip but on the sworn testimony of three reputable witnesses. And this is that Miss Lizzie, the day before the murders, went into a pharmacy not far from her home and tried to buy prussic acid.

A lady who knew Miss Borden for many years assures me that she was timid, shrinking, and quite lacking in initiative or adventure. Yet she also tells me of a week-long house-party, for an entire theatrical troupe. Miss Borden hired the house, paid expenses for the party, and attended it herself, because of her admiration for the leading lady. Surely, that is a departure from the traditional shyness of the New England spinster.

Was she quite without rancor or venom? One informant tells me that she was. Another, entirely deserving credence, tells me a story of Mr. Justice Moody, of the United States Supreme Court. Mr. Moody, before going on the bench, was assistant prosecutor in the case of Commonwealth vs. Lizzie A. Borden. After the trial was over, and Miss Borden had been acquitted, amid the ecstatic cheers of all the agitators for "Women's Rights," Mr. Moody one day received a package by mail. It was from Miss Borden, and contained copies of all the official photographs in the case—including the gruesome pictures of the dead victims. A note accompanied the gift, in which Miss Lizzie said that she thought that Mr. Moody might like to have these pictures, "as souvenirs of an interesting occasion."

One more story—undoubted fact. It comes from a friendly source, that is, from a believer in Miss Lizzie's innocence of murder. The teller of the tale was a witness to the incident. Miss Lizzie, some years after her acquittal, visited two sisters who owned a farm in the country. In her presence, these ladies always avoided unpleasant topics of conversation. For instance, keeping in mind the ancient precept of courtesy that in a family in which someone has been hanged, one does not speak of ropes, the two ladies always were careful to say nothing about axes or hatchets. Although the Borden murders were undoubtedly committed with a small hatchet, the word "axe" got into the case—probably because of the popular rhyme:

> *Lizzie Borden took an axe*
> *And gave her Mother forty whacks—*

As Miss Borden and her hostesses walked about the farm, one of the sisters pointed to an old shed, tumbledown and decayed.

"Look at that wreck," said she. "Tomorrow I'll have Mike pull it down and cart it off."

Miss Lizzie's sudden and enthusiastic response made them gasp. She exclaimed:

"You don't need to get Mike to do it. I could do it now. Gimme the axe!"

TABLOIDS called them "The Murder Trust," but to a careless observer they were a group of scrubby-looking young men who used to meet at Tony Marino's. Actually, they did possess distinction which merits a title of some kind.

There was Tony Marino himself, Dan Kreisberg, Harry Green, a taxi-driver; and Joe Murphy, formerly in the scientific line, but now acting as bartender for Tony. Then there was Frank Pasqua, who, although only twenty-four, was already known as proprietor of what my social correspondents tell me were "the most luxurious funeral parlors" on East 117th Street.

Two or three nationalities were represented in the little coterie, and although the oldest man of all—Kreisberg—was only twenty-nine, they had a variety of knowledge and experience. When they were together, intellect played upon intellect; one mind would strike another, as flint strikes against steel, and there was sure to be an interchange of thought—of original, suggestive thought. Provocative—that's what it was. There was good talk at the old Mermaid Tavern, and there was conversation worth hearing at Tony Marino's in the winter evenings.

Marino's speakeasy, at 3804 Third Avenue, was a quiet

sort of place, where everything went along in the same old rut. Aside from the murder of a fellow called Tough Tony Bastone, nothing happened for a long time. Why he was murdered does not appear in the record of this case, and I doubt if we need go into it. If a man allows himself to be called Tough Tony, it is apt to incite some of his friends.

"Tough, are you? Well, are you tough enough to take *that*?"

Perhaps the somber and rather refined atmosphere of the speak was due to the loss of one of its bright figures—Betty Carlsen, the blonde sweetheart of the proprietor.

Some time in the spring—May, I believe—Miss Carlsen died, and was buried in Washington. The medical examiner certified alcoholism and pneumonia as the causes, and this is not disputed. However, if (as ill-natured Bronx gossip insists) the first of these was mere temporary insensibility, and if it was treated by stripping the patient naked, leaving her in a room with all the windows open, and, further, throwing cold water over her, then the pneumonia was, as one might say, superinduced.

It is further alleged that there was a prompt collection of $800 life insurance, which went to Marino or some of his colleagues.

Time flits fast in the Bronx, and things that happened back in the spring of 1932 are hopelessly lost in the mists of iniquity. No one can say whether Betty Carlsen's death was the first of a series, or whether it belonged to a series at all. Old residents sit, during the early autumn afternoons, in the pleasant surroundings of Crotona Park and refresh their eyes with the sight of the beds of scarlet cannas. But they refuse to discuss events prior to December of that year.

In that month, by every sign, there was an important

conference at Tony's. The boys wanted to talk life insurance. The subject has a perpetual fascination. So long as insurance companies offer to bet hundreds, perhaps thousands, of dollars that this man, or that, will *not* die, there are sure to be sportsmen to arise and say,

"We'll take some of that."

The police, the district attorney, and a grand jury all asserted that Tony's friends went into life insurance in a very practical way.

Peering about for a prospect, the associates were delighted by Michael Malloy, an old customer of Tony's. His thirst was immense, but his buying ability limited, and he often had to wait late and long to be treated. He was about forty, he had been a stationary fireman, but now he was merely stationary—at the bar.

"He looks all in," mused Tony. "He ain't got much longer to go, anyhow. The stuff is gettin' him."

The brethren listened with respect to this diagnosis of their leader, and their eyes brightened as they looked out from the back room. You see they were all specialists in their different ways. Tony was a general business executive, with advanced knowledge as to the difference between an ordinary souse and someone in the last stages of delirium tremens. Harry Green, the taxi-driver, had a good topographical knowledge of the region and could act as chief of transportation. Murphy, who had formerly rated as a chemist and was now bartender, might be expected to advise on toxicology. Pasqua's profession, as an undertaker, was just too good to be true, while Kreisberg was not only a consultant but a practical field-worker in robbery and assault. Perhaps never were there so many experts to concentrate upon one middle-aged, debilitated stationary fireman.

The first thing was to get Malloy properly insured. You are not supposed, so I understand, to insure people behind their backs—at least, not for large sums. But they got an $800 policy from the Metropolitan Life, and two, for $494 each, from the Prudential. This made Malloy worth $1,788, but there were double indemnities in case of death by accident.

"*In case* of accident!" said they, with solemn stateliness, that evening as they honored the toast and set their glasses down.

"In case!"

Then the toxicologist was told to shoot the works.

When the tide began to flow, what did Malloy think? Perhaps he decided he was already dead and in Paradise. For in the speakeasy where he had hitherto been doled out drinks on a severely cash basis, the highballs began to roll on the ground. It was:

"Fill her up again, old-timer!"

"Take another, with the boss' compliments!"

"Sure—on the house; this'll do yer good!"

In two or three days, aside from a crick in his elbows from working both arms too fast, Malloy was blooming like a daffodil. He looked ten years younger. And the boss realized that this business was ruinous. Orders were issued to the dispenser, and the Killing of Michael Malloy —as this great saga of the Bronx will be known in the future—entered upon its legendary, its mythical phase. What they gave him to drink depends upon which old gossip you talk with. Tales are told of pints of wood alcohol tossed off, with another on the hip, to take home. You may believe, if you care to, that turpentine and horse liniment were quaffed with the gusto which ought to greet Berncastler Doktor and Romanée Conti.

After a carouse of this incredible nature, Malloy would stagger out into the night. Next day, around noon, the associates would gather, with a sheaf of newspapers, and strain their eyes looking for something like this:

"Elderly Man Found in Street, Thought to Have Been Struck by Lightning."

But the door would open and Malloy would walk in, chirping like a cricket. He would give Murphy his regular sign, and remark genially:

"Boy! Ain't I got a thirst?"

By the last of January, the little group were becoming pessimistic. There were signs of mutiny and disaffection, and a general demand for a balancing of the budget. As one influential member said:

"What's this guy woit'? He's woit' seventeen hunderd, ain't he? An' what's my cut? Two or t'ree lousy hunderds! An' look at this time an' trouble an' frettin' meself sick over him. Already, I'm in the hole on this boid!"

Everyone agreed. Some members were suffering headaches and eyestrain from too close application to the newspapers—reading the death notices, in hope of good news. The undertaker had his throat bound up in flannel and could speak only in a croak. He took the gloomiest view of himself and thought that he was probably in for the flu and early death. And it was all contracted in performance of duty. Four nights earlier, he and the taximan had waited until Malloy was comatose, then taken him to a suitable spot near the Zoo—not far from the yaks' corral—removed his coat and shirt, poured cold water over him, and left him there. It was in the course of this operation—on a raw night, in a storm of sleet—that the undertaker had caught tonsillitis.

All to have Malloy arrive, next day, with the remark:

"Gimme some of th' old regular, me lad! Say, th' coverlid slipped down last night. I got a wee chill. Ah, these head-colds; you better look after 'em, I'm tellin' you. . . . What say to another shot of th' same?"

At their next meeting, the chemist-barkeeper would naturally have been the one to suggest trying "pee-toe-maines."

"What's them?" somebody asked.

"They're things that get into spoiled food, an' make yer sicker'n blue hell. If you get the right dose, you never come back."

So a box of sardines was opened and left around, until the most skeptical had to admit that they were spoiled. But when the executive committee looked at them, no one could see any pee-toe-maines. The workers were not in the mood, anyhow, for piffling measures, so they chopped the cover of the sardine tin into fine bits, added a few carpet tacks, mixed these with sardine hash, and constructed sandwiches.

But, exactly like Rasputin when the Russian aristocrats gave him poisoned cake, Mr. Malloy came up hankering for more.

"Appetizin'," he murmured, as he washed the sandwiches down with a pint of whatever kind of deadly nightshade he was being served at the time.

Shortly after midnight, on January 30, a patrolman found Malloy at the corner of Baychester Avenue and Gun Hill Road. The police say he had been put in the middle of the road—standing or lying—and then run down by Green's taxi. At the hospital, he was found to be suffering from concussion of the brain, perhaps a fractured skull, and certainly a broken shoulder. In addition to "alcoholism."

Tony and the boys read the papers for a week. At the end of the week, Malloy entered the speakeasy, with the first protest they had heard him utter. It was:

"I'm dying for a drink!"

You see, at the hospital, they hadn't given him any real man's beverage. Only milk and cocoa, and that kind of muck.

Evidently, the Tony Marino Association had picked a person who, for invulnerability, made Achilles look like a water lily. What they needed was an understudy, some-body who would be responsive to their attentions. They found a man—the police, at last accounts, did not know his name—and put a card in his pocket with the name of Nicholas Mellory, which was what they had called Mal-loy in the insurance policies. Then they ran this substitute down with the taxi; ran him down once, and were about to do it again when some other motorist happened along and scared them away. The substitute recovered from his injuries in the Lincoln Hospital.

The insurance club had now ceased to be interested in money. Professionalism was a thing of the past; they wanted to play the game for its own sake. Some statisticians reckon that they spent $1,875.31 on a $1,788 man. They offered two men—McNally and Salone—at first, $200, then $400, to run Malloy down with a car. This was refused.

On Washington's Birthday, Malloy was put to bed in a room on Fulton Avenue. He was no drunker than usual, simply insensible. A rubber tube, connected with a gas-tap, was placed in his mouth. And in the morning, Mr. Pasqua, the undertaker, was called in. His first step was to "contact" a doctor in the matter of the death cer-tificate.

The physician certified death by pneumonia. And for this service it was alleged—and denied—that he received $100. At any rate, it was unfortunate for the doctor, who was indicted as accessory after the fact. As he is an ex-alderman, it is satisfactory to know that he left the court without a stain.

Mr. Murphy, the ex-chemist, succeeded in collecting $800 insurance. Agents came around to press still more upon him, but he could not be found, and his friends were reticent with his address. This, as it turned out, was because he was in jail. And it made the police inquire about Malloy's death, and find that a number of his entertainers were already locked up on various charges. Green for carrying a gun, Kreisberg on account of a holdup, and Murphy as a material witness in the old, old murder of Tough Tony Bastone. And so, in the Bronx County Courthouse, they were all tried for killing Malloy.

And, in the end, the State imposed the gravest penalty of the law on two or three of the associates—merely for killing a $1700 man.

Michael Malloy, the all-but-indestructible, was called as a witness. They found him twelve feet deep, in a dismal part of Ferncliffe Cemetery, out in Westchester. Although Mr. Pasqua had rendered a bill for $400 for his services, the attentions which poor old Malloy had received did no credit to the most luxurious funeral parlors on East 117th Street. The unconscious object of plots which would have fatigued the Borgias had been put in a $10 coffin and smuggled below ground in a charity grave which cost $12. He had died from illuminating gas, not from the cause named in the certificate, and he bore the scars of his taxi "accident."

Only in one respect did his pursuers seem to give him

a kindly thought. In the Indian fashion, as if for comfort on the voyage to the happy hunting grounds, they had left a small plug of tobacco in his trousers pocket. But it may be doubted if even this was an act of grace. Just an oversight.

FOUR
INFAMOUS NAMES

I. JACK THE RIPPER

A QUEER thing about the most celebrated murderer in the world: nobody knows his name. To the questions, who was he? how many people did he kill? why did he kill them? what happened to him in the end? only one answer can be given.

And it is that we do not know.

It sounds grotesque, but there is no certain legal evidence as to the murderer's sex. Man or woman—we have no positive knowledge.

Someone, probably a newspaper writer, invented the killer's notorious nickname: Jack the Ripper. In the black hours before dawn, he hideously slaughtered at least five forlorn women. People still remember, with shuddering horror, those foggy autumn days and nights in London, and the bellowing newsboys:

"Another horrible murder! Murder! Mutilation! Murder!"

Jack the Ripper is a perpetual topic of interest, forever coming up in the newspapers. The stolen child, Charley Ross, is always good for an item in the American press, but the fame of the Ripper is international. Wedekind put him in a play. Most readers of fiction know that somber novel *The Lodger*, by Marie Belloc-Lowndes, which Lord Haldane is said to have reread every year. Probably he did this because the novelist regarded murder as a dignified subject, and surrounded it with terror, instead of treating it as a trivial puzzle.

No one who writes about the Ripper agrees entirely with anyone else. For their failure to catch the murderer, the London police were bitterly and unfairly attacked. England was shocked by the mere existence of such a monster, so the London journalists, with patriotic impulse, seized every pretext to attribute Jack the Ripper to some other country.

The number of murders committed, and the length of time the murderer was at work, vary in each account. Conservative writers say the five crimes began with the killing of Mary Ann Nicholls, on the night of August 31, 1888, and ended nine weeks later, with the frightful slaughter of Mary Jeanette Kelly.

The victims were street-walkers, of the most degraded class. At first, the murders took place outdoors: it was easy for a man to lure one of these destitute women into an alley or court of the kind then so plentiful in the London slums. There, in the dark shadows, he would cut her throat with a knife, and indulge his mania for other mutilations of the body, which increased as the murders went on.

Nicholls was found lying across the gutter. She had been slashed with a long-handled knife, wielded by a person with "a rough anatomical knowledge," since he attacked all the vital parts. No part of the body, however, was missing.

A week later, Annie Chapman was found in a backyard, with her head nearly cut off. More than a dozen persons, within earshot, had heard nothing. Jack the Ripper had carried out further mutilations, so that "a certain organ," as the papers described it, had been abstracted. He had taken two brass rings from her fingers, a few coppers and trinkets from her pocket, and carefully laid them in a row at her feet.

The next victim was a local celebrity known as Long Liz. Her real name was Elizabeth Stride. The Ripper was interrupted in his work by a man who drove a pony cart into the yard. The pony shied as he entered the yard—probably at Jack the Ripper, who was in a dark corner behind the gate. When the driver of the cart jumped down and lifted the woman's head, the blood was still pouring from her throat.

This interruption annoyed the Ripper, so that he went forth and, within an hour, lured Catherine Eddowes into a lonely alley. Here, he was able to proceed at leisure. After the throat-cutting, he extracted the left kidney, and "another organ"—presumably an ovary—nicked the lower eyelids of the dead woman, tore off part of her apron, and wiped his hands and knife on it.

Jeanette Kelly was the only one killed indoors; she was also the only one possessed of youth and any pretense to good looks. She lived with a man named Barnet in a squalid place called Miller's Court. Mr. Barnet had approved her conduct, as that of a prostitute who was "straight and decent." But she had tried his patience, departing from the paths of straightness and decency, and bringing home, to sleep with her, "an immoral woman." So the puritanical Barnet had left her to her sins.

On the night of her death, Kelly had been heard, by someone in the house, singing "Sweet Violets." At what time she admitted her murderer is not known, but the crime was undiscovered until the next morning, when people looked into her room through the window. A

Scotland Yard official, Sir Melville Macnaghten, an old Etonian, and therefore not given to overstatement, says:

"The operator must have been at least two hours over his hellish job. A fire was burning low in the room, but neither candles nor gas were there. The madman made a bonfire of some old newspapers, and of his victim's clothes, and by this dim irreligious light, a scene was enacted which nothing witnessed by Dante, in his visit to the infernal regions, could have surpassed."

Her naked body, or what remained of it, was lying on the bed. The murderer had cut her throat, opened the body, and removed most of the internal organs, which he distributed here and there about the room. He had also cut off her nose and ears. In this case, however, he had carried away with him no part of the body, which damages the theory that these crimes were committed for the purpose of collecting anatomical specimens.

The Ripper took many chances, and always slipped through the hands of the police. Many persons were detained; the papers talked about a Polish Jew, an American sailor, a Russian doctor, and anyone, so long as he did not "remain an Englishman." Someone with "a knowledge of surgery," or someone else with "a houseful of big knives" was always under suspicion.

Mr. Leonard Matters, a journalist, has investigated the facts with great patience and intelligence, adventuring afterwards into what appears to be sheer fiction, with a story about "the satanic Dr. Stanley." This diabolical physician is supposed to have died in Buenos Aires, making a "deathbed confession" that he was Jack the Ripper.

The "deathbed confession" bears about the same relation to the facts of criminology as the exploits of Peter Rabbit and Jerry Muskrat do to zoölogy.

Four years after the Ripper murders, a Dr. Neill Cream

was hanged in London for poisoning four women. As he stood upon the drop, so runs the alluring tale, he started to speak. The executioner's hand was on the lever. The doctor said:

"I am Jack the ——"

But, at this moment, the lever was pulled and the body shot down.

Unfortunately, one of those tiresome devotees to truth looked into Dr. Cream's history and found that he was in prison in Illinois, throughout the period of the Ripper murders. That wise and humane Governor of Illinois who commuted Cream's life-sentence—with the result that the convict went out and committed four more murders—had not yet performed his beneficent act of clemency. And a man cannot cut women's throats in London if he is behind the bars in Joliet—no matter how "sinister" he may be.

Now, in our own time, comes a distinguished investigator of crime, Mr. H. L. Adam, with something better than guesses and gossip. He has made public a number of interesting parallels between the career of Jack the Ripper and a known man.

One day, shortly after King Edward had ascended the throne, Inspector Godley of Scotland Yard arrested a London innkeeper—a man who called himself George Chapman. This publican had a dark and ferocious mustache, and a career which matched the mustache. He was wanted for murder by poison.

Inspector Godley and Inspector Abberline had spent months and years in the pursuit of Jack the Ripper, and although that case was thought to be closed, Abberline now greeted his assistant with the words:

"You've got Jack the Ripper at last!"

For the moment, however, they were engaged in un-

covering the series of offenses which Chapman had committed under his own name—no, not his own name, for
that, as they soon learned, was Severin Klosowski. This
man had been born in Poland. He came to London, at
the age of twenty-three, and worked as a barber. He married a girl from his own country, and after a time went
with her to America. He tried barbering in Jersey City,
but in about a year they returned to London.

He spent the next ten years as a barber, as shopkeeper,
and finally as tavern-keeper. What concerned the police
were his "marriages" with Annie Chapman (whose last
name he assumed), with Mrs. Shadrach Spink, with Bessie
Taylor and with Maud Marsh. Curiously enough, one of
the Ripper victims was also named Annie Chapman.
These ladies were profitable to him, either because he
took over their savings, or because he made them work as
barmaids. At least three of them died, painfully and mys-
teriously, by poison. Finally, the doctors began to think
something might be wrong, so Chapman was put on trial
for the murder of Miss Marsh.

He wrote complaining that he was being "unjustly
criticised and falsly Represented," and added that he was
"an American orphend of good family"—which he certainly was not. Let us consider what Chapman had in
common with Jack the Ripper.

1. It is pretty well established that Jack the Ripper had
a knowledge of anatomy, and some degree of surgical
skill. Chapman had been assistant surgeon in a Polish
hospital.

2. The Ripper murders began in 1888, in the Whitechapel district. That was the year of Chapman's arrival
in London, and the place of his residence. His wife of
that period was still living at the time of his arrest for the
later murders—the poisonings. She remembered the Rip-

per murders, and told the detectives that at that time her husband was often out until 3 or 4 in the morning—for what purpose, she did not know.

3. The messages received by the police, and supposed to be from the Ripper, contained "Americanisms," as well as certain bits of gruesome humor. Chapman was addicted to both. In comment on this it may be said that the "Americanisms" (in the opinion of the London journalists) were the use of the word "boss"—he began his letters "Dear Boss"; and other phrases like "just for jolly" as in "next time I shall clip the lady's ears off and send to the police just for jolly." To one officer he sent part of a human kidney, remarking that he had fried and eaten the other part.

4. The Ripper murders ceased in London in 1891 and '92. Chapman was then in America, where similar murders took place "in the locality of Jersey City."

5. The only reliable description of the Ripper came from someone who saw Kelly in company with the creature who probably murdered her. It was of a man thirty-four or thirty-five years old, five feet six inches tall, of a dark complexion, with a dark mustache turned up at the ends. This is a good description of Chapman, who always looked older than his years.

Of these points, the only one which I believe fails altogether, is that of the letters and their "Americanisms." London journalists are not on sure grounds when they discuss American slang. But whether the messages received at the time came from the Ripper, or not (and it is now pretty generally agreed that they did not), they were surely *not* written by Chapman. One of them was reproduced in the *Daily Telegraph*. Handwriting, spelling and grammar are all beyond the powers of that grotesque Polander, as exhibited in his authentic epistles.

As to the Ripper murders in America, they have passed into the creed of the English writers. After a number of attempts, I have found only one which resembles the Whitechapel crimes. The slaying of a wretched woman, "Old Shakespeare," in a water-front hotel in New York, in April, 1891, was greeted by New York papers with the query: "Has Jack the Ripper arrived?" For this crime an Algerian, called "Frenchy," was convicted. He was found insane, but after ten years was released, and sent back to Europe or Africa. As to Chapman, it can only be said that he was living in Jersey City at the time.

The other parallels between Chapman and the Ripper remain unshaken. The one great likeness between them is that they were both addicted to the secret, senseless and cruel murder of unoffending women. The great difference between them is in their methods. Would the monster who raged through Whitechapel, with his great knife, like a Malay running amuck, afterwards content himself with stealthy poisonings? The probable answer is no; and this difference between the Ripper and Chapman seems to me practically destructive of the theory that they were the same.

Whatever your decision as to Chapman's identity with the Ripper, it is academic. The murder of Miss Marsh was sufficient, and upon Chapman has been executed the utmost penalty of the law.

II. CHARLEY PEACE

IN QUEEN VICTORIA'S glorious days, when Mr. Gladstone and Mr. Disraeli were rival statesmen, there might have appeared in a London newspaper, an advertisement like this:

CHARLES PEACE

Retired Murderer

England's Leading Burglar

Mr. Peace wishes to inform his friends that he is established in Peckham, where he is living respectably by day & nefariously by night. Houses stealthily entered & looted. Mr. Peace carries arms & never hesitates to kill policemen. In addition to his nocturnal pursuits, he practises many other arts of Peace: viz., the writing of epitaphs & mortuary verse; mechanical inventions of all kinds; solos on the one-stringed fiddle. He is accomplished in public recitations, having given the grave-digging scene from *Hamlet* before some of England's public schools. He is also skilled in methods of escape & of disguise, being able to change his appearance by facial contortion & thus hoodwink the police.

No such advertisement appeared, since it was never a part of Peace's plan to attract attention. But he had a sardonic vein, which might have made him enjoy seeing such a thing in print. It is all quite true.

For two generations of Englishmen, Charley has been the master criminal; the Dick Turpin of the nineteenth century. His name is as well known in the British Empire as Jesse James's in America. He was a murderous thief; a lying, lecherous ruffian; a brutal killer when his opponent was unarmed; a sniveling, sanctimonious fraud when he

149

faced a Judge in Court. In short, the typical criminal of all times and all countries.

Nevertheless, he had qualities which for fifty years have delighted England's literary men, and caused both Sherlock Holmes and Raffles to regard him with affection. The irony of the name, Charley Peace, gave him a start over all his fellow criminals. I am compelled to admit that America has had nobody like him. He is a grotesque out of a Dickens novel, and, by comparison, Jesse James was a machine-made desperado by some hack-writer of "Westerns"; while John Dillinger was the crude modern product of the cinema.

Peace, characteristically, was born in a place called Angel Court (in Sheffield) and for a time followed his father's profession of lion-tamer. He soon branched out into a pleasing variety of trades. On the legal side, he was a peddler, a skilled wood-carver and picture-framer, and the inventor of gadgets like folding ladders and artificial fingers. At the same time he practiced the humble calling of pickpocket, sneak-thief and porch climber.

His rise from such petty beginnings to the proud eminence of Britain's premier housebreaker was not meteoric. The path was long and thorny. Between his twentieth and forty-fifth years he must have spent more than half his time in jail; there were few of England's prisons in which he had not done a stretch.

As with many notable persons, Peace's great period was short. It began in 1877, when he was about forty-five. He had committed two incidental murders, and these returned to plague him. He nicely exemplified De Quincey's precept that "many a man has dated his ruin from some murder or other, that perhaps he thought little of at the time." The second of these murders is beyond question; about the first there is some mystery.

In August, '76, somebody was burglarizing a house in
Whalley Range, near Manchester. An energetic policeman, named Nicholas Cock, tried to interfere, but was
shot and killed. For this murder, two brothers named
Habron were tried, with the result that one of them was
convicted and sentenced to death, but was finally sent to
prison for life. One of the spectators at the trial was
Charles Peace, who, two or three years later, and under
queer circumstances, confessed that he, and not Habron,
had killed Policeman Cock. I think that the confession is
a trifle dubious, but such a murder was quite in character
for Peace, and the Government, having been uneasy
about Habron, willingly seized the opportunity to pardon him, and give him £800.

The other murder was not done in the practice of his
profession but as the result of an *amour*. Charley's love-
life was extensive and picturesque; he succeeded in ac-
quiring one wife and a strange assortment of doxies,
concubines and fancy girls. Men who were comely of
face and irreproachable in character were amazed at the
ease with which this old gargoyle, who was forever in
and out of jail, led a troupe of women at his heels.

His legal mate was a widow, one Mrs. Ward, with a
son named Willie. As Mrs. Peace, she had two more children, and it was the death of one of them, little John
Charles, which caused Peace to write one of his best
elegies. As he was then in prison, he never saw his son,
but from his cell he lamented:

> *Farewell, my dear son, by us all beloved,*
> *Thou art gone to dwell in the mansions above,*
> *In the bosom of Jesus who sits on the throne,*
> *Thou art anxiously waiting to welcome us home.*

Some of the orthodox among Charley's biographers have suggested that little John Charles had a long wait.

Living, for a while, in Banner Cross Terrace, Sheffield, Peace had for neighbors a Mr. and Mrs. Dyson. Mrs. Dyson, who was an Irish woman of about twenty-five years, was "buxom and blooming." Peace asserted that she was one of his conquests; Mrs. Dyson insisted that their relations were proper, and restricted to such incidents as her acceptance of a small ring, and being photographed with Peace at a fair. She denied that she frequented a public house called the "Yorkshire Stingo," or that she had been drunk at the "Halfway House." She might have been "slightly inebriated." The extent of Peace's love affair with Mrs. Dyson is not important; there is no doubt that, as a neighbor, he was a perfect nuisance, cordially disliked by Mr. Dyson.

In a back-yard squabble, one evening, Charles Peace shot and killed Mr. Dyson, climbed over a wall and disappeared. Known henceforth as "The Banner Cross murderer," Peace vanished from sight.

He was now under the ignominy of using an alias, and the necessity of going in disguise. With this double handicap, he was nevertheless about to enter upon his golden years.

In a semi-detached villa in Evelina Road, Peckham, there was established a household which, I suspect, had much to do with starting that legend about the lives of middle-class families in semi-detached villas, to which English writers have devoted so much satire.

The basement rooms were occupied by "Mrs. Ward" and her son Willie. Mrs. Ward was really Mrs. Charles Peace. The apartments upstairs were devoted to the mas-

ter of the house, "Mr. Thompson," and a woman friend
of his. This lady was presented, of course, when the
curate called, as Mrs. Thompson. That the curate did call
there can be no doubt, since Mr. Thompson regularly
attended Sunday evening services. Mrs. Thompson's real
name was Susan Grey, although she had often been
known as Mrs. Bailey. She was rather a pretty woman,
with fair hair and brown eyes, but with two unfortunate
failings. As the man who knew her best remarked:

"She is a dreadful woman for drink and snuff; she
snuffs half an ounce a day; and as for drink I have paid
as much as £3 in two days for her."

In "Mr. Thompson," who described himself sometimes as a dealer in musical instruments, and sometimes as
"a gentleman of independent means with a taste for scientific inventions," few of his friends and none of the
police would be likely to recognize Charley Peace. He
had shaved off his white beard, dyed his hair, darkened
his face with walnut juice, and put on spectacles. On occasion, he would appear in the street in the full glory of
black coat, top hat, velvet waistcoat, with a walking-
stick, gloves, and a fox terrier. Usually, however, he preferred not to assume the guise of a youthful gallant, but
to pose as the genial, elderly buffer. This was easy for
him, as he always seemed to be far older than his years.

The "Thompsons" entertained the socially desirable
of Peckham at evening musicales. The refining influence
of domestic pets was not lacking since Peace kept cats,
dogs, rabbits, guinea pigs, canaries, parrots and cockatoos.
The ladies sang and played the piano, while Charley performed on the violin, or entertained with anecdotes and
recitations.

The Russo-Turkish War was going on, and Mr. Peace,

an ardent pacifist, often discoursed, eloquently, about war as proof of the failure of civilization.

After the musicale was over, and the guests had gone, after Mrs. Thompson had been found to be secure in the house, and not dangerously wandering abroad, convivial and talkative, the villa would appear to be plunged in virtuous slumber. In fact, the real work was beginning.

When midnight approached, Peace harnessed Tommy, his pony, into the trap, and set out on his nocturnal business. With a good set of burglar's tools in a violin case, and a revolver in his pocket, this pious Sunday evening churchgoer set out to crack some crib.

For nearly two years the solitary burglar plundered houses in the suburbs of South London. Sometimes he went as far away as Portsmouth and Southampton. Wanted, all this time, for the murder at Banner Cross, he created terror throughout a wide district, and earned a reputation which nobody has ever surpassed. In the value of the loot, by modern American standards, the hauls were not great. It was the persistence, the daring and the ingenuity of the raids which attracted admiration. Peace was no bad gymnast: he had a Houdini-like ability to squeeze through narrow spaces and twist out of policemen's hands. He could distort his face and defeat identification. And his mechanical skill made locks and bolts fly open.

One moonlight night, in the garden of a substantial house in Blackheath, Peace had the bad luck to encounter a dauntless bobby, named Edward Robinson. Peace began to shoot, but Robinson ran in, despite a bullet through his arm, and presently had the burglar on the ground, where he held him till other officers came. At the station, they had no idea what a rare bird was in their hands.

It is in dispute whether it was Mrs. Thompson, "the traitress Sue," who gave away his identity, but soon he was on trial as John Ward, *alias* Charles Peace, for attempting to murder Policeman Robinson. For this crime he was sentenced to prison for life—a rather superfluous proceeding, since he was still to be tried for the murder of Mr. Dyson.

He made one more dramatic escape, wriggling out of a policeman's grasp, and jumping out of a train window, *en route* from London to Sheffield. But he only succeeded in knocking himself unconscious. He was at last reduced, in Court, to his usual expedients of groans, moans, tears, pious snufflings and outcries against the injustice and tyranny of the law. While he was in the condemned cell, awaiting execution for the Dyson murder, he made, to a clergyman, the confession that he, and not young Habron, had murdered Policeman Cock.

It must always be a little doubtful whether this confession was genuine, or if it had its roots in some tortuous notion either of gaining time or arousing sympathy for himself.

Peace was executed by the famous hangman, Marwood. On the gallows, he made a sanctimonious speech to the newspapermen. But, in his cell, half an hour earlier, the real Charley Peace is revealed in conversation with his warders. He sat down to his breakfast, speaking to his guards about his state of grace, and the value of Christian resignation. Then he paused suddenly and looked up from his plate.

"This is bloody rotten bacon!"

After breakfast, the hour of eight approached: the time for the execution. He was permitted to visit the lavatory, where he smoked his clay pipe with deliberate calm. After a while a warder reminded him that time was flitting, and knocked on the door.

Said Peace:

"You're in a hell of a hurry—are you going to be hanged or am I?"

III. J. P. WATSON

HOLMES, this is marvelous!"
        "Elementary, my dear Watson!"
How often have the parodists of Conan Doyle repeated these imaginary remarks, supposed to have passed between the great detective and his admiring friend!

In London, when Holmes and Watson set out together in a hansom (Watson with his old service revolver in his pocket), it was well for criminals and evil-doers to hunt their holes.

The curious fact seems to have escaped that select class of readers who enjoy old tales of real crimes, that these revered names, Holmes and Watson, were, quite by chance, adopted in America by two sons of Satan, who enlisted not under the flag of the children of light, but under the banner of the foul fiend.

Mr. Holmes of Philadelphia, and Mr. Watson of Los Angeles may have been America's most lavish practitioners of the appalling art of wholesale murder.

When the hangman in Moyamensing Prison conducted the former of these men to his just punishment, it had been discovered that his real name, as entered on the rolls of the Universities of Vermont and Michigan, was Herman W. Mudgett. He had done well to adopt the steely title of H. H. Holmes; it was better suited to this lantern-jawed person who strolled about the country, slaying the old and the young, and who kept in Chicago a strange building, called "Holmes' Castle," where pretty typists sometimes entered, never more to be seen by anyone, except as well-articulated skeletons dangling in a row in the closet.

The career of "Bluebeard" Watson even more fully deserved the attention of the great investigator of Baker Street. After the law officers and newspapermen of California had uncovered enough of his rascality to hang about eleven men, they rested from their labors. They were all out of breath.

During four exciting weeks the district attorney of Los Angeles County had not ceased to tear his hair. Every morning, the good Angelenos turned to their *Examiner* or their *Times* to see under what new name Mr. Andrews (*alias* Hilton, *alias* Gordon, *alias* J. P. Watson) was in possession of bankbooks or marriage certificates.

Each noonday train brought down to the City of Our Lady, Queen of the Angels, another indignant woman from San Francisco or Sacramento or Seattle, full of well-justified suspicions that she was one of the multitude of wives of the mousy little fellow then fidgeting in the County Jail.

And each eventide, half a dozen men, named Gordon or Harvey or Lawrence or something else, telegraphed in from Florida or Massachusetts or Ontario or Kansas to protest because they were being confused with the "monster" whose grisly exploits in the lonely cañons west of San Diego were slowly coming to the light of day.

In the spring of 1920, in that pleasant section of Los Angeles called Hollywood, there dwelt a lady of austere mien, named Kathryn Wombacher-Andrews. Mr. Wombacher had passed from her life, by act of God, or Court's decree—I know not which—and now Mr. Andrews, her second husband, began to mystify her by absences of two weeks at a time.

Like many other innocent persons who have unconsciously stood on the brink of the steaming pit of Sheol, Mrs. Wombacher-Andrews did not look the part. Had you met her on a street car, and observed her rather ascetic countenance, you would have concluded that she was on her way to address the Woman's Club of Pomona, on "Helen Hunt Jackson: Her Place in American Literature."

You would not have guessed that she was about to consult the Nick Harris Detective Agency, and thereby raise the lid off a very active section of Hell.

She had no special complaint against her husband, so she told the handsome Mr. Nick Harris. She just wanted to know why an employee of a trust company in British Columbia (as he had assured her he was) should now and then vanish for a fortnight.

"He is always a gentleman," she said. "Remember that. He is a clever man, and intellectually bright. We met in Seattle. I was a business woman, and tired of living alone. So we were married last November. At Christmas, his Company transferred him to Los Angeles; so we moved here."

Mr. Harris began his search, helped by the police, and soon picked up Mr. Andrews, who had—quite unjustly—become suspected of a bank robbery. The officers, immensely interested in the contents of his valise, altered their suspicions to burglary and then to bigamy. They might have proceeded to barratry and even bigotry had not the reticent prisoner given indication that he had something really serious on his mind. He did it by an unsuccessful effort to cut his throat with a penknife.

This happened during what the elated reporters called a "night-ride" to San Diego. Police officers were convey-

ing him thither to discover the truth about all these bankbooks, held in the names of "Walter Andrews," "H. L.
Gordon," "C. N. Harvey," *et al.*, and carried in his bag-
gage, together with some marriage licenses, indeterminate
in number, but thought by the police to be excessive.

While he was recovering from the slight wound in his
throat, and while the newspapers, after many suggestions,
were fixing upon his name as "J. P. Watson"—because it
was as good as any other—there was much running to and
fro, much gossip of this and that, and a few modest ad-
missions by the diffident little polygamist himself.

The district attorney became aware that he had in
his keeping one of the most widely married men of modern times, whose seraglio was scattered from the Canadian provinces to the Mexican border. Many of these
ladies were still fretting out their days in the light of the
sun, but an amazing number of them had been stealthily
buried by the prisoner.

Mrs. Wombacher-Andrews learned that a good many
women were, so to speak, her sisters under their skins.
Some of them came buzzing into Hollywood, and decid-
edly got under *her* skin.

What, asked the newspapers, could Watson tell about
Mrs. Alice Ludvigson, whom he married under the name
of Lewis Hilton? Or Irene Root Gordon, of San Francisco? Or Bertha Goodnick, of Spokane? Or some fifteen
or sixteen others, from Kate Pruse, of British Columbia,
to Anna Merrill, of Massachusetts?

In short, the papers sang an unrhymed "Ballade of Lost
Ladies." It had to be unrhymed: not even François Villon
could have done much with a name like that of the wife
from Vancouver—Myrtle Briggs Fritch.

There was also "the unidentified body found last sum-

mer in Martinez Cañon"; an unnamed lady carried to the
morgue in this town, or found floating in such and such
a harbor. There was his room in a hotel at Santa Monica,
taken under the name of "James Lawrence," and embel-
lished with a lot of furs, a Paisley shawl worth $1500,
and "a rich widow from Victoria who had a date to meet
him on the beach."

Meanwhile, sang the editors of the Los Angeles papers,
where was Margaret Myers Stokes of Portland, Oregon?
And has anybody here seen Irene Erickson of the
Alameda County Hospital? Where are the Four Ladies
of Tacoma who were all married to him at the same time?

After keeping everybody in a perfect feeze for nineteen days, Mr. Watson made a statement. It was sufficiently astounding to bring him back on the front page,
with a seven-column head:

BLUEBEARD WATSON CONFESSES

Many people thought he had really "come clean" at
last—a thing which this grimy little fellow never did in
his life.

Yet, uttered in his deprecatory manner, this partial
confession was not without its points. He said he had
married fifteen women, and murdered four of them.
Later, he raised the number of marriages to eighteen and
the murders to seven. He described six murders in detail.
The names of two of the eighteen brides were, he said,
unknown to him, and always had been. A later estimate—
not made by Watson—raised the number of marriages to
twenty-six.

His method was this. Going to and fro in Canada and
the United States, driving his little car up and down in
them, he would frequently put a newspaper notice in the
matrimonial columns:

PERSONAL: Would like to meet a lady of
refinement and some social standing, who
desires to meet middle-aged gentleman of
culture. Object matrimony. Gentleman
has nice bank account as well as a considerable roll of Government bonds.
H. L. Gordon,
Hotel Tacoma.

Such a notice would be promptly answered, say by
Mrs. Jennie Leighton, who would write a long letter,
confessing to a previous marriage when she was only a
child of fifteen. She would also admit 147 pounds, dark
hair, pretty teeth, and a "starved soul."

Mr. Gordon-Watson would reply, opening his letter
rather formally, to "Mrs. Jennie Leighton," but pro-
gressing rapidly in warmth of diction until, at the fifth
line, he was calling her "Girl of My Dreams."

He would assert that, in addition to his bank account
and his roll of bonds, he had other advantages, including
"certain personal traits which have been considered different from most of my sex." He was rather vague about
them, fearing to be thought "conceited."

His form letter, of which he had dozens, all typed,
added:

*I am in the thirties, have brown hair, blue eyes and fair
complexion. Weigh 150. Am 5 ft. 7 in. tall. I believe in
the better and elevating things in life.*

(Police records say that he rather underestimated his
age, which was 42, and overstated his weight, which was
135.)

By this exchange of letters, it was easily settled and
Jennie Leighton (like a swarm of Irenes, Kathryns, Ger-
trudes, Ninas and Myrtles) would speedily become Mrs.
Gordon (or Harvey or Huirt or Andrews or Watson).

Then they started cruising about in his car. He told
some of his wives that he was in the secret service, and

consequently had to travel all over the country on con-
fidential missions.

Most of his wives had savings, or Liberty bonds, and
these were promptly transferred to his care. He always
combined business with pleasure, and his strict attention
to the profits of the game (as with other men of his kind)
discounted the earnest efforts of alienists to classify him
as a person suffering from a "compulsion neurosis."

He had, in his bag, letters addressed to fourteen women
in Canada and England, and scores of sheets of paper
signed at the bottom with women's names. The latter
were to be filled in by Mr. Watson with wills, or with
letters to reassure the relatives of these women—after they
were dead.

In his confession, he described how one of his wives
fell out of a boat into a river; how his efforts to recover
her failed, and how he thought it unwise to report the
"accident." How Bertha Goodnick perished in a lake
near Spokane; Alice Ludvigson in a lonely wood in
Idaho; and Betty Prior near a place he called "Plum," in
the State of Washington.

As for Nina Lee Deloney, he drove her to the vicinity
of Long Beach, California, killed her with a hammer, and
buried her in the hills near El Centro.

He may have committed bigamy in Canada, but like all
American criminals, he was exceedingly careful not to be
guilty of murder in the Dominion. Canadians have observed something which is highly mystifying to the crim-
inologists of the United States: that "compulsion neu-
roses" do not seem to make people commit murder in a
country that promptly punishes that crime on the gallows.

It was to the burial place of Mrs. Deloney that Watson
gladly guided the officers. In a sense, he had the law by

the throat in California and, in return for his confession, had been able to wangle a promise of nothing worse than a prison sentence.

Word had reached him that the State of Washington might view him with an unfavoring eye, and he was already shivering in fear that he might suffer the death penalty.

On his own confession, he was sentenced to life imprisonment at San Quentin. It was recorded that he heard the sentence "with deepest gratitude." It was also recorded that his fellow-prisoners, as he entered the yard, spat upon him. Perhaps they felt a sense of injustice when they remembered that so many others, who had been guilty of much less cruelty, had not been treated with consideration, but had mounted the famous thirteen steps to the gallows.

After all the researches of the newspapers, Watson remains a mystery. Within a few days of his committal to prison, the papers ceased to call him Watson, and referred to him as "Joseph Gillam." He had been vague about his origin and early life; telling the truth when it might serve his interests, but lying most of the time. Even his vaunted confession began in this discouraging fashion:

Question: "What is your name?"

Answer: "I do not honestly know."

To the end, Mrs. Wombacher-Andrews (Wife No. 23, according to some computations) continued the most fortunate of all. She accompanied No. 19, a Mrs. Elizabeth Williamson of Sacramento to Santa Monica—perhaps to run down the "rich widow from Victoria."

Mr. Nick Harris, who sat between the ladies in the car, recorded their conversation. Said Mrs. Williamson:

"I used to sit up at night and put up jelly, so he could

take a jar or two in his grip, when he went on those trips."

Mrs. Wombacher-Andrews spoke:

"Dearie," she said, "was it currant jelly?"

"Yes," replied the other.

"Well," replied Mrs. Wombacher-Andrews, "he used to bring it all to my house, and we would eat it."

Then all three of them gazed sadly at the golden sun, sinking into the Pacific behind the palms of Santa Monica.

IV. PETER KÜRTEN

PETER KÜRTEN may have been the worst man who ever lived. He has claims to that eminence. But his career had one beneficial effect. It did much to scatter that great cloud of fog and fluff which gathers around the study of crime and criminals. In the final disposal of his case, the law returned to realism.

Soon after the War (and, as some people would have us believe, because of the War) a peculiar type of murderer arose to notoriety in Germany. Nations whose murderers favor poison as a method, assert their moral superiority over the Germans for that reason. And, we are told by an experienced newspaper correspondent in Berlin, Margaret Seaton Wagner, that the Germans return the compliment, and affect surprise and disdain for the poisoners of England and Italy.

At all events, Herr Denke of Münsterberg, who killed about thirty men and women—and pickled them—used weapons which could hardly be called subtle. A pickax was one of them. Herr Grossmann of Berlin, who disposed of an indefinite number of women ("scores" of them), carried on "an illicit trade in meat." And Herr Haarmann of Hanover placed in the river, near his house, enough bones to make twenty-six complete skeletons of young men.

The careers of these men explain why, in medieval times, folk concocted the myth of the *werewolf*. Our ancestors were as much puzzled as we are to account for cases of frightful inhumanity, and so came to believe in men—and women—who at night could put off human and assume bestial form. After committing their shocking crimes, they resumed, at daybreak, their human bodies.

That the fourth of these great modern *werewolves* was ravaging the countryside, dawned upon the people of Düsseldorf with the discovery of the body of a murdered child named Rose Ohliger. This was in February, 1929. For more than a year, thereafter, murders and murderous attacks terrified Düsseldorf and astonished Europe.

Women, walking in parks and lonely places, were stabbed or strangled or killed with blows of a hammer. These assaults were varied in their methods and details; they included children, young girls, middle-aged women, and, in at least two instances, men; and they seemed so to differ in purpose that the police were confused. In their scientific desire to fit the murderer into this or that class— the "Ripper," or the "sex-maniac," or something else— the detectives could not believe that one man was at work, but thought they had to find four criminals of different types.

Two little girls would be killed and a woman would be murderously assaulted on the same day. Girls would be stabbed or half strangled, and left to recover and tell the detectives of a polite man who had offered to escort them through some lonely place, and had then suddenly attacked them with a knife, a pair of scissors, or a noose. Chief Inspector Gennat, from Berlin, was baffled fully as much as was the detective-novelist, Edgar Wallace, who came and lived in Düsseldorf, to be near the scene.

Some of the police, who completely "went Hollywood," dressed up a lay figure in the clothes of one of the victims, and carried it to cabarets and dance-halls, in the wild notion that its appearance might cause the murderer to confess!

During fifteen months, 9,000 people were questioned in Düsseldorf alone, and, in the country at large, more than 900,000 accusations were investigated. The murders went steadily on. Four hundred graphologists, astrologers and other experts in hanky-panky, offered their services. The police were actually in receipt of letters from the real murderer, telling where the body of a victim would be found.

The world was horrified, more than forty years ago, by the four or five crimes of Jack the Ripper in London. But after the "Düsseldorf vampire" had been at work for a year, and his murderous attacks numbered over thirty, with the police still at sea, there was natural indignation.

The scientific methods of the detection of crime in Germany have been offered—and justly—for the admiration of the world, but in this instance, police in London, Paris and New York must have grimly observed that the German detectives are not superhuman.

Someone (was it De Quincey?) said that society is at the mercy of a murderer who is remorseless, who takes no accomplices and who keeps his head.* For a long time the Düsseldorfer observed these rules. While the police were compiling their card-indexes, or trotting around the night-clubs with their mannikin, the murderer was living at home with his wife, more or less prosaically and normally, although sometimes putting a strain upon her good nature, by rousing her at 3 A.M., to take her for a walk in the park, to hear the birds sing.

"He knew," she said, "every bird by name and could tell them by their song."

At last, this nature-lover made a wee bit of a slip. He did not completely murder Maria Büdlick. This girl, a

* Miss Dorothy Sayers, in her novel "Unnatural Death," attributes this saying to me!

stranger in town, was picked up at the station by a gentleman, who, with all the solicitude of an agent of the
Travelers' Aid Society, offered to conduct her to a girls'
hotel. The way, however, seemed to lead through a
lonely park, which Fräulein Büdlick sagely refused to
enter. While they were arguing about it, another gentleman approached (a little *werewolf* music, here, please)
and rebuked the first man for seeking to lead an innocent
maiden astray. With lofty words he bade the marauder
begone, and the marauder (whose name is unknown to
history) slunk off, like the dastard that he was.

The new gentleman, whose manner was still more respectable, gracious and kindly, was now accepted as
Maria's escort. First, he suggested that she might care to
come to his apartment for rest and refreshment, since she
was obviously tired, hungry, and without any place to
stay for the night.

She promptly accepted, and went with him to the
fourth floor of a good-looking apartment house. His
apartment was one room only, but his entertainment of
the girl took the perfectly moral form of a ham sandwich
and a glass of milk.

Then, at about eleven o'clock, they set out again for
the girls' hotel. This time the path led to an alarming
region—through thick woods, and to a place—had she
known it—called the Wolf's Glen. His attentions now
declined from the harmless sandwich-and-milk stage, to
enforced kisses and then to chokings. She fought him off,
and during the struggle, he inquired:

"Do you remember where I live? You might be in
want, and I could help you."

Maria Büdlick hastily replied that she did not remember. This was nearly, but not quite true.

Her assailant let her go, with no further molestation,

and two days later she was able, with a little trouble, to find the street, and point out the apartment of the polite choker.

The police arrested Peter Kürten.

He was forty-seven years old, but, owing to his skill with powder-puff and rouge, was able to make most women take him for less than thirty. He and his wife were casual laborers, the one who happened to be employed cheerfully supporting the other. Frau Kürten knew nothing of her husband's murderous activities. She had merely been resigned to such of his weaknesses as were known to her: his addiction to early morning bird-walks, and his frequent affairs with other women.

Of Kürten's forty-seven years, twenty-one had been spent in prison. He had been sentenced seventeen times for theft, fraud and "brutality." One term, of seven years, from 1913–1921, covered all the period of the War, and shakes Mr. William Bolitho's theory that these "mass-murderers" are the result of war or militarism.

Far from being a soldier, Kürten had avoided military service by desertion. The idea that war implants in the minds of naturally good men a desire to commit murder, finds little support in actual observation of notorious criminals. From Charley Peace, the philosophical pacifist, who announced his horror of war, through G. J. Smith who killed his wives for profit, while his countrymen fought in France, to Kürten, the deserter, the most infamous killers are often found among the slackers and peace-at-any-price men. They eloquently denounce war, while they engage in private assassination.

Kürten had committed arson twenty-two times; and made twenty-three attempts to strangle people, in addition to stabbings, bludgeonings, hammerings and drownings. When he went, for the last time, on trial, he was convicted for nine completed and seven attempted murders. He was bloodthirsty—not in the figurative but in the literal sense. It does not appear that he was given to cannibalism.

Those to whom Kürten's career is unknown will say that the story is incredible, and that if one quarter of it were true, then Kürten was a roaring madman. On the contrary, his memory of his crimes was correct to the minutest detail, and his confessions of all these events were corroborated beyond the shadow of doubt.

He was not tried until nearly a year after his arrest, so the demand of the modern criminologist that such men be studied was fulfilled to the heart's desire. The leading experts of a nation distinguished for the learning of its alienists and psychiatrists kept him under observation for months. With the usual dissent of some of the alienists, the final decision held him sane and responsible.

His crimes, except for one, were all premeditated. He did not act under that "uncontrollable impulse" dear to some criminal lawyers and their assistant alienists. Professor Karl Berg testified that Kürten "was master of his own resolutions." He was "all attention at the moment of carrying out the deeds, ready to take cover at the moment of danger." He showed a high degree of intelligence, while the facial characteristics of the criminal (Lombroso's "stigmata") were absent. He acted—in public—like anybody else.

He *looked* like anyone else. People who think they can recognize "a murderer's eyes" or "a degenerate's face" had been seeing Kürten every day.

German criminal law at that time, at all events, was careful and merciful. A strong element of public opinion disapproves of capital punishment. But after all the psychiatrists had finished, after every *Gerichtsmedizinalrat* had had his innings, they were reduced to the expedient of acting with ordinary common sense.

They brought out an ancient guillotine and cut off his head.

THE GREAT
CHOWDER MURDER

NEW YORK'S major attraction in the spring of 1896 was a vivacious lady who went by the *nom de guerre* of "Mrs. Fleming."

Ellen Terry and Henry Irving were at Abbey's Theatre, where Sarah Bernhardt followed them. May Irwin was playing "The Widow Jones," and De Wolf Hopper "El Capitan." At Koster & Bial's you could see the new invention, Edison's Vitascope. All these, however, received but tepid attention, while Mrs. Fleming was filling two columns on the front pages and turning away crowds at Recorder Goff's court.

So much moral turpitude to the square inch had never been displayed before. So many respectable-looking people had never before been spattered with scandal. And the wellspring and source of all this scandal was, strangely enough, a pail of clam chowder. It seems to justify the belief of every New Englander that the New York kind of clam chowder is never to be trusted.

Mrs. Fleming's real name was Miss Mary Alice Almont Livingston. She was Miss Livingston when she had the first of the series of babies which annoyed her family and moved the sob sisters to gusts of tears. She was still Miss Livingston when, one hot August morning, she sent her mother that queer gift of clam chowder. And—so said a Grand Jury—not nice chowder, at all.

Mary Alice's father was Judge Robert S. Livingston. He was a grandson of the last lord of the Manor of Livingston, and had been a county judge in Dutchess County. His estate was at Almont, on the Hudson, where, until his death at the age of eighty-seven, he lived as a country gentleman. As the Judge was eighty when he married her mother, the birth of the little girl was greeted with congratulations from the goodhearted, but with spiteful comments from the cynical. Indeed, when trouble arose over the Judge's will, someone proposed to question Mary Alice's paternity. This was not done.

On the Judge's death, his estate of eighty-five thousand dollars was left in trust for his daughter. His widow had the use of it during her life. The widow was free to marry again, and she promptly took as a second husband a gentleman who bore, ironically, the soothing name of Bliss.

From the time when she was twenty, Mary Alice's love affairs gave her mother, her stepfather, and her half-brothers and sisters a good deal of concern. Her adventure with Henry Fleming was notable for the birth of her first child, her moral victory in securing a judgment against her lover in the sum of seventy-five thousand for breach of promise, and, shortly afterward, the death of Mr. Fleming. It does not appear that the money was ever paid, or that Fleming's death was other than natural. Shortly afterward, Mary Alice began to call herself Mrs. Fleming.* She felt, somehow, that she just had to.

* She must, by no means, be confused with Mrs. May Agnes Early Fleming (1840-1880), the widely admired author of "Unmasked; or, The Secret Marriage"; "Guy Earlscourt's Wife"; "Lost for a Woman"; "Pride and Passion"; "Norine's Revenge; or Sir Noel's Heir"; and "The Gypsy Queen's Vow."

About an interlude with a lawyer named Lewis the chronicles say little. She brought a breach-of-promise suit against him. It was astonishing, the regularity with which her suitors' promises were breached.

Next came Ferdinand Wilckes, a young German with a sandy beard. He was in the coffin business. His flirtation with Mary Alice was no mere matter of nods and winks; already, on the day when the main story opens, it had resulted in two children.

The great day, the great Chowder Day, in the families of Fleming and Bliss was the last Friday in August, '95. The personages were arranged as follows: Mrs. Fleming, with little Gracie, her eldest, and the two younger children (offspring of Mr. Wilckes) dwelt at the Colonial Hotel on 125th Street. At the same hotel lived Mr. Bliss, her stepfather.

A few streets distant, in a flat on St. Nicholas Avenue, was Mrs. Bliss, who had secured a divorce from Mr. Bliss. It was a perfectly friendly divorce, and Mr. Bliss not only contributed to the support of his former wife but dropped in for an occasional game of tiddledywinks.

Of Mrs. Fleming's three lovers, Mr. Fleming was in Heaven; Mr. Lewis had vanished, none knew whither; while Mr. Wilckes was living somewhere in New York, worrying about the depression in the coffin trade, and—it has to be concluded—coming up to see Mrs. Fleming sometimes.

With none of the Blisses was Mrs. Fleming on friendly terms. They were not excessively narrow people; one or two illegitimate babies they might have overlooked, but with Mary Alice, as they pointed out to her, these events could no longer be classed as mere accidents.

She was badly in need of money. Mr. Wilckes was moaning about the coffin business, alarmed lest for want of cash it might slip from his hands. Mrs. Fleming had asked the courts for part of her father's estate, which Mrs. Bliss still enjoyed. The request was refused, and the attempt only increased the family bitterness.

She called little Gracie Fleming, aged twelve or thirteen, and her playmate, Flossie King, who was eleven. She saw that they were polished up and spotless, with all their ribbons in place, and then sent them on an embassy, bearing gifts, to Grandma Bliss. Gracie carried the chowder. And Flossie carefully balanced a beautiful lemon-meringue pie.

The two little girls, walking sedately through the street, form a picture over which we who are tenderly sentimental must love to linger. There was something neighborly about it; something which suggests the warm-heartedness of the small town, not the callous indifference of the great city.

The little girls handed their gifts to Mrs. Bliss, and came bounding home.

"I hope you didn't touch any of Grandma's chowder, Gracie?" inquired Mrs. Fleming.

"Oh, no, Mamma!" was the reply.

I think she told the truth. Surreptitious tippling from a pail of cold clam chowder, was not a vice of children in the nineties.

Mrs. Bliss had a sort of high tea at four that afternoon, and partook of both chowder and pie. Within a short time she was very sick; and at 11 P.M., in spite of a doctor's efforts, she was dead.

"I have been poisoned. That chowder and that pie were poisoned. I was sick ten minutes after eating them. They were sent me by a relative, who will inherit a large sum of money when I am dead."

Such, repeated again and again to the doctor and other

bystanders, were the ante-mortem statements of Mrs. Bliss. A chemical expert, Dr. Scheele, examined the remains of the pie and the sediment in the chowder pail. The pie was proper enough, but the chowder contained large amounts of antimony (from tartar emetic) together with traces of arsenic. He found the same poisons in the stomach of the late Mrs. Bliss.

An air of constraint marked that lady's funeral. Mr. Bliss bluntly asked his stepdaughter if she had murdered her mother. Mrs. Fleming, as blithe as circumstances would permit, was escorted to and from the grave by two heavy-looking men—the kind that, on the stage, always establish their authority by the silent exhibition of a police badge.

When the last mourner had departed, these men gently intimated to Mrs. Fleming their painful duty.

"Oh, *arrested!*" said she. "What a bore!"

And after a silence, on the way downtown, she added:

"I do hope they will let me out before February. You see, I shouldn't like my baby to be born in the Tombs."

By February, however, the authorities had transferred her to Blackwell's Island, not then made into a place of hope and cheer by being renamed Welfare Island. And it was there that little Gussie, the third of Mr. Wilckes' children, was born.

Judge Livingston's eighty-five thousand dollars might now come into the possession of Mary Alice. And her claim to that estate enabled her to engage some astute lawyers, headed by a great defender of accused persons, Charles W. Brooke. It was their task to see that no conviction for murder interfered with a happy inheritance.

When the murder trial began, in May, the case for the State seemed strong. No one except Mrs. Fleming had

any known motive to kill Mrs. Bliss; she had sent to her
mother poisoned chowder, and of this her mother died.
It was true that nobody caught her buying poison or saw
her putting it into the chowder. But circumstances appeared black indeed.

It was in a trial like this that the abilities of Mr. Brooke
were conspicuous. He announced fourteen lines of defense. Among these were the suggestions, first, that Mrs.
Bliss committed suicide; second, that she died of heart
failure; third, that she died of Bright's disease; fourth,
that she died of arsenic superinduced by bismuth, pre-
scribed by a physician.

Next, he powerfully argued that whatever she died of,
it could not have been the chowder, since in all probability little Gracie and Flossie dipped into it on the way
to Grandma's, and see how well they were!

Then, having proven the absolute purity of Mrs. Fleming's gift by the healthy condition of Flossie and Gracie,
he next announced that the chowder was really a teeming
nest of the deadliest creatures known to science; that is,
ptomaines.

This word was then new to the public, and Mr. Brooke
made the courtroom ring with it.

The human race, he let the jury understand, was beset
by these cunning little hellions, and in nothing else did
they so contrive to cluster, in no other form of food did
they propagate so rapidly and reach such virulence, as in
clam chowder. For many months New York restaurants
had to remove this broth from their bills of fare.

At the end of the trial, there had been so many lines of
defense that nobody could agree what the defense was.
In addition to the ptomaines, Mrs. Fleming's lawyers
made a determined attack upon Dr. Scheele. The evi-

dence of this learned chemist was very damaging to the prisoner, but it happened that he had been concerned, at Albany, in some legislation which annoyed the brewers, and that he was also sympathetic with some anti-Semitic movement.

His foes, therefore, were many, and to them the guilt or innocence of Mrs. Fleming was of minor importance compared with their desire to make the Doctor look foolish. They gave the defense every aid and comfort, and Mrs. Fleming was often cheered in beer gardens.

For five weeks, Mr. Brooke displayed the arts of the advocate in their sublimest forms. He was an impressive person, able to become pink in the face with mild indignation, scarlet with anger, or deep purple with apocalyptic rage. These colors played across his handsome face like a Tyrolese sunset as he depicted the State of New York in the guise of a pack of wolves and a flock of buzzards, bent on drinking the blood of "this willful child."

With sobs, which were echoed from the prisoner and the jury, he described the wrongs suffered by his client— "this willful child." (Mrs. Fleming was then thirty-seven.) Of course, no one could foresee that within a few months Mr. Brooke was going to treat this petulant lass as if she were grown up and responsible. At least, he sued her for part of his fee.

The jury, worn out and often put to sleep in the hot June afternoons, were probably impressed by Mrs. Fleming's wide-open, blue-eyed expression of total innocence. It had been proposed to have her hold little Gussie in her arms during the trial, but for some reason this was not done. The jury took twelve hours to discuss the case, but then reported her "not guilty." Recorder Goff was "stunned" by the acquittal, but all the sob sisters sang together and Mr. Brooke shouted for joy.

Thus, for Mrs. Fleming, everything ended happily. Later in the summer, she received her inheritance, and the newspapers discussed whether it had been diminished by twenty or thirty thousand dollars for the cost of her defense. But for the small trouble with Mr. Brooke over his fee, there were no other legal duties for her, except when somebody dragged Mr. Bliss into court over the matter of a paltry three hundred and seventy-five dollars. Then his stepdaughter cheerfully came forward and gave testimony which, if true, would have convicted Mr. Bliss of gross perjury.

After that, as I am told, the only public appearances of Mary Alice were in the brighter spots along Broadway.

One judicious reporter remarked that hardly anyone connected with the case escaped with reputation "un-smirched." He added a list of smirched reputations. Mrs. Fleming's indiscreet love letters to Mr. Wilckes had been read in court, and their contents seemed to blacken the characters of herself and most of her relatives.

Mr. Wilckes, when called as a witness, was forced to hide behind his constitutional privileges to escape smirching. He was, by the way, a mild-looking man who wore a broad black hat of the Western politician pattern and invariably carried an umbrella.

A theosophist, employed by the *World* to trace the earlier incarnations of Mrs. Fleming, had discovered her previous existences, from ancient Egypt to the present. She had first met Mr. Wilckes, it seemed, in the twelfth century, when he was a Viking, and already had a blond beard.

There were, according to the judicious reporter, two persons whose reputations had not been smirched. This was due merely to their good luck, not to merit. It is impossible to say exactly who they were, since he refrains from giving their names. He cautiously describes one as "a well-known elderly financier" and the other as "The King of the Dudes of Harlem."

THE
THIRD PASSENGER

WHAT do you do if you see a red-faced and hatless man running toward you, hoarsely bellowing: "Murder!"

If he waves his arms at something behind you and roars out:

"Stop that man! Murder!"

And if he continues to wave, to pant and to perspire, as he rushes past you—if he continues to yell for someone to stop that man, or stop that car, or carriage—what, as I asked before, do you do?

You look over your shoulder, and there, certainly, are a number of men, as well as cars or carriages. Some of them are hurrying.

If you are a prompt and bold sort of person, quick to believe anything you hear, and eager for excitement, you start to run and to shout, and perhaps you catch and collar the hurrying man.

And he turns out to be an innocent gas inspector. You look round for the original shouter, and find that he has gone away, chuckling over the success of his joke.

Or it may be that you are nearly run over by a car in which are two men with a motion-picture camera. One of them calls out to you:

"Get out of the way, feller! Don't yer see we're taking pitchers?"

You realize that you have at last got into the movies, but will not get any glory out of it. Only abuse.

So probably, being of a doubting cast of mind, you do not join the red-faced man who is screaming about murder. You draw aside as he runs by, and say:

"What's all the shoutin' for?"

And thus, perhaps, you miss undying fame; someone else gets his name in the papers and pockets a reward.

Two or three policemen once made exactly this mistake. They looked at the shouting man and remarked:

"You're crazy!"

Then they went on directing traffic, or walking their beats, or whatever they were doing. And they must have suffered agonies when two other policemen suddenly jumped into public notice by arresting the most notorious criminal of the year, and finally appearing as important witnesses before the Lord Chief Justice himself.

In the year 1875 these skeptical policemen were posted along the way leading from the Whitechapel district of London, across London Bridge with its stream of traffic, and into Southwark. One pleasant September afternoon a man, all out of breath, came running along these streets vainly trying to interest the police in a four-wheeled carriage which always kept a little ahead. The police laughed at him. But he pounded on.

At last, at a place called the Hen and Chickens, in the High Street, Borough, the carriage stopped. The Hen and Chickens seems not to have been a tavern, but a building devoted to business of various kinds.

There were two persons in the carriage. One was a broad-shouldered man wearing a tall hat and smoking a big cigar. The other was a chorus girl named Alice Day.

She was an attractive little creature, wearing all the frills, ribbons, and petticoats of that period and, probably, carrying a parasol. There was another occupant on the front seat, but neither Miss Day nor the driver knew it. The driver sat up on the box, with his blanket and his whip, apparently quite unaware of the shouting man who had chased him all the way.

The pursuer, whose name was Stokes, sighted two more policemen, and running up made one more attempt.

"For God's sake," he croaked out, "go after that man with the tall hat! There is something wrong."

The officers saw the man, who had alighted from the carriage, entering the building and carrying a large parcel. He was letting himself in with a key. They ran across, and one of them followed him into the Hen and Chickens. The other spoke to Miss Day in the carriage. She stepped out and stood on the sidewalk, all of a flutter. The man who had carried in the parcel now returned to the carriage, followed by the policeman. He had lifted out another parcel when the officers began to question him:

"Do you live here?"

"No."

"Have you got any business here?"

"Yes, and you have not. Why do you interfere with me? I am only going in to see an old friend of mine."

The policemen now pushed him toward the inside of the building, and he went, herded by them and carrying the second parcel. On the way he turned to them.

"Look here. Say nothing about this, ask no questions, and here is fifty pounds for each of you."

They got him in an old deserted shop in the building, where they found the first parcel, which they laid out on a dusty counter. They told him to take off the wrappings and let them see what he had.

"Don't open it," he implored. "Pray don't look at it, whatever you do. Don't touch it!"

The officer was now busy with the cover.

"I'll give you a hundred pounds—I'll give you two hundred, and produce the money in twenty minutes—if you will let me go."

But the wrappings were already pulled aside. . . .

Two minutes later the officers came out again, one of them leading their prisoner, who was still carrying one of the dreadful bundles in his arms. He tried to throw it away from him, but he was put into the cab. An officer then returned for the other parcel, and the carriage, with all its occupants, was driven to the police station.

Alice Day said:

"Well, Mr. Wainwright, this is a fine thing you have done for me!"

But Mr. Wainwright puffed his cigar and said nothing. Soon the horrified girl clutched him and cried:

"For God's sake, tell them what I know of this! I know nothing!"

And Mr. Wainwright obediently said:

"She knows nothing."

The police were not so sure. Who was Mr. Wainwright, and who was Alice Day, and why was she in that carriage? Who was this other frightful passenger? There was reason enough for Mr. Wainwright to smoke a cigar; he should have smoked two. And who was Stokes, who had run all this distance from the other side of the river?

Henry Wainwright was not recognized near the Hen and Chickens, but it was soon found that he was known to everybody in his own neighborhood. Big, breezy, jolly and hearty, he was regarded as an important man and an all-round good fellow in the Whitechapel Road. Here he and his brother William carried on their business as brushmakers.

They had inherited some money from their father, and this set them up in business and enabled Henry to cultivate the arts at his leisure. Making brushes and mats is a dry sort of occupation; but Mr. Wainwright, although at one time a lecturer on temperance, was no fanatic.

He seems to have spent a good part of his time inviting people to have a drink; encountering actors, whom he greatly admired, in the street and asking them in for a glass of sherry. As for the ballet girls at the Pavilion Theatre, next door to his factory, they never had to suffer the tortures of thirst. Going home in groups or singly, after rehearsals, if they were lucky enough to meet Mr. Wainwright they were sure to be asked into a public house and refreshed with a pint of beer or a glass or two of port.

In a conversation which took place, at a later date, between Alice Day and the Lord Chief Justice of England, his lordship showed great interest in these little parties, leaning over the bench in kindly fashion and asking for full particulars. Even chief justices can be quite human when drinks and chorus girls are mentioned, although this one was ordinarily a rather stuffy old person. He was that Sir James Cockburn who stamped angrily out of the Geneva Tribunal when the Alabama decision went against him.

It was not a mere interest in chorus girls which animated Henry Wainwright. He was stage-struck. Recitations, speeches, dramatic impersonations, far beyond the ability of the usual brushmaker, were his solace and delight. He loved amateur acting. He gave addresses to

schools and church institutes, and readings from humor-
ous authors. He went into politics a little, and was also
one of the supporters and dupes of that absurd impostor,
Arthur Orton, who went about the country wheedling
money out of poor and rich, under the pretense that he
was Sir Roger Tichborne being deprived of his "rights."

Wainwright was happy when he could give a supper
at his own house and invite the actors and actresses from
the Pavilion. In his comfortable home, where he lived
with his wife, four children, and servants, he loved to
entertain his theatrical friends. They ate and drank merrily, and perhaps even enjoyed the recitation by their
host which always followed the supper. Probably he had
the lights lowered before beginning one of his favorite
poems: Thomas Hood's "The Dream of Eugene Aram"
—now almost forgotten. Certainly he chilled the blood of
all those little actresses as he rolled out the melodramatic
stanzas with tremendous force, lingering with especial
delight upon the purple patches which tell

> *Of lonely folk cut off unseen,*
> *And hid in sudden graves;*
> *Of horrid stabs, in groves forlorn,*
> *And murders done in caves. . . .*

> *He told how murderers walk the earth*
> *Beneath the curse of Cain,*
> *With crimson clouds before their eyes,*
> *And flames about their brain:*
> *For blood has left upon their souls*
> *Its everlasting stain.*

The poem goes on to describe the horrors which beset
Eugene Aram in his dream; to tell in his own words of the
nightmare of the dead body of his victim which constantly rose against him:

There was no time to dig a grave
Before the day began:
In a lonesome wood, with heaps of leaves,
I hid the murdered man.

And all that day I read in school,
But my thought was otherwhere;
As soon as the mid-day task was done,
In secret I was there;
And a mighty wind had swept the leaves,
And still the corse was bare!

When at last the poem ended, the lights were turned up again, and the ladies were easily persuaded to have another glass of wine and the gentlemen some brandy and soda.

"Oh, Mr. Wainwright," we can imagine one of the actresses exclaiming, "you fair give me the creeps! Do you suppose that murderers suffer remorse like that? They *must*—look at Macbeth! How foolish Aram was not to hide the body where no one could find it!"

And everyone began to chatter again. How pleasant was the contrast between Aram's distress and their own comfortable situation in Mr. Wainwright's hospitable dining room! Jolly, kind-hearted Mr. Wainwright! A good fellow, said all the men.

"And so good-looking!" murmured the girls.

There is more than one curious coincidence about this favorite recitation of Mr. Wainwright's. It was for years given by Sir Henry Irving, and later by his son, Harry B. Irving, who appeared in many of his father's tragic rôles. And it is Harry Irving to whom so many writers on crime are indebted, not only for his histories of the Wainwright and other cases, but for the scholarly care which dignified everything he wrote.

Wainwright was good-looking in the style of that day and place, and he was altogether too successful with ladies. The house where he gave these parties, in Tredegar Square, was not his only establishment. Three or four years before that September afternoon when he took his strange drive over London Bridge with Alice Day—and that other—he had met, at an outdoor pleasure resort, a pretty blonde girl of twenty years. Her name was Harriet Lane.

Mr. Wainwright and Miss Lane became great friends, and soon were lovers. If the way to her heart and hand did not lead up a church aisle, she at least insisted that there must be an imaginary church somewhere in the romance. She put a notice in a paper to say that Harriet, ninth daughter of John Lane, had been married to Percy King, Esq., at St. Mary's. There are about sixteen churches in London with St. Mary as part of their name, so it would be a busy person who would examine the registers of all of them to see if such a marriage had really taken place.

Harriet Lane, now calling herself Mrs. King, was a clever, sprightly girl, very fond of nice clothes. She had been, when she met Wainwright, a milliner and dress-maker. During the next two or three years "Mr. and Mrs. King" lived in St. Peter's Street and in other places. They had two babies. Only a few persons knew that Percy King and Mr. Wainwright were the same man.

Then the brush business began to decline. Wainwright had to have a meeting of his creditors and make what terms he could. Also, he had to mortgage his warehouse. His brother William, one of his largest creditors, with-drew from the business.

Harriet and her babies, hitherto generously supported, began to suffer. Her income was steadily cut down and she often had to call on the pawnbroker. Also, with increasing frequency, she tried the public house to see what consolation could be found in drink. Her friend Miss Wilmore was one of those who knew who Percy King really was, and she could be relied on to help Harriet and often to take care of the children.

At last Harriet had quarrels both with her lover and her landlady. She began to call at the brushmaker's place on Whitechapel Road, and assure everybody that, no matter how he treated her, she would always be true to her Henry. This was annoying.

One day in September, 1874, Wainwright bought a box of chloride of lime, which he conveyed to a warehouse, part of his works on Whitechapel Road. On the next day, a Friday, Harriet Lane wrapped up a nightdress and said good-by to Miss Wilmore, telling her that she had an appointment with Henry Wainwright. Late that afternoon three workmen who were employed near the warehouse heard three pistol shots which seemed to come from some of the deserted buildings on the brushmaker's premises.

Two days later Miss Wilmore came over to inquire anxiously about Harriet. Wainwright told her that he had sent Harriet to Brighton—doubtless for a rest and the sea air. A few days after that he came with some sad news. Harriet had not been true to him! Beguiled by the gayety of Brighton and the fascinations of their young friend Teddy Frieake, she had fled to the Continent with Teddy. They might even get married.

Now, Miss Wilmore did know a young fellow called Teddy or Edward Frieake, who had once called on Harriet. When he was inquired for, it was found that, instead of being on a frisky trip to Paris, he was going soberly about his business of auctioneer in London. Curiously enough, a letter came to Miss Wilmore, signed "E. Frieake," telling all about his elopement with Harriet. It ended gayly:

"We are just off to Dover."

Teddy Frieake told Mr. Wainwright that if that was his idea of humor it was not appreciated. Said Teddy:

"This is a very serious imputation to cast upon my character, and if it got to the ears of the young lady I am engaged to, it will very likely ruin my happiness."

But the ready and affable Wainwright laughed it all off. He assured Teddy that "it is not you at all, but another fellow of the same name." Teddy insisted that this was rather curious; there were not so many Frieakes around loose. As he put it:

"Mine is not a Brown, Jones, or Robinson name."

But finally all inquiry ceased. Mr. Frieake's sweetheart was reassured; Teddy himself had his ruffled feelings soothed; and the docile Miss Wilmore actually seems to have been convinced. She continued to care for Harriet's babies, Wainwright paying for their support. Old Mr. Lane made a few feeble inquiries, but soon let the matter drop. When you have nine daughters it is hard to keep checked up on them all. No doubt someone was caring for Harriet, somewhere.

Nearly a year went by, and still Harriet did not reappear. Henry Wainwright's business affairs did not improve. One of his buildings was burned down, and he quarreled with the insurance company, which refused to settle. He sat in public houses, drinking more and more, but not getting any great amount of cheer out of it. I do not think that he now recited Eugene Aram at all. Meanwhile Thomas Wainwright, another of his brothers, had set up an ironmongery business in the Hen and Chickens

building on the south side of the Thames. There were in
this building some deep old cellars, dark and secret places.

As the anniversary of Harriet Lane's disappearance
approached, two disasters fell upon Wainwright. He
went bankrupt, and the mortgagee of the warehouse fore-
closed and prepared to take possession. There had long
been something peculiar about that place. An unduly
curious dog which had been sniffing around there disappeared very quickly.

On September 11, a year to a day since Harriet Lane
had gone to keep her appointment in Whitechapel Road,
Wainwright asked a young man named Stokes, a former
employee, to help him carry a parcel. Stokes agreed, and
the two went to the warehouse together. Wainwright
produced two heavy parcels wrapped in cheap oilcloth—
the material which in England is called American cloth.
These parcels were exceedingly offensive, and the un-
kindest cut of all came when Alice Day testified that she
noticed an unpleasant smell in the carriage, but "thought
it was the American cloth."

Wainwright and Stokes with some difficulty carried
the two parcels along the street, looking for a carriage.
Finally—making one more mistake—Wainwright himself
went for the cab. Stokes, his curiosity aroused, opened
one of the parcels slightly, and saw a human hand. He
covered it up quickly, and waited in terror and consterna-
tion for his employer to return.

Then, still perplexed, he helped Wainwright put the
two parcels into the carriage and saw him drive away.
He recovered his courage and began his pursuit, pausing
when the carriage would stop, and hiding in doorways.
He saw Wainwright meet Alice Day—it was an accidental meeting—and invite her to "take a ride over Lon-

don Bridge." She accepted, and became one of the most curious examples of the "innocent bystander."

At last Stokes' mind awoke to the fact that he had to do something more than follow the carriage. He began to shout, to appeal to police for help, and to work himself into a wild-eyed, panting, incoherent sleuth hound who almost saw his prey escape.

Inside the carriage, Alice Day had a rather gloomy joy-ride. Wainwright gave her a paper to read and said:

"Don't speak to me; I'm thinking."

She must have wondered why she was asked to come. It was like Wainwright's selfish disposition that, apparently for the purpose of giving the expedition a harmless aspect, he inveigled the girl into this trap, thus causing her arrest and detention for more than a week and nearly getting her tried for murder.

When Henry Wainwright and his brother Thomas were tried, the evidence against Henry was too strong to be explained away. Thomas' part in the plot seems to have been that he wrote the letter to Miss Wilmore signed "E. Frieake," and that he may have impersonated Teddy on the occasion of the call on Harriet. He also helped buy the "American cloth" and other things, including a spade and a "chopper." Luckily for his own neck, he did not take part in the ride over London Bridge.

How could Henry Wainwright have been so stupid as to make the three or four blunders of that September afternoon? Like many murderers, he was a vainglorious, egotistical person, clever rather than really able, and had come to feel a contempt for the intelligence of everyone because he had fooled a few. If a murderer is really skillful, of course we never hear of him nor suspect him at all. But he is usually a cruel egotist, and it follows that he is also, for a good part of the time, a big fool.

The best that his lawyers could argue for Henry Wainwright was that the body was not that of Harriet Lane; or, if it was, she had committed suicide and he had taken fright.

The identity of the mutilated remains was established in several ways: teeth, hair, and other indications. One of Wainwright's lawyers, pressing old Mr. Lane as to his ability to recognize the pitiful fragments, did his client poor service by making the old man recall that Harriet had a scar on her knee, caused by a burn when she was a child. It was found and the identification was complete.

Wainwright was found guilty and condemned to death. His brother Thomas, convicted as an accessory after the fact, was given seven years. Each tried to implicate the other as principal, but at the end, after many denials, Henry Wainwright admitted the justice of his sentence. Stokes gained a reward which was to him a small fortune. He got thirty pounds, which enabled him to set up in business.

As for Alice Day, it would be pleasant to say that as soon as she was let out of jail theatrical managers began offering her engagements, that she prospered, changed her stage name, and finally rose to celebrity. But I am afraid I do not know that. It is safe to believe that the Pavilion Theatre kept a place open for her, welcomed her back, and that she was one of the chief attractions of their chorus. If she ever accepted any more invitations to go for rides, she must have looked carefully to see what was on the front seat of the carriage.

The chief person in the tragedy, Henry Wainwright, made his last appearance one dark cold December morning in the yard of Newgate Prison. A waning moon shone overhead; that and a flaring gaslight gave the sixty witnesses their light during the brief and dreadful event.

He looked at the group of spectators and muttered: "Come to see a man die, have you, you curs?"

As with many and many other brutal murderers, his last moments were remarkable for the fact that he bore himself with dignity and courage.

BIRTH OF THE
BRAINSTORM

ALL that he seemed to be was a man with a red nose and a plug hat. Yet he was the first Protector of the American Home. His was the first "brainstorm," the first case of "dementia Americana," that divine rage which makes *homo Americanus* go berserk when the Honor of Womanhood is assailed.

It was a late November afternoon in 1869, and the scene was the office of the New York *Tribune*. The illustrious person who had the purity of American Hearths and Homes in his keeping was sitting in a dark corner.

Even then, of course, there had been "triangle murders"; husbands had shot or stabbed the betrayers of their honor. The insanity defense was not unknown. But the "uncontrollable impulse" was now about to be illustrated for the first time in New York, perhaps in America. Here, in the person of the man in the plug hat (his name was Dan McFarland) was the pioneer of that great army of shooters and stabbers who wait around with a gun, or sharpen their knives for weeks, only at last, in the presence of the victim, to have "everything go blank," or suddenly to "see red."

When everything stops going blank, or when they see, once more, some other color instead of red, there is a dead man on the floor.

BIRTH OF THE BRAINSTORM 197

Darkness had fallen and the street-floor office of the *Tribune* was lighted by gas. Only two or three men were there. One was a stranger, looking at the files. The advertising clerk, a boy of sixteen or seventeen, is more interesting, for his name was—and is—Daniel Frohman.

When I suggested to Mr. Frohman that he might remember the incidents of that afternoon, he replied:

"Certainly I remember them!"

His tone suggested that it was rather silly to intimate that one should forget the details of an event merely because it happened sixty-seven years ago.

"I knew McFarland," said he, "and I knew that it was possible that he was waiting for Mr. Richardson."

Albert Richardson, war correspondent, was one of the owners of the *Tribune*.

"Once or twice before," continued Mr. Frohman, "I had warned Richardson. I said, 'Mac has been hanging round to-day.' And this afternoon I knew that Richardson was apt to come in about five o'clock, to get his mail, before going up to the editorial rooms. So when I saw the door open and Mr. Richardson come in, I tried to tip him a warning. I started to lean across the counter and say, 'S-st! Look out!' But before I could even attract his attention, 'Bang!' the gun went off right in my ear. McFarland had crept up behind me and fired.

"Richardson looked at Mac for an instant, without saying a word; then went outdoors, entered the building again from the Spruce Street side, and walked upstairs to Whitelaw Reid's office. In the excitement, McFarland ran out through the Nassau Street door. When I saw Mr. Richardson again, he was lying on a sofa up there and the doctors were with him."

The wounded man had walked up four flights of stairs, lain down on the sofa, and calmly asked someone to send for a doctor. After a short delay and an examination, Richardson was taken to a room in the Astor House.

The bullet had pierced the liver, the stomach, and an intestine. His condition, as the physicians realized, was hopeless.

The pretext for this murder was that Mrs. McFarland, who had recently divorced her husband after a separation of two years, was intending to marry Richardson. The real reasons for it were that McFarland was a failure, embittered against everybody; an habitual drunkard, made savage rather than merry by drink; a sponge, indebted for his living to his wife and his wife's friends.

After ten years of it, Mrs. McFarland wearied of putting her husband to bed when he was drunk and getting punched in the eye next morning when he had a hangover, of supporting him and their children, and listening to his blubberings when he had a fit of repentance.

After she had left him, and before she got her divorce, she agreed to marry Richardson as soon as she might be free. For this offense, she and Richardson had been under the threat of McFarland's vengeance. Once he had crept up in the dark, as they walked along the street together, and fired shots at both of them. One bullet had wounded Richardson slightly.

The newspaperman was not wanting in courage—as his Civil War career proved—but he knew it was useless to go about armed. It was not McFarland's way to shoot it out in the open; his delicate sense of honor led him to spring suddenly out of dark corners.

The Richardson-McFarland quarrel had been a subject for New York gossip for two years, or ever since the first shooting. Now it became a national scandal of the first water, especially as the wounded man was known—and liked—everywhere in the country. Dozens of eminent persons sent telegrams of sympathy. The American press was almost unanimous in denouncing McFarland as a cowardly murderer. The only exceptions were a few New York papers whose politics led them to think that any misfortune to a *Tribune* man was probably all right.

McFarland had studied at Dartmouth and in Paris, but the only use of his learning he ever made was to get appointed Professor of Logic, Belles-Lettres, and Elocution in Brandywine College in Delaware. This did not last long, for the whole college burned up one night. He had been admitted to the Massachusetts bar, but never practised. Meeting, in New England, a precociously brilliant girl of nineteen named Abby Sage, he persuaded her to marry him. Within three months he pawned his watch to pay their hotel bill and sent her back to her father. He was always willing to borrow five dollars from old Mr. Sage, a laborer in Massachusetts.

Abby Sage was one of the great number of women who have an ambition to write for publication. There was this peculiarity about her writings: editors in both New York and Boston were willing to publish them and pay for them. This was convenient when her children wanted something to eat.

Mr. McFarland's only contribution to their welfare was to cry into his beer, tell the bartender that his wife failed to appreciate him, and to curse out "old Greeley and the *Tribune* crowd." The black sin which old Greeley and the *Tribune* crowd had committed against McFarland was twice to get him a job in a city office.

But Abby Sage had another ambition: to go upon the stage. And even this did not seem absurd when no less a person than Edwin Booth approved it and gave her small, but nevertheless speaking, parts in his company.

"Make no mistake," Mr. Frohman emphasizes, "about

Richardson and Abby Sage. There never has been a finer or higher-minded man or woman. Richardson was kind to the people who worked for him and honorable in all his dealings. A brilliant man."

Albert Richardson's reputation was based on solid achievement. His books—on Civil War experiences and on the West—were vivid and popular.* They are thoroughly readable, to-day. On account of his escape from a Southern prison, he had emerged from the Civil War with the glamour of romance about him. There was no more widely known war correspondent in America.

McFarland's immediate grievance was based on an intercepted letter to his wife from Richardson. She had already left her husband and was contemplating divorce. If the text is correct as given out by McFarland, it is undeniably a love letter, which might be interpreted to mean intimate relations between the two. It started McFarland upon various kinds of attack: first, letters in the papers, assailing Richardson; then, a suit for forty-five thousand dollars' damages; and finally, to assure the world of the purity of his motives, two shootings.

His first use of the letter is illuminating: the key to his character. He wandered about with it, reading it to people in saloons and to policemen on the street, any acquaintance or stranger who would listen. Then he went to the notorious Brick Pomeroy, owner of *Pomeroy's Democrat*, and tried to sell the letter to him for a hundred dollars.

Brick, on the witness stand, testified,

"He said the letter contained full particulars of the debauchery of his wife by Mr. Richardson, of the *Tribune*; he stated that Mr. Greeley and others of the

* The Field, The Dungeon, and The Escape" (1865) and "Beyond The Mississippi" (1869).

Tribune were running a free-love establishment [laughter] and that I, by publishing the letter, would make a sensation, and enable me to get even with Mr. Greeley."

The high-minded Brick declined the offer.

As soon as Richardson was shot, Mrs. McFarland came to New York and helped take care of him. Her divorce had been granted in October. For a week he lay, in torment, dying. On December 1st, papers printed this notice:

> Married. At the Astor House, Nov. 30. By Rev. Henry Ward Beecher, assisted by Rev. O. B. Frothingham, Albert D. Richardson of New York, to Abby M., eldest daughter of William Sage of Boston.

He survived for about twenty-four hours, and died at five o'clock in the morning of December 2nd.

Four months later, when Richardson was buried and forgotten, his widow was set up as a target for the batteries of mud which were being prepared by McFarland's defense.

This defense was led by a truculent lawyer named John Graham. Its first assertion was that McFarland was raving mad and hadn't the faintest idea what he was doing; its second, that he acted from an "uncontrollable impulse" (everything "going blank"); and its third, that he was a Paladin of Purity, striking in behalf of all that was chaste and holy in America.

The "uncontrollable impulse" was dwelt upon day after day. Thirty-six years later, in the Thaw trial, it was being called a "brainstorm." But Mr. Graham had still other strings to his harp.

McFarland had been born in Ireland, therefore this persecution of him, by a trial for murder, was one more outrage upon th' ould sod. Mr. Graham announced from time to time that while the breath was in his body, Ireland should suffer no wrong, and this display of courage was loudly applauded by a claque which filled the court.

Next, McFarland was a faithful henchman of Tammany Hall. And what had he done except shoot a dirty, black Republican? The ruler of New York at that time was Boss Tweed, then at the height of his power.

Finally, this was a splendid chance to tell the world that the chief Republican newspaper was managed by people who were all "free-lovers"—and worse.

So McFarland's junior counsel, Mr. Spencer, began with a ferocious address in which he excoriated Mrs. McFarland's women friends. One of these was the wife of a *Tribune* editor, and another was a writer for that paper. They were actually a lot of rather gushing but harmless girls, who had exchanged long letters with Abby Sage.

Their burbling epistles, mostly about her stage career and her good fortune in joining Booth's company, had no more to do with the case than had the lives of Antarctic penguins; nevertheless all the letters were read in full. Mr. Spencer described the *Tribune* ladies as "panders and procuresses." He went so far in his enthusiasm that he found it wise to apologize next day.

Mr. Graham growled and snarled. In court, he quoted the Bible and long passages of Latin. Outside, in the corridors, he descended to more familiar discourse, as when he met one of the prosecuting attorneys, old Judge Davis, there. Mr. Graham's remarks on this occasion were:

"God damn you! I can lick two of you, God damn you!"

Such were legal amenities in days when, we are often told, gentlemen were devoted to the stately, old-fashioned courtesies.

After more than a month of Mr. Graham's bombast, the jury acquitted McFarland—as everyone expected. The court rang with cheers, and the women who were waiting to kiss McFarland had to form in double lines.

Abby Sage Richardson had to be content, for the rest of her life, with the respect and friendship of the intelligent. She died in Rome, in 1900, although she had lived in America most of the time since the tragedy. She was the author of a number of books, and she both wrote and adapted for the stage.

Mr. Frohman speaks of her as "probably the best reader of plays I ever had."

"She made dramatic versions of Mark Twain's 'Prince and the Pauper,'" said he, "and of Agnes and Egerton Castle's 'Pride of Jennico,' and of novels by Stanley Weyman. She could read the manuscript of a play, or read a novel, and then put on four pages of note paper a précis which would tell me whether or not I wished to produce it. She was a woman of great ability, and, besides that, a most lovable person."

Soon after his acquittal, McFarland, the Paladin of Purity, followed great Orion, sloping slowly to the West. In what state he lived, I do not know, but the rest of his career was similar to that of many protectors of virtue who have been released by juries amid cheers and kisses. He never "saw red" again; indeed, had he been successful in scaring forty-five thousand dollars out of Richardson, or even wheedling a hundred out of Brick Pomeroy, probably he would never have seen red at all.

In the West, he went in for serious drinking, for which his means were limited but his application perfect. He managed, without difficulty, to drink himself to death.

BERTRAM
THE BURGLAR

THE burglar's profession has been commercialized and robbed of romance. To-day, if your wife's pearl necklace is stolen, you do not send for the police. They would merely hector the gardener, the chauffeur and the cook. Instead, you call up an insurance company, and two days later a mysterious little man saunters in with the necklace.

Simple as that! And only costs a few thousand dollars a year.

In 1860, 1870, or 1880, a burglar had some pride. He wore a black mask, and came tiptoeing upstairs at 2:30 A.M. In one hand, he carried a revolver; in another hand, a dark lantern smelling of whale-oil; in another hand, a bottle of ether and a sponge. Sometimes you heard him creeping about; usually it was when you came out of the ether that you learned he had called.

You found that he had taken, and carried away in a sack, eleven teaspoons, the ice-water pitcher, the baby's porringer, your wife's mosaic earrings and brooch, your second-best watch, your shirt-studs and black jet cuff buttons, your gold cravat pin (a tiger's head, with ruby eyes) the wax calla lily under glass, from the parlor table, a copy of the Rev. Dr. Lord's lectures, and the ambrotype portraits of Uncle Henry and Cousin Susy.

In my native city of Newburyport, where Bossy Gillis (like Bryan Duff in the poem) "no longer rules* as lord upon the hill," there was, long ago, a picturesque burglar who did things in the best tradition. And he added little touches of his own, such as setting out the chessmen on the open pages of the family Bible, to show he had been there.

One night he ran whang into a charge of buckshot, and when they bore his lifeless form into the police station, everyone was amazed to discover that he was an African citizen, wearing a pink silk undershirt. Swank of that kind, in the underworld, was a novelty in the 1860's.

Twenty-six years ago there was an attempt to revive the old customs. Springfield, Massachusetts, was the scene of the revival, and for two summers the city experienced some bizarre sensations.

Householders, coming indoors from their verandas, and ascending to their bedrooms, would find a tall, masked man, studiously collecting trinkets from the dressing tables, or peering into purses and wallets. He would point a revolver at the intimidated family, and suggest that they help him find something valuable.

Sometimes, on a lean evening, he had to be content with the lady's rings, a two-dollar bill, and a tearful assurance that there wasn't any more. Once, however, he eased $40 out of two women; and again, when he had been found lurking in the bathroom, he pursued his discoverer, a maiden lady, to the front door, and with his revolver induced her to ransom her life and liberty for $60.

Altogether, from beginning to end, he accumulated a considerable amount of plunder. Along with this he took many pieces of cheap jewelry and other rubbish, and this fact was enlarged upon, at a later date, when a determined

* Mistake; he does rule there. But it's Newburyport's mistake.

effort was made to show that he was just a mischievous fellow, who needed only to be humored. Of course, he was not an expert burglar, on the grand, modern scale. He was more dangerous than that.

He revived the ancient notion of hiding under the bed. There he would uncomfortably linger, for an hour or more, patiently waiting for the lady, on the upper side of the mattress, to get to sleep. Restraining the tendency to sneeze, which must come from such close association with the lint which gathers under a bed, he would at last betray his presence.

Then there would be agitation on the part of the lady, checked by threats with the revolver, and after the transfer of any convenient jewelry or money, he would bid the victim good night, and vanish. His conduct toward one or two of his hostesses was plainly indecent, but these facts were mercifully hushed up, on the day of reckoning, so that he should not be prejudiced before the jury, who were considering a still graver crime.

Once or twice, he thrust his black mask and his revolver into an evening party of whist, and once he adroitly shot out the lights in order to get away. Once, on Christmas Eve, and after an appeal from the mother of a family, he tenderly refrained from stealing the children's Christmas presents. Probably he said that nothing would prevail upon him to harm "the kiddies." I think he was just the kind of person to say "kiddies."

Once he conversed, at length, with two maidservants, one of whom he surprised as she sat, simply attired in her nightdress, reading a magazine. Then, thinking of business, he descended to the floor beneath, and stole the pocketbook of the master of the house. From another man, he declined a goldpiece—after he had noticed that the owner had taken an identifying glance at the date of it.

But he did not confine his persecutions to women and timid householders. One night, in the open, he held up a motorman, Mike Gilhooley—no less—shot him in the leg, and robbed him of his money—about a dollar. Dr. L. Vernon Briggs, in an essay, mentions the fact that it was a small sum, as if that made the affair rather a treat to the motorman. The caliber of the bullet removed from Mr. Gilhooley's leg was .38, so that may have compensated him for any disappointment he felt at not having handed over a whole week's pay, instead of one measly dollar.

One night, the burglar hastily slid down a ladder to escape from a house, ran across a garden and dropped a locket: his own locket, with his initials B.G.S., and portraits of his mother and sister. This was found, but, by a tragic error, no use was then made of the information.

Mr. B.G.S. realized that he had left a dangerous clue behind him, and for six months refrained from his raids. Then, on a night in March, 1910, he ventured out once more; took his revolver; adjusted a black handkerchief over part of his face; removed his shoes; and entered the home of a Mrs. Dow, who sat, trying to do a picture puzzle, with her two daughters and a guest, Miss Martha Blackstone.

These women were alarmed when the burglarious figure entered the room and demanded their money. Two of them screamed and tried to escape, whereupon the burglar shot Miss Blackstone through the heart, and with another shot wounded Miss Harriet Dow in the head. Then he departed.

It was afterwards argued, by those who felt the warmest sympathy for the burglar, but only irritation toward his victim, that Miss Blackstone was inconsiderate to have

screamed. It seemed that he never liked people to scream
while he was robbing them. If Miss Blackstone had understood this, everything might have been different and
much pleasanter.

I have never heard, by the way, that Mr. Gilhooley
screamed. He simply tried to run away.

The clue of the locket now enabled the police to arrest
Mr. Bertram G. Spencer, a married man of twenty-nine,
who had been supplementing his fair earnings by day,
with these forays by night. He promptly made a complete confession of the robberies and murder, and this
was corroborated by identification by some of his victims, and by his possession of the revolver, the mask, and
a satchel of loot.

Bertram, henceforth, was not a popular character in
Springfield, where the life of Miss Blackstone, a worthy
school teacher, was regarded, by conservative opinion,
as rather the more valuable of the two. As a conspicuous
and brutal killer, however, Spencer enlisted the warm
support of a minority, who for more than two years
adopted every device for his preservation.

The only possible plea was insanity: that he did all
these things, such as carrying the revolver, putting on
the mask, and robbing these houses, because of an "ir-
resistible impulse." Spencer adopted the idea with enthusiasm, and began to wag his head, roll his eyes and
scream curses at all his "enemies."

The first doctor who saw him at it—a humble, general
practitioner—promptly told him to "stop faking," and he
instantly obeyed.

One or two of the heap-big, *pukka* alienists from Boston, steeped in the lore of Vienna, fell for his maneuvers,
and the result was a long, costly and rather disorderly
trial, held in order to prove the obvious fact that Spencer

had murdered Miss Blackstone and that he did not need to do it. Alienist disputed alienist, and the prisoner roared and frothed and yelled his abuse.

The jury heard an account of nearly a year passed by Spencer, after his arrest, in a State Hospital, under observation. They learned that his play-acting, there, had gradually subsided, as the electric chair had seemed to have become a remote possibility. They saw his mimicry commence again, when the law held him responsible for his act. And, in the end, the jury refused to be bamboozled.

That he was "mentally defective" was as much as his alienists could say for him. It had not been noticed by his employers, nor by his superiors when he was in the Navy. Everyone agreed that he sometimes had a nasty temper.

Anyhow, it is almost as annoying to find a "mental defective" under your bed, to be robbed by him of your pocketbook, or to have him put a bullet into your thorax, as if it were done by the most high-powered psychiatrist who ever sat up all night reading the works of Dr. Brill.

SOB SISTERS EMERGE

MARIA BARBERI had become angry with her lover. He still refused to marry her—although, by all the laws of God and man, he ought to have done that at any time for more than a year. She got a razor, an unpleasant, jagged razor, which looked as if it had been used not only to sharpen pencils but to open tin cans.

The faithless one—his name was Domenico Cataldo—was sitting in a bar-room, playing cards with some friends. Maria crept up behind him, and very efficiently cut his throat. In doing this, as any newspaper reader knows, she observed the conventional limit of the gash—it was "from ear to ear."

Cataldo, thoroughly dismayed, rose from his chair and rushed into the street. Pausing in front of the bar-room, at the corner of Avenue A and Fourteenth Street, he remarked:

"I die!"

And, falling upon the pavement, he instantly made good his statement. The police led Maria away to prison.

With her family, a few years before, Maria had come to New York from southern Italy. She met Cataldo in the street. Her father warned her against the man, but his allure was great. He had four hundred dollars in the bank, and to this he added as much more—from what source I cannot tell you. He and Maria set up housekeeping (disregarding all omens) on Thirteenth Street.

From time to time, so said Maria, Cataldo uttered a promise of matrimony. But he said less and less about it, and finally, on the day of the throat-slitting, expressed the utmost contempt for the holy estate. His exact words were:

"Only pigs marry."

This obviously incorrect assertion seemed to need no reply. Maria, however, found it exasperating. So she had recourse to the crushing rejoinder of the razor, and now Cataldo was in the morgue, and she was in the Tombs.

Three months later, in July, 1895, Maria sat in court, wearing her usual bovine expression. On the bench, as in all proper murder trials of that period, was Recorder Goff. This old Irish gentleman, with his white beard and gentle voice, has gone down in tradition as a "hanging judge." This is because he had the idea—even then curiously antiquated—that the criminal law does not exist to be made into the likeness of a monkey.

The first trial of Maria Barberi was brief. There could be no denial of the killing. The character of Cataldo was discussed, but the Recorder simply told the jury that the question for them was not whether the dead man might have been a saint or a devil. It was: had Maria deliberately murdered him? They conferred for one hour, and answered that she had.

Not long afterward, Recorder Goff sentenced her to death. He was presently to learn that the law not only can be made into a monkey, it can be transformed into a three-ring circus, with a cageful of baboons.

The newspapers presently discovered that if Maria were executed in the electric chair, she would be the first woman so to suffer. Straightway, the founts of emotion were unsealed; the sob sisters were gathered together; and for a year and a half there beat upon Sing Sing Prison, upon the Tombs, and upon the Criminal Courts, the rolling billows of a mighty ocean of mush.

The Governor might have chosen the expedient of commuting the sentence to a term of years in prison. But the law still held that Maria was a murderess; while to all the hysterical folk in the land, the death sentence had converted her into a heroine, a broken blossom, and a martyr of the tyrant Man. Nothing but complete exoneration would satisfy: to punish her original prosecutors, Maria must not only be set free, but walk on roses.

When she went into court for sentence, the *Tribune* noted the group of sympathizing women: her aunt, the Contessa di Brazza Savargnon, and others. She—I think the *Tribune* means the aunt, and not the Contessa—was frisked as she entered court and found to be carrying a stiletto with a blade five inches long. During the second trial, it would have been most unpopular to record that any of Maria's supporters went so well heeled.

The *Tribune*, however, coldly refrained from ecstasies about Maria Barberi, and even said something about "sentimentality run wild."

The Contessa di Brazza Savargnon announced that, for her part, she intended to leave no stone unturned in her efforts to secure justice for Maria. The Contessa's participation gratified the newspapers, and helped to lift the case out of the lowly atmosphere of Avenue A.

People began to send in petitions and write wrathfully to the newspapers. The story of Maria's blow for oppressed womanhood had rallied the advocates of "Women's Rights" and inflamed the country. On the same day, groups of people as widely separated as "the Italo-Americans of Texas" and the summer boarders at the Griswold

Hotel, near New London, sent red-hot messages to the Governor of New York. Austin Corbin and Colonel Bob Ingersoll began to boil.

The sentence was denounced as a "ferocious absurdity." An indignant native American, resident of Connecticut, wrote in to say that as women had had no part in making the laws, they were not responsible to the laws —a theory which must have delighted the noble army of shoplifters. This gentleman added, as a clincher, that in writing his letter he had used an inkstand which once belonged to "the great Garibaldi."

One man, in Fort Scott, Kansas, sent to the Governor of New York demanding transportation to Sing Sing so that he could be electrocuted instead of Maria. Being about to die for her, he could not be expected to pay his fare too.

In August, the hot and silly season, the whole country seemed to be exploding with indignation toward that callous set of brutes, the male citizens of New York. Five or ten years were subtracted from Maria's age, and she was called "this child of fifteen." That she had voluntarily lived as Cataldo's mistress for more than a year, was, of course, quite ignored, and she was described as a Lucrece, desperately striking in defense of her "unsullied purity."

The massed chivalry of Arkansas arose, and in a petition signed by the Governor and all the state officials, apprised Governor Morton of New York as to the correct conduct of a man of honor.

Instead of some short cut, like a commutation of sentence, Maria was granted another trial, to which she came in November, 1896—two weeks after Mr. McKinley's election to the Presidency. This trial is thought to have marked the first great emergence of the sob sisters. They were already in existence, but never before had they been given a chance to utter such a universal moan, or to compose so many columns of unmitigated tripe. It is to be admitted that some of the worst of the sob sisters, as well as those who directed it all, were really brothers.

The *Journal* and the *World* were contending for supremacy. The *Journal* had an artist who, every Sunday, drew a picture of a nauseous boy in a yellow nightgown, and the *World* had an artist who also drew a nauseous boy in a yellow nightgown, and although the color of those nightgowns was extended, in popular phrase, to cover both papers, there was still no decision as to which was the better. Each claimed ownership of the "Yellow Kid."

Both papers set out to convert into a great human tragedy a murder trial which contained neither mystery, nor romance, nor legal or social importance. The conduct of the lawyers was perhaps equally footling, and the result illustrated the ability of the public to go—for one month—perfectly cuckoo about something for which they do not care a solitary damn.

No reporter, no artist, could endow Maria with beauty. She was squat in face and in figure. The newspaper illustrations at that time could make even Mrs. Langtry look like a scarecrow, and to little Signorina Barberi they did cruel justice. Nor was it discoverable—in spite of rumors—that "the stork was hovering over the Tombs." So the reporters had to content themselves with a lesser bird: Maria's canary, which was in a cage in her cell. His name was Cicillo, and he and the Contessa di Brazza Savargnon flutter in and out of the story.

After a few preliminary accounts of Maria in her dungeon (the solitary sunbeam that fell on the cold stones —tears of the lonely girl—the dawning of hope—"a prayer and all is bright again") the newspapers allowed the trial

to begin. Justice Goff was no longer presiding. Messrs.
McIntyre and Lauterbach were cast for the parts of
First and Second Ruffian—that is, they represented the
People. Messrs. Friend, House and Grossman, for the
defense.

Maria had learned English in her sixteen months at
Sing Sing. She was supported in court by the "Tombs
Angel," a being whom the newspaper artists made to
look as gloomy as the gates of Tartarus. Her function
was to restore Maria from time to time by means of
"peptonoids," of which she had a bottle in her pocket.
Everybody who read the *Journal* or the *World* knew
how often, and at what times, the Angel slipped Maria a
peptonoid.

Maria had crocheted a silk purse, not out of the traditional sow's ear, but from the orthodox material, and also
a chatelaine bag. She ornamented them both with jet
beads, and gave them to "Lawyer Friend." The *World*
also showed large-scale views of Maria's ears. It discussed
Lombroso's theories, and asked: Is she a degenerate?

The defense was "psychical epilepsy." Mr. House
described the prisoner's life, and her family history in
Italy for three generations. Her ruin had been accomplished by means of drugs. In the 1890's no girl was ever
ruined except by drugs. Sometimes the rascal put the
drug into her soda water; in especially wicked instances,
into beer. Maria had been ruined both ways.

A genealogical chart was produced: it showed that
Maria was descended from the Barbellis on one side and
Bonfantis on the other. Both families were full of insanity
and epilepsy. The lawyer mentioned other allied families, all lunatics. Maria had an uncle who was an "exhi-
bitionist"; he used to take his friends to a tavern, treat

them to drinks all round, get himself drunk, and then, tearing his clothes off, run down the street shouting.

Cataldo had "insulted" the girl for days. Finally, everything "went blank," and Maria killed him.

What these newspapers thought about her is undiscoverable. On the same page with articles recounting her sweetness, her prayers, her Christian kindliness, would be enlarged plans of the palms of her hands, with especial emphasis on her "degenerate thumb" and her "abnormal nail."

Astrologer Bache cast her horoscope, and the papers reproduced it. The progressive Luna had reached the evil Uranus, while Mars and Neptune by transit were retrograde. So there was danger of "ultimate collapse," but while her life would be spared, she would hardly escape "a milder touch of the law." This looked as if the stars in their courses were hedging, and even so they guessed wrong.

Maria's mother, a grim old lady in a mantilla, gave evidence. The headlines for that day were "Tortured in Court. Mother Gives Way. 'Oh My Head!' She Moans." This was because she was cross-examined.

Maria was a witness in her own behalf. The artists were waiting for this. She sat under the mural painting of the Three Fates, in the Supreme Court Room, and the pictures all showed the skull in that painting as ominously near Maria's head.

Question (by Mr. House): Maria, were you a good girl before you met Cataldo?

Answer (in a whisper): Yes.

Don't cry, my dear, said Mr. House.

Maria had her handkerchief to her eyes, but wept very little.

That afternoon, Mr. McIntyre, for the prosecution,

refrained from cross-examination. So she kissed his hand and told him that, the very first night at Sing Sing, she had prayed for him. This was the first of many kissings, and the artists drew pictures of them all. Mr. McIntyre, although a great, big, strong assistant district attorney wearing a bowler hat, was all broken up. He moved aside —thirty sob sisters marked him well—and "something like a tear" glistened in his eye.

Next day, however, he questioned her at length. So she "Wept on Stand" and "Collapsed in Cell." (Pictures both of the weeping and the collapsing.)

The high spot of the eighteenth day of the trial came as a surprise. Angelo Piscopo, friend and neighbor, was testifying as to Maria's infirmities. Nobody had suspected Mr. Piscopo's accomplishments as an actor of the Grand Guignol school. When he was asked about the prisoner's fits, he suddenly uttered a dismal howl and gave such an imitation of epilepsy that two of the sob sisters became hysterical and had to be removed from court, while the Tombs Angel ran out of peptonoids.

The next day was given over to social pastimes and amenities. "Lawyer Friend" had his forty-third birthday. Maria gave him a silver lead pencil and a letter full of gratitude. The other members of the bar—on both sides—united in buying him a fine luncheon and a large basket of red roses. All—as Captain Andy Hawks would say—all one big, happy family. Afternoon tea was served in the Tombs for Maria and other guests. Mrs. Sarah Bird poured.

Around Mulberry Bend was being sold a street ballad:

> 'Tis not for me to speak aloud
>   On lofty themes. I tell
> As one among the lowly crowd
>   How young Maria fell.

Swift as a flash a glittering blade
Across his throat she drew,
"By you," she shrieked, "I've been betrayed:
This vengeance is my due!"

Behold her now, a wounded dove:
A native of a clime
Where hearts are melted soon with love
And maddened soon to crime.

Meanwhile, greater days were preparing. The more costly methods of wasting time were yet to be employed. Outside, expert alienists were pawing the ground and shouting ha! ha! among the trumpets. There were five great doctors on each side. So all day long the noise of battle rolled.

Dr. Hrdlicka, one of Maria's doctors, was asked by Mr. McIntyre if, when he measured Maria with Benedict's instruments, he knew that Professor Langer of Vienna had found them to be .07 of a centimeter short. Said the Doctor:

"I didn't use Benedict's. I used the *compas d'épaisseur* of Glissière, the cephalometer of Anthelme, and the bregma indicator of Broca."

"Oh," said Mr. McIntyre.

The following day, the lawyer put over a fast one and nearly evened the score. He showed the Doctor some unlabeled charts and plans of human craniums, and almost trapped the learned scientist into branding as "abnormal" President Grover Cleveland, Senator David B. Hill, George Vanderbilt, and Judge Gildersleeve, who was presiding over the trial.

Finally, all topics of conversation having been exhausted, the lawyers and doctors were reduced to discussing whether baldness and premature gray hairs are signs of degeneracy.

After about a month of this solemn balderdash, at a public cost of two or three hundred dollars a day, the jury deliberated for one hour and acquitted the prisoner. There were more kissings and embracings.

"My dear, I never doubted for an instant that you were a good, honest girl," said the prosecutor.

The *World* and the *Journal* each reproduced her autograph letters of thanks to the editors. She was offered five hundred dollars a week by two or three dime museums. Her return to the Tombs was a triumph.

> "Let me in, let me in!" the girl cried, beating with her chubby hands against the grating. She laughed loudly. There was no ray of triumph, of jubilation in the laugh. She was a baby, free again, playing like a baby at going to prison. Keeper John Hurley opened the grating.

When she got in, all the warders had to be kissed. The Contessa had been mislaid, but someone at last reached her by telephone. Maria greeted her over the wire.

"Hello, the Contessa!" she cried. "I am so glad!"

Outside the Tombs, the crowd continued to cheer.

Cicillo, the canary, for some reason, did not get out that night. A day or two later, Maria, accompanied by "Lawyer Friend" and a shoal of reporters and artists, made a special visit and recovered him.

Meanwhile—the papers recorded it, but drew no inferences—over in Brooklyn, one Mrs. James Dockery had found Mr. Dockery too tiresome. She cut his throat with a razor, and he was removed to an emergency hospital. According to later reports, Mr. Dockery was in "a highly critical condition."

MR. BRAVO'S
BURGUNDY

DINNER at Mr. Bravo's, "The Priory," Tooting Beck Common, Balham. Mr. and Mrs. Bravo, and the *confidante*, Mrs. Cox. A family dinner, at 7:30, in the Bravo residence, "a stucco structure of bastard Gothic," surrounded by a lawn, rose bushes, melon pits, strawberry beds, fruit trees, a pinery and a vinery. In short, an Englishman's suburban villa in the year 1876.

We see this trio on an evening in April, waited upon by the butler, Frederick Rowe, who, like his master, decorates his face with side-whiskers. The dinner is whiting, a roast of lamb, poached eggs on buttered toast, and vegetables, followed by bloater-paste, probably as a savory. No sweets are mentioned, and everyone, afterwards, took care to say there was "no spinach." Bravo took what the others did, except that he ate no fish.

The wine is interesting. The butler had decanted the usual allowance for the meal: two bottles of sherry, a bottle of Marsala, and a bottle of Burgundy. Mr. Bravo had had a pint of claret with his luncheon in town, and a glass of wine when he came in from his ride before dinner. Now, with this meal, he drinks his customary three or four glasses of Burgundy. Nobody else takes this wine.

Mrs. Bravo and Mrs. Cox had not been without vinous comfort during the day. Mrs. Bravo—who was in delicate health—had a solitary luncheon at home, and, with it, champagne—I suppose a pint. Yet, considering what has been attested about her, I would not put it past her to get away with a quart, and tell the butler to keep his mouth shut. (She spent the afternoon reclining on a couch.)

Mrs. Cox had been away since breakfast, house hunting, but she had been shielded against drought by a pint of sherry which she carried on her hip—or whatever was its Victorian equivalent.

Yet these two sedate ladies now drink two bottles of sherry—and this was no special occasion of festivity. Just a quiet home dinner.

After their meal, they go to the "morning room" and while they are there, drowsing slightly, let us consider them and their histories.

Mr. Bravo is a barrister of about thirty; the much-indulged stepson of a wealthy man. He is not overfond of the law, but desires the distinction it may bring him in the form of a seat in Parliament. He fusses about his health a good deal, and fosters a childish temper which makes him fly into a tantrum if the soup is cold. Or if the soup is hot. Rather a petulant tyrant towards his wife, he submits to some ridiculous commands from her: for instance, he wears, because she says it "becomes him," a red flannel contraption, "a cross between a kilt, a sporran, and a pair of bathing drawers" which has "as many strings as a harp." It makes him feel, he says, "as if I had stays on my stomach." It was supposed, in some mysterious way, to be healthful.

He and his wife have been married less than five months. She is a small and very pretty woman, with remarkably beautiful chestnut colored hair. When she married Mr. Bravo, she was the widow of a Captain Ricardo.

Her life with him had had its pleasant intervals, during the Captain's periods of sobriety, but his three or four attacks of delirium tremens had so marred their happiness that they separated. When Captain Ricardo died, leaving his young widow an income of nearly £4000, there was no reason to pretend grief.

She traveled with her companion, Mrs. Cox, and her physician, Dr. Gully; she bought "The Priory"; she met Mr. Bravo and married him; and they settled down at "The Priory" which, first of all, she made over to her new husband. He insisted that he must "sit on his own chairs."

Upon one important matter, Mrs. Bravo had her way. And that was the presence at her side of Jane Cannon Cox. This hard-sided, steel-spectacled, old battle-ax was an absolute necessity to the young and pretty Florence Bravo, and, like it or not, her husband must accept her as a member of the household.

Mrs. Cox was from Jamaica; a widow with three sons, who were away at school. Provided with a pleasant home, good cooking (*vin compris*), no very heavy duties, and £100 a year, Mrs. Cox was assured of her comfort, and quite naturally, would not care to have things altered.

Yet Mr. Bravo continued to regard Mrs. Cox as rather an extravagance. Although heir to a fortune, he had only a small income, with casual allowances from his step-father, and he felt in duty bound to conserve his wife's money.

Said Mrs. Bravo, at a later date:

"He was pressing me to put down my garden and my cobs—my two great hobbies—and turn away Mrs. Cox, to save. He thus hoped to save £400 a year."

About a month before this dinner, he had begun to agitate about Mrs. Cox, when a curious incident happened. On his way to the train one morning, directly after breakfast, he was taken violently sick—so sick, that, as he told his stepfather, he feared people would think he had been drunk the night before.

The attack had lasted only part of a day, and he was now in his usual good health. Yesterday, Easter Monday, he had marked out a court for lawn tennis, and had spent the day teaching Mrs. Cox's little sons (there for the holiday) this new game. (He wanted to play on Sunday, before the boys came, but Mrs. Cox objected.) And to-day he had taken a ride, on his cob "Cremorne," before dinner.

He came in hot and bothered—the horse had bolted with him—and Mrs. Bravo commanded the housemaid to prepare a warm bath for the master. It is a bit odd to notice that in this household, where wine flowed free, they were parsimonious with the water: Mr. Bravo bade Keeber, the housemaid,

"Leave the water in the bath, as it will do for me in the morning."

The three sat in the morning room for half an hour or so before their early bedtime. Conversation did not sparkle. Mr. Bravo muttered about aches and pains: the result, he thought, of trying to hold in his fiery horse. Mrs. Cox was gloomy on her own account: her relatives in the island of Jamaica had been suggesting her return, and both Mr. Bravo and his stepfather seemed to think it a good idea. They were trying to separate her from darling Florence. And Mrs. Bravo was again suffering from thirst. Evidently they did not take coffee and cordials after dinner at "The Priory." She asked Mrs. Cox to get her another glass of sherry.

They all went upstairs, Mrs. Cox bringing the sherry up from the dining room. During Mrs. Bravo's indisposition her husband was occupying another bedroom, while Mrs. Cox and Mrs. Bravo slept together. The sherry did not assuage Mrs. Bravo's dryness, and as soon as she was undressed she sent the maid downstairs for another glass of wine. Marsala, this time. Mr. Bravo, on his way upstairs, saw the servant with the Marsala and rushed into his wife's room, exclaiming—in French, because of the maid's presence:

"You have sent for more wine; you have had nearly a whole bottle today!"

This was an understatement; Mrs. Bravo must have been a daughter of the three-bottle-men of old, and was living up to her heritage.

She made no reply and, as she said, "was asleep in ten minutes"—a statement easy of belief.

Shortly afterwards, Mr. Bravo emerged on the landing, in his nightshirt, shouting:

"Florence! Florence! hot water! hot water!"

Mrs. Cox and the housemaid rushed to his assistance. He retreated to his room, where he was violently sick. Mrs. Bravo was roused from her slumbers, and found Mrs. Cox rubbing the sufferer's chest with camphor. They procured emetics; they sent the menservants for doctors.

The history of the next fifty hours is altogether distressing. Mr. Bravo, to every physician who saw him, was plainly dying from the effects of an irritant poison. He was usually conscious and often in agony.

To every doctor who questioned him as to what he had taken, his only reply was "laudanum." This, he said, he had rubbed on his gums to cure neuralgia. They assured him that laudanum could not account for his symptoms. At last, worn out with their queries, the dying man retorted:

"Why the devil should I have sent for you, if I knew what was the matter with me?"

Mrs. Cox who was very active, in and about the room, suggested that he had taken chloroform, but this did not strike the physicians as probable. At last, some hours after the beginning of the illness, Mrs. Cox took one of the doctors aside and told him that when she first reached Mr. Bravo's room, he had said to her:

"I've taken some of that poison, but don't tell Florence."

The astonished doctor hurried back to Mr. Bravo, who said that he remembered no such remark. During the two days and nights that remained to the wretched man, he and his wife bore themselves as any married pair would do who were passionately in love with one another. No one who knew him believed that he would commit suicide; everybody who saw Florence Bravo was convinced that her grief and distress were genuine. Before his death, Mr. Bravo said:

"I am going to appear before my Maker, and I have told you the truth. I have taken nothing but what I have told you."

The inquest revealed that he had been killed by antimony, in the form of tartar emetic. The coroner sat at "The Priory," and the proceedings had the air of an endeavor to hush everything up. The verdict was:

"Poison—antimony, but we have not sufficient evidence under what circumstances it came into his body."

Mr. Bravo was buried, and his widow and her faithful companion went off to recuperate at Brighton. Mrs. Bravo was now convinced that her husband—"poor Charlie"—had committed suicide. And Jane Cannon Cox seemed secure in her position.

But no one else was satisfied. Questions were asked in

Parliament; a Government investigation was held; and finally another inquest was ordered. This tore the lid off everything, including poor Mr. Bravo's coffin, which was exhumed.

For twenty-three days the eyes of England were on a small room in a stuffy little Balham hotel, where were gathered all the great lawyers of the land, including the famous solicitor, Sir George Lewis, who represented the Bravo family, and made everyone unhappy by his withering cross-examinations.

Butlers, ladies' maids, grooms, physicians, chemists and all the members of all the families had their bad quarters of an hour. Mrs. Cox had five days of it.

This lady had been gradually enlarging her original story of Mr. Bravo's declaration, until it took this form:

"I have taken poison *for Dr. Gully.* Don't tell Florence."

Now, lawyers, in their uncompromising search for truth, are never so eager as when the path leads them to expose the ways of a man with a maid, or, better still, the escapades of two people who are married, but not to each other. Then, their pure enthusiasm becomes all the more commendable, especially when the scandal has little or nothing to do with the point at issue.

What was dragged bit by bit out of the humiliated and tearful Mrs. Bravo, and out of the apparently reluctant Mrs. Cox was a complicated story. The Bravos had quite honestly exhibited to each other the skeletons in their respective closets.

"He told me," testified Mrs. Bravo, "that he had kept a woman, before marriage, at Maidenhead for four years, and I believe he continued her an annual payment after marriage, and owed her or her sister £500."

There was also a child—Katie—by this woman, and the

dying Charles Bravo had asked his wife to take care of her. She had evidently agreed.

On his part, he had found it hard to contemplate with equanimity his wife's excursions into primrose paths. Yet, before marriage, she had told him frankly that in the year following the death of Captain Ricardo, she had conceived an indiscreet affection for her old family physician, Dr. Gully. The extent of this affair was slowly wrenched from Mrs. Cox by Sir George Lewis. The cross-examiner was not content with Mrs. Cox's description of it as an "intimacy" but insisted on the phrase "criminal intimacy," and he bore down with like persistence upon Mrs. Bravo, until that lady had, once or twice, to leave the room, weeping. In 1876 it was "not nice" to discuss these things in public.

It appeared that Dr. Gully, with Mrs. Bravo, chaperoned by Mrs. Cox, had traveled in Europe, but that there had been at least one excursion—to Kissingen—when the chaperon was left at home.

Mr. Bravo nevertheless had insisted on marrying Florence, and had promised to say nothing more about her adventures. He repeatedly broke his promise, only to be reminded by his wife that she was faithful to her agreement: she never mentioned "the person at Maidenhead."

The ingenious Mrs. Cox was now suggesting that Charles Bravo, suddenly overcome with grief at his wife's pre-marital escapade, two years earlier, had condemned himself to a death by slow torture through swallowing a dose of antimony. As a student of forensic medicine, he knew the effects of that distressing drug.

Dr. Gully, a fat, little, bald-headed hydropathic physician of sixty, had to set the seal on his professional ruin by coming to the inquest, and, under oath, groaning out the words:

"Too true, sir; too true."

This was when his examiner charged him with his affair with Mrs. Ricardo—now Mrs. Bravo.

He couldn't "perjure himself like a gentleman" as it would have been useless anyway, and only increase the danger that he might go to the gallows as one of Mr. Bravo's murderers. He had kept his agreement never to see the lady after her second marriage—kept it until she called him into consultation during Mr. Bravo's illness. She esteemed the physician, in addition to the admiration she felt for the man. He had never proposed marriage to her for the reason that his wife, albeit ninety-three years of age, was nevertheless his wife.

Ribald public opinion, which at this time held that Mrs. Bravo had conspired with her *confidante* to bedevil her husband's wine, expressed itself in the rhymes:

> *When lovely woman stoops to folly*
> *And finds her husband in the way,*
> *What charm can soothe her melancholy*
> *What art can turn him into clay?*

> *The only means her aims to cover*
> *And save herself from prison locks*
> *And repossess her ancient lover*
> *Are Burgundy and Mrs. Cox.*

The long, long, inquest was inconclusive. It is said, in this case, that "the police know who did it," and, for once, this saying is right. The verdict was murder,

"But there is not sufficient evidence to fix the guilt upon any person or persons."

The jury did *not* say "some person unknown."

That the Burgundy was poisoned is not, to-day, acceptable to everyone. Mr. William Roughead thinks that, if it had been so, Mr. Bravo would have suffered from its effects before going upstairs. He thinks it more likely that the water-bottle in Mr. Bravo's room had been doc-tored—by somebody who nipped upstairs for that pur-pose.

Writers and lawyers have absolved of guilt both Mrs. Bravo and Dr. Gully. That leaves exactly one person who might be interested in Mr. Bravo's death, and it is con-sidered sporting not to name her: merely to make un-mistakable hints.

If Mrs. Cox thought that she had laid the ground for a life of peace with darling Florence, she was disappointed. Mrs. Bravo was not greatly pleased by darling Jane's revelations as to Dr. Gully. And, crushed and humiliated by the whole experience, Mrs. Bravo died within the year.

So Mrs. Cox had to return to Jamaica after all. And I think that whatever happened to her served her right. The law could not prove that she put anything into Mr. Bravo's water-bottle. But we know—on her own confession—that almost on the last day of his life, she bilked him out of his Sunday tennis.

PART TWO

OTHER STUDIES

THE CURIOUS DRUCES

IMAGINE that a mysterious stranger turns up at your door, some night, and hands you a letter. He was told to give it to you, he says, by an old man with a long black beard, who wore a long black coat. You look at this letter and it says that you are sole heir to half a million.

An "eccentric millionaire" named Abner Waffle, who died twenty years ago in a lonely cabin in the California mountains, left you his vast fortune, which now amounts to $500,000. The will, and all the other "papers" which will bring you the money, are buried in a black box 250 yards southeast of the Washington Monument.

What would you do? And what would you say to the mysterious stranger? Well, I think you would conclude that he, or someone, is trying to pull your leg, and that it is all leading up to a touch. For you never heard of Abner Waffle, and if there was any such man, there is no earthly reason why he should have left *you* all that money. And even if there was an Abner Waffle, and he did make you his heir, why should he go about things in this cockeyed manner, burying the will in the ground? If he wanted you to have his money, why make it hard for you to get it?

You would probably tell the mysterious stranger that

you were not buying any wooden nickels, and to be off about his business immediately.

But among every ten men or women, there seems to be one or two who will believe a story like this. And even try to bolster it up for himself. Such a man will remember that he heard his grandmother say that she had a third cousin who once went to California. Perhaps this was Abner! Thinking it over, he remembers that his grandmother said that this cousin was "peculiar."

This clinches it, and, in all probability, the hopeful "heir" to the Waffle fortune is picked up by the police two or three weeks later, digging holes in the grass around the Washington Monument.

The "heir" does not find the black box, because some one got there ahead of him, and the box is now sunk in the Mississippi River.

Probably the "heir" has raised enough money to hire a lawyer—one of the lawyers who take such cases on speculation—and pretty soon all kinds of things begin to happen. The affair gets into the papers, and for months and years there are yarns about the "Waffle millions." For the original half-million quickly grows into "millions"—millions upon millions!

Strange people begin to turn up in the lawyer's office. Curious looking men from far-away places, and funny little old ladies. Valuable witnesses—if only their stories are true! Some of them—in spite of their oddities—seem to be honest folk. And they can tell all about Abner Waffle; they knew him personally, and often heard him say he intended to leave his fortune to his third cousin's grandson, and mention his plans for keeping the will buried underground, in a black box. This was to baffle his "enemies."

And so this goes on for years; the legend grows, and

its age makes it more and more respectable. And though no one ever finds Mr. Waffle, either dead or alive; and no black box is dug up, or fished up either, yet the belief in these things has a long, long life. Many people are sure it must be true; because they have "read about it in the papers so often." They live and die, firm in their trust that the "lost heir" to the Waffle fortune has been deprived of his sacred rights, and is a badly used man.

Well, there never was a "Waffle" case, but there have been other real cases, which were much more romantic. Almost always, at the bottom of them is the idea that somebody is being kept out of his "rights," by wicked enemies—rich and powerful people who stop at nothing.

And curiously enough, these stories flourish nowhere better than in "sober and conservative" England.

So leaving the Waffles behind, let us turn to the real English family of the Druces, and their mysterious history.

To understand the adventures of the Druce family, we have to go back into history, and trace the rise of an entirely different family—people named Bentinck, with whom the Druces were to be most curiously associated.

In 1688 there came to England, a gentleman from Holland named Hans Bentinck. He was one of the advisers of the Prince and Princess of Orange, later William and Mary of England. King William always thought better of his father's people, the Hollanders, than of his mother's, the English. So he brought a few of his more reliable Dutch friends along, for the sake of their sound advice.

Mr. Bentinck was raised to the peerage as Earl of Portland. It was the beginning of a great family; great, at least, in that they became owners of a vast amount of property. The next Earl was made a Duke and I think it is the sixth of these Dukes who is head of the family today.

The Dukes of Portland, and their sons, have served in the Army, or occasionally gone into politics. One, in the time of George III served briefly, and ingloriously as Prime Minister.

The best thing they did was to marry. It may not be fair to say that they always married for money, but somehow it happened that the girls they fell in love with had a tremendous amount of it. Their own estates were valuable, and one of the ladies who married a Portland brought with her a tidy little dowry amounting to £180,000 a year.

The principal home of the Portlands is Welbeck Abbey, near Sherwood Forest. The fifth Duke held the title from 1854 to 1870, and it is his peculiarities, real or imaginary, which helped make the Druces both famous and mysterious.

There is a story about one of the Portland family, which may or may not be true. If it were true it might account for some of the oddities in their conduct. It is that, more than a hundred years ago, one of the sons of the Duke of that day was an officer in the Army. He was called Lord William Bentinck, or perhaps Lord John or Lord George Bentinck. William and George and John have been favorite names for the sons, and these names have been repeated again and again. This young second-lieutenant was stationed, with his regiment, at a seaport, like Dover or Plymouth. He and his brother officers were keeping it up, one night, at their mess, and drinking heartily.

They were making bets about various things, and one of the officers bet Lord John twenty-five guineas that he wouldn't dare go out into the street and propose marriage to the first woman he met.

He took the bet, and a minute or two later they all went outdoors—whooping. Down the narrow, rocky street they ran plump into a little black-eyed barmaid, who was scuttling home from her day's work at the inn, with a pitcher of beer for her father. One of the officers took the pitcher away from her, and they all stood around, while Lord John, taking off his hat, and making a courtly bow, asked her, with perfect gravity, and only one hiccup, to do him the honor to be his wife.

When he had finished, one of the other officers—who perhaps had a side bet, and was interested in the affair —told the girl her suitor's name, and explained to her that if she said "yes," she would probably become Duchess of Portland, one day, and go to London and see the Queen.

So Peggy, the barmaid, did not just giggle: "You go along with you, Sir!"

She took the matter into serious consideration—for five seconds—and then she gave her answer. They hunted up a parson, and Peggy the barmaid, before she went to bed, was Lady Peggy.

Whether she and her husband ever became Duke and Duchess of Portland does not matter. They contributed at least one son to the noble line, and that son, or his son, did become Duke. Then, new and surprising things began to happen in the dukedom.

For the Bentincks, solid and respectable Hollanders, had been marrying sober and respectable English women, and you could tell just where they and their children would be, and what they'd be doing at any hour of the day.

But while Peggy was a perfectly well-behaved bar-maid, she had a lot of strange ancestors: smugglers, poachers and miscellaneous rapscallions. Their vagaries were in her blood, and took odd and amusing forms. The results were not smugglers nor poachers nor barmaids, but neither were they the usual kind of Dukes.

William John Cavendish Bentinck-Scott never expected, as a young man, to become Duke of Portland. He had an elder brother who was Marquis of Titchfield.

Young William John had a good time. He was a fearless horseman. For a while, he was a lieutenant in the Army, like that ancestor of his who is said to have married the barmaid. His elder brother died, and William John became Marquis of Titchfield, and heir to the dukedom.

About this time—he was thirty-four—he fell in love with the actress, Adelaide Kemble, but when he proposed marriage to her, she had to tell him that she was already secretly married. Perhaps this was "the sorrow of his life," which caused him to do all the peculiar things of his later career.

Just what these peculiar things were is in dispute. Some of them we know as facts; others are matters of gossip. He became Duke of Portland in 1854, when he was about fifty-four years old. With the title, he became master of an enormous fortune, which he could use as he liked.

One of the things that he liked, and one which we know he did, was to spend great sums, perhaps half a million dollars a year, in digging in the ground. He kept gangs of men—sometimes fifteen hundred of them—at work, for eighteen years, and dug big apartments underground. There were subterranean ballrooms and picture galleries, connected by miles of tunnels. They are at Welbeck Abbey, to-day.

One of the peculiar things which gossip declared that he did, was a little out of the ordinary. At times, so ran the tale, he would become weary of being the Duke of Portland, at Welbeck Abbey. Then he would jump into his carefully closed and heavily curtained carriage, which would be taken on board a flat car, and carried by rail up to London. Here he would be driven to his town house in Cavendish Square. There was a long tunnel under this house, and into this tunnel the Duke would pop. At the other end of this tunnel was the Baker Street Bazaar.

When the Duke came out in the store, he was another man. At home, he wore only "side-burns" as facial decoration, but somewhere on his dark and mysterious journey he had pulled on an immense lot of fuzzy brown whiskers. Thus he became Mr. Thomas Charles Druce, proprietor of the Bazaar.

Everyone in London knew him as Mr. Druce. And when the day was over at the store, he would take the omnibus for his other home, where there was Mrs. Druce, and some young Druces.

After a few weeks of Mrs. Druce, and the omnibus, and after he had supervised the store, and kept the floor-walkers and salesladies in order, he would get his fill of London. Then he would reverse the process, go back through the tunnel, shedding the full beard *en route*. Next day the Duke of Portland would be at Welbeck Abbey again, walking about in his tunnels there and surprising his workmen by his sudden appearances, as before.

It all showed what can be done, if you have plenty of good underground passages, and are clever with disguises and false whiskers.

Everyone knew that there was a Duke at Welbeck Abbey. Hundreds of people knew Mr. Druce who owned the Baker Street Bazaar. But what nobody suspected, what nobody even suggested for years and years, was that these two men were one and the same.

There are many other reported peculiarities of the fifth Duke of Portland, which, like his identity with Mr. Druce, rested upon gossip. His fondness for privacy, his tunnels underground, his closed carriages, the enormous glass canopy over his gardens at his London house, were accounted for in various ways. People said it was because he had been disappointed in love. Or, it was because he had an incurable skin disease which made him sensitive about being seen. It was because he was a leper. And it was because he was overcome with remorse for the death of his younger brother.

This brother was Lord George Bentinck. He had been one of the famous racing men; the winner of great prizes on the turf. But one day, five or six years before his brother became Duke, Lord George, while taking a lonely walk in the country, fell dead of a heart attack.

The story got about that the brothers had quarreled over a woman, and that the elder, William John, had killed the younger. It also was said that Lord George had been poisoned by Dr. Palmer, another racing man, who in later years became notorious as a poisoner. Both stories were rubbish, but they illustrate how many yarns were told about the Portland family.

It was also said of the Duke that "he hated tobacco, women, and anyone dressed like a gentleman." He arrayed himself in a curious fashion: a long brown cape, an extremely tall hat nearly two feet high, with a broad brim. He also wore a white tie and a high collar. He carried a tremendous umbrella while going about his estate at Welbeck. And what struck everyone as odd, was that in dry or in wet weather he always tied strings about the bottoms of his trousers legs, as workmen used to do.

He did spend a great lot of money—in all over £2,000,-000, so it is said—on his tunnels and subterranean rooms.

All around Welbeck Abbey there protruded from the ground great glass "bull's eyes" which lighted these places by day. At night they were lighted by gas. The rooms were beautifully planned and skillfully constructed, and the big gallery housed a magnificent collection of pictures.

The Duke, with his money, was neither wicked, selfish nor crazy. He gave large sums to charity. At the time of the Crimean War his contributions of money and supplies to the soldiers were generous. And finally, by his digging and building operations, he gave employment to thousands of men at the highest current wages. Anybody could always get a job at Welbeck.

And if he seldom spoke to his servants, but communicated his orders in writing; and if he liked to do such fantastic things as to be driven about the country in a carriage that looked like a hearse, with heavy black hangings, drawn by six ponies and driven by boys, that was his own business.

All the time of the Duke's life, or nearly all of that time, there certainly seemed to be a Thomas Charles Druce, carrying on in London or elsewhere. Carrying on, is right, for he appears to have been a bit of a rogue, and in some ways more like the wicked nobleman of romance than a plain and honest tradesman.

This figure of mystery was married, in 1816, at Bury St. Edmunds, to a girl named Elizabeth Crickmer. Her family thought she was much too good for young Druce, who was a draper's assistant. But Druce thought that he was too good, for after living with her four years, he vanished like a ghost. Deserted his wife and their two children, George and Frances.

For fifteen years nobody knows what he was up to, but at the end of that time he came to light as a salesman at the Baker Street Bazaar; apparently highly respectable, but actually living in sin with a woman named Annie May.

In the manner of the wicked, he flourished like the green bay tree; was promoted and promoted again; taken into partnership, and at last, in 1850, he was sole owner of the big store.

Ever since he was able, he had supported his two legal children, George and Frances. George, after going to sea and trying railroading, went to Australia, where he married, had a son, and died. On this son of George's you must keep your eye. His name was George Hollamby Druce of Australia.

Mrs. Druce, the former Elizabeth Crickmer, died in 1851, and her husband then set his house in order by marrying Annie May. They had already had one son, named Herbert, and about four months after the marriage to Annie May—which was a very secret ceremony, indeed—had a second son, Walter. It is easy to see why they did not advertise this wedding.

Finally, in 1864, old Thomas Charles Druce, being then a little over seventy years of age, became ill and died. He was buried in his family vault at Highgate Cemetery.

And, of course, if the story about the Duke and the tunnel and the false beard were true, then the Duke would have died, too. But strange to say, the Duke seemed to be as well as ever—still burrowing in the ground in Welbeck, and driving around with the six ponies drawing his little pleasure-hearse.

Mr. Druce left £70,000. His will made provision for his only widow, Annie May; gave £1,000 to legitimate son George of Australia; and left the rest of his money to Annie May's children, Herbert and Walter—the first being born out of wedlock, and the latter, by a narrow margin, born in wedlock.

In 1879, fifteen years later, the Duke died, and his cousin succeeded him. The Duke was buried, not at Welbeck Abbey, but in London—although not in the cemetery selected by Mr. Druce. I think the Duke was buried at Kensal Green. I have had the curiosity to look up the account of his funeral in *The Times*. The ceremonies were without ostentation, and there is no reference to anything whatever which might have been thought eccentric or queer in the life of the dead man.

For the next twenty years, while Mr. Herbert Druce carried on the Baker Street Bazaar with great success, you are to suppose these two old gentlemen (The Duke and Thomas Charles) are lying in their different graves, that is, if there *were* two old gentlemen. In the other case, there was one old gentleman resting in *his* grave. And, in that event, what was in the other grave?

Annie May's second son, Walter Druce, died in 1880, leaving a widow, and, I think, a son and daughter. These children do not matter greatly, but the widow does matter. She is another great figure in the mystification, and she is known as Anna Maria Druce. It seems to be a fact that in cases like these, men may play rascally parts and foolish parts, but the rôle of chief trouble-maker, is usually reserved for a determined woman, who is perfectly sure she is right, and who mistakes her own whims and fancies for inspiration from on high.

Such a lady was Anna Maria Druce. Although she had been well provided for, she began, after her husband's death, to peer into the history of his family. She discovered the date of old Thomas Charles's second and secret marriage, and that it was later than the date of birth of her husband's elder brother, Herbert. *She never found out* that old Thomas Charles had been married once before, and that he had legitimate descendants by that marriage.

That news would have upset her apple-cart at the beginning.

But if she could disprove the will of 1864, Herbert would be dispossessed; all would be as if there were no will; and Walter, or his heirs (herself and her children) would inherit the entire estate. She seems to have been ignorant of the Australian Druces.

In 1898 she went to the proper court in London and expressed her desire to have the coffin of old Mr. Thomas Charles Druce dug up, so that she could have a look into it. Her reasons, she said, were that he did not die in 1864, but became insane, and was hustled off to an asylum, where he was confined under the name of "Dr. Harmer." He had actually lived, she said, for nearly twenty years after his supposed death.

"Interested parties," said Mrs. Anna Maria, were responsible for this outrage, in order to grab the old man's estate. And she left little doubt that she meant Mr. Herbert Druce, her brother-in-law, who was still living in 1898, the time of this petition.

She added that two people had told her that in 1864, when old Thomas Charles died, they had been told to strip some lead off the roof of his suburban home. And what could anybody possibly want of lead except to weight a coffin for a mock funeral? That was all that lay buried at Highgate—two hundred pounds of sheet lead.

Moreover, another suspicious circumstance, there was no doctor's signature on the death certificate—only that of the sinister elder son, Herbert Druce. This was quite true; no doctor had signed the certificate, but at that time the law did not require it.

The Court was impressed, and issued the order for exhumation. But Mr. Herbert Druce, evidently determined to keep his evil deeds underground, entered an objection, and stopped the proceedings. He had some unaccountable objection to having his father's body dug up for the edification of Anna Maria. The few people who heard of it gathered a very unfavorable impression of Herbert Druce.

Anna Maria had only told part of her wonderful story to the Court. She knew that such a story would get more attention from newspapers. So she went to the newspapers: to *Lloyd's Weekly News.*

In this paper, apparently, was printed for the first time, thirty-four years after the supposed death of Thomas Charles Druce, and nineteen years after the death of the Duke of Portland, the story of the extraordinary pranks which these two old boys—or this one old boy—used to play. All about the tunnels and caverns; all about the lead in the coffin, and what not. The marriage in 1851, Anna Maria told the newspaper reporter, was not between Thomas Charles Druce and Annie May, but between the Marquis of Titchfield (as the Duke was then) and a lady who was the illegitimate daughter of the Earl of Berkeley. And finally, said she, the Duke first had a mock burial of Mr. Druce, and then had himself shut up in an insane asylum!

This was highly to the taste of everybody in England who read the spicier newspapers.

Thousands of people hurried out to Highgate to look at the vault which did not contain Thomas Charles Druce, but only the sheets of lead. And they all groaned over the wickedness of rich old Herbert Druce, and the bad conduct of the rich Portlands, who were keeping Anna Maria and her son Sydney and her daughter, whatever her name was, out of their rights, when if there were justice in the land, they would be Dukes and Duchesses, and riding in their own little pony-hearses.

Instead of this, they received nothing at all from the ducaı family, except that the daughter—so said Anna Maria—had inherited the family skin disease.

Mrs. Anna Maria, balked the first time, tried again. Once more, she got a Court order to open the grave, and again Mr. Herbert Druce interfered. He was backed up in this by the cemetery company, who feared that people wouldn't enjoy being buried there if they were in danger of getting dug up at anybody's whim. And Anna Maria's supporters, that is, all the people in the land who got their information from sensational newspapers, were more than ever convinced that somebody was trying to cover up something. Dirty work somewhere!

Three years later Anna Maria was at it once more. This time she attacked the will. And now there came an ominous rumble from Australia. George Hollamby Druce, grandson of the first marriage, sent his attorney to Court, and said that he, too, wanted to have the will revoked. He explained who he was, and, of course, if his claims could be established, and if Anna Maria's story about the lead in the coffin were true, he would walk away with the money, the dukedom and everything, while she would be left holding the bag.

Anna Maria began to rage like the seven sisters of Jezebel. George Hollamby Druce, she said, was an "impudent, audacious, and absolutely ignorant impostor." He was no relation to the Druce who was the duke, but merely the grandson of a Druce who was a draper.

She testified at this hearing, after being warned as to perjury. She swore that she saw her father-in-law ten years after his supposed death. But the sworn statements of doctors and nurses who attended old Thomas Charles, in his final illness, together with the testimony of Mr. Herbert Druce that *he saw his father dead in his coffin,*

convinced the jury that there was nothing in her contentions. They said that the 1864 will of Thomas Charles
was all right, and Mrs. Anna Maria Druce vanished from
sight.

She was heard of only once again, when she was sent
to an asylum for the insane. But the fire that she had
kindled went on burning, and George Hollamby Druce
was prevailed upon by something or somebody to come
to England and lead the charge in person.

He took his time about it, but finally he came over
with his lawyer. He published one or two pamphlets in
which he adopted, with some variations, most of Anna
Maria's contentions. He also founded two companies,
G. H. Druce, Ltd., a company which sold shares at one
pound each, and another called the Druce-Portland Company. In this way he collected a considerable amount of
money, and it is sad to say that much of it came from
domestic servants.

By 1907, G. H. Druce was ready for the fray and his
method was to go right at the chief offender, Herbert
Druce himself. A summons was issued, bringing Herbert
into Court on a charge of perjury, for swearing that he
saw his father lying dead in his coffin.

At last, the sympathizers of the "rightful heir" thought,
they were going to smoke the rascal out. And in October,
1907, at the police court, they had the satisfaction of
seeing the head devil in person. He proved to be a mild-
looking old gentleman, with a long, gray beard, like one
of the Prophets. He was in feeble health, and had to recline or partly recline in the courtroom, while having the
pleasure of hearing himself described as a criminal liar, a
corrupt and fraudulent person, and a practitioner in all
sorts of rascality.

One of his real offenses, although it could not be

named in an indictment, was that he was disappointing all the newspaper readers and inquisitive persons in the British Empire, and other countries, in their desire to dig down into the ground and find out what was really in that coffin in Highgate Cemetery. This had become a passion.

The Australian claimant produced three of the queerest witnesses ever seen in a Court, and their testimony shows something of the strange workings of the human mind and conscience.

Robert Caldwell, native of Ireland, seventy years of age, a resident of Staten Island, N. Y. was the first of these.

He told a peculiar story of his meeting with the Duke of Portland, and of a wonderful cure which he effected upon the Duke's nose. A number of people seemed bound to concentrate upon the Duke's nose, although others said there was nothing at all the matter with it. Mr. Caldwell was rewarded for this cure by a gift of £5,000. He saw the Duke for weeks, both at Welbeck, and in London —where he always wore a false beard and was called Druce. He—Mr. Caldwell—swore that he stage-managed the fake funeral of Druce, and put the lead in the coffin.

At the hands of an acid English barrister, Mr. Caldwell had an uncomfortable time during his cross-examination. The lawyer asked if Mr. Caldwell were not known as "the great American affidavit maker" and Mr. Caldwell had to admit that some ill-disposed persons did call him that. At the time of the theft of A. T. Stewart's body in New York, Mr. Caldwell tried to sell an affidavit to the *New York Herald* for $10,000. Mr. Caldwell seemed to be at his best when there was any funny business going on with a dead body. The barrister pointed out other peculiarities in Mr. Caldwell's testimony, and suggested

that at the time of the cure of the Duke's nose, Mr. Caldwell was really in Ireland. This Mr. Caldwell hotly denied. It was a brother who sometimes "impersonated"
him.

There followed a witness called Miss Mary Robinson.
She came, it seemed, from a big tobacco plantation in
America—the "Green Hill plantation near the Alle-
gheny Mountains." She had passed much time traveling
between England and America, and was a great friend
of Mr. Druce, and also of Mr. Charles Dickens, the
famous novelist. She remembered Mr. Dickens' funeral
in Westminster Abbey. It was nearly forty years before,
but the mere recollection caused her to weep. Mr.
Dickens had told her that Druce was the Duke. There
has always been an undercurrent of suggestion that "The
Mystery of Edwin Drood" by Dickens, had in some
vague way become mixed up with the Druce mystery.
Mr. Druce, said Miss Robinson, used to take part in plays
at Mr. Dickens' house at Gadshill—enacting, whiskers and
all, the part of the Grandmother in "Little Red Riding
Hood."

When Miss Robinson returned to America she passed
her time in "the Chicago district" occasionally running
over to Newfoundland—probably for the afternoon. She
met Mr. Dickens there, also, and he got her a position
with Mr. Druce as "outside correspondent"—whatever
that was.

Another old lady, Mrs. Margaret Hamilton, whose
memory got better as she grew older, also testified as
to her father's acquaintance with the double personality
who was sometimes Druce and sometimes the Duke,
and she related a lot of risky stories about both of them.
There is one quality about "inside information," which

some people claim to possess, about this subject or that. It is invariably scandalous.

Meantime, the Court had decided that it was necessary, in the interests of justice, that the Druce grave should be opened. The Government gave consent; so did the cemetery; and so did Mr. Herbert Druce. When it was known that he had at last given permission many a wiseacre said:

"Ah, the old sinner! He'd better!"

In England, they do not disturb the dead in their graves in a light-hearted and casual manner. In fact, the procedure is long and ceremonious, and hedged about with every precaution of the law. So much was at stake in this case, that more than usual care was taken. It was agreed by everyone that if the coffin contained the sheets of lead, the contentions of George Hollamby Druce were partly sustained, and his claim to the Druce estate, if not to that of the Portlands, was greatly advanced.

On the other hand, if the coffin should contain the body of Thomas Charles Druce, as his son said it did when it was buried, then the whole claim, and all the tales of the masquerade and the double life were knocked higher than a kite; the bubble was pricked; the game was up; and all the Anna Maria-George Hollamby contentions would have gone—phooey.

For days in advance, workmen were in the cemetery, moving the monument, which weighed several tons, and erecting a shed over the vault, to protect the operations from the eyes of the crowds.

At five o'clock of a dark winter's morning, next to the last day of the year, and in a cold storm of rain and sleet, the final work began. Dozens of stalwart London policemen guarded the cemetery and kept the public away. Mr. George Hollamby Druce, the claimant, arrived in a high hat, and demanded entrance. He was turned away, and was soon in a rage as high as his hat. Lawyers on both sides were admitted. Dr. Pepper was the great personage of the ceremony; he was there as the representative of the Government. There were one or two distinguished physicians who were experienced at conducting autopsies. There were present two Scotland Yard inspectors, including Sir Melville Macnaghten. There were two reporters and no more. Workmen, electricians, and photographers were inside the inclosure.

Gravediggers removed the sod and mold from the lot. Workmen with crowbars eased up the great flagstones which covered the vault, and carried them away on rollers. The coffin of Mrs. Druce—Annie May, I suppose, not Elizabeth Crickmer—was first disclosed. The stone slabs at the side of the vault were taken out and numbered, so as to be replaced in order.

Then appeared a tiny coffin which was supposed to contain a baby, a grandson of Thomas Charles. Near it was resting a great coffin, which was believed to be the one for which they were searching. Proceedings were halted, and photographs were taken of the three coffins as they lay in place.

The biggest coffin was an old-fashioned affair, covered with cloth, and studded, "panel-style," with brass nails. The plate was scrubbed and dusted, and revealed the inscription:

Thomas Charles Druce
Esqre
Died 28th Decr.
1864
In his 71st year

There was a brass cross above and below the lettering. Another photograph was taken of this, and then the great coffin was raised by means of a derrick, and conveyed by rollers, to a small shed nearby, where the witnesses and the doctors gathered. The gravediggers withdrew, two workmen came in, and with powerful pliers unscrewed the lid. There appeared an inner, leaden coffin. Measurements were taken and noted, the officials calling off the figures and a secretary taking them down.

A workman now cut through the lead all around the outer edge of the upper surface. The lid was next removed, bringing away with it the top of the innermost wooden shell. Then there was displayed a shrouded figure. The wrappings were opened, and there lay an aged, bearded man.

At that moment, and in the dead silence which ensued, one could imagine a noise like that of rats, as all the claimants, false witnesses, and deluded folk, scurried away.

Mr. Thackrah, a business associate of the dead man, stepped forward and said solemnly:

"That is Thomas Charles Druce."

Later, the physicians performed an autopsy and further corroborated the identification, by proving the correctness of the evidence as to the cause of death.

At the hearing, next week, in Court, the Magistrate said:

"How the myth ever arose that confounded Mr. Druce with the Duke of Portland, it would be idle to speculate."

The case he added, is "one more striking proof of the unfathomable depths of human credulity. . . . Mr. Herbert Druce leaves the Court with his character for truthfulness absolutely vindicated."

No one knows, to this day, exactly how the story began. There may have been some village gossip which arose shortly after the death of Thomas Charles Druce, and while the Duke was living. Then Mrs. Anna Maria, greedy for more than her share of the Druce estate, discovered, in her pryings, the fact of Herbert Druce's birth before the marriage of his parents. He was a harmless old man, who was not to blame for the accident of his birth, but Anna Maria proposed to make him suffer for it, and, of course, perform this mean action with an air of great righteousness—in the interests of her "fatherless children"—and other sentimental humbug.

Her mind went to pieces later, when she was balked of her purpose, but there is no evidence that it was affected at the time she began her suits. She was merely a willful nuisance.

The Duke of Portland and Thomas Charles Druce, had lived their separate lives, and died their separate deaths, fifteen years apart, and had been buried in their separate graves.

Nothing ever happened to show that the Duke and old Mr. Druce knew, or even saw, each other.

As for George Hollamby Druce, the claimant from Australia, he seems to have kept on the safe side of the law. His contentions, added to Anna Maria's notions, had been caught up by the credulous; had tempted others into crime; and in the end brought distress to many people. After it was over, the Australian claimant had to meet the stockholders of his company, and tell them that the cupboard was bare.

The police were already after Mr. Caldwell, "the great American affidavit maker." He had taken the precaution of sailing to New York. When he arrived, he fought extradition, for perjury, until he could have himself safely shut up in an insane asylum, which he greatly preferred to an English jail.

Miss Robinson got four years for perjury, and Mrs. Hamilton got eighteen months. Miss Robinson admitted that she had sworn to all her fantastic whoppers in the hope of getting £4,000 for them. Mrs. Hamilton had received £400 for bearing false witness, but she stuck to her lies to the end. She got a light sentence on account of her age.

And, unless I am greatly mistaken, you can find in England to-day, hundreds of people who will wag their heads when the Druce case is mentioned. For there are always those who will not credit the truth, even though archangels come down to testify. And these folk will tell you:

"There's a lot more about that case than has ever come out."

But what it is, they could not possibly tell you. They prefer to be mysterious—and look wise.

A THOUSAND POUNDS
A MINUTE

WHEN Max Steuer stood in front of the jury box at the Mitchell trial and for ten minutes seemed to lead the twelve in silent prayer, there was nothing novel about it. That is his usual manner. He does not shout and yell at juries. Instead, he almost takes the nearest man by the lapel of the coat, leans over, and whispers:

"Don't mention this out loud, and I'll tell you what really happened."

There appeared to be a conspiracy of silence at the opening of the trial. Newspapers were aware that the United States was about to try Charles E. Mitchell on the charge of evading his income tax. But a spectator got the impression that some pussy-footed elders in a church were looking into the conduct of one of the deacons, who was suspected of cutting didoes.

Judge Goddard had a bad cold. So had Mr. Medalie, the Federal District Attorney. And they simply did their best to help Mr. Steuer pull a thick, wet blanket of silence over the transactions.

They couldn't hear what he was saying. The Judge gave up trying to hear. The reporters couldn't hear, and the spectators might as well have been ten miles away. The stenographer was clearly in trouble. But Mr. Steuer, his shoulders bent, his arms somewhat in the position of "parade rest," continued to face the men in the box as if he were weeping at an open grave when the first clods begin to fall.

You could tell by the delighted expressions in the eyes of the prospective jurors that something was being uttered, something mystic, wonderful; and that they enjoyed it. This was a great experience for them, this secret communion with the celebrated attorney whose time, like that of the railway guard in "Alice," is worth a thousand pounds a minute.

Little by little, it leaked out in court-room gossip what Mr. Steuer was saying. He was telling the talesmen his ideas of a good juror to try this case.

It was no ordinary trial, and it was plainly useless to ask the usual questions. That was why the Judge abandoned the usual methods in a United States Court and let the two attorneys run the pantomime to suit themselves. That was why the first stab at selecting a jury lasted all one dreadful day, until 7:30 P.M. They were looking into each talesman's philosophy of life; trying to discover his views about wealthy people, about Wall Street bankers, and about income taxes.

Mr. Steuer expressed a fondness for unbiased, impartial men, who were willing to give another human being a square deal and no more. Persons who had been gypped in the failure of the Bank of United States were not good in his sight. Neither were those to whom the presence of a man who owned a town house, as well as one in Tuxedo and another at Southampton, might cause bubbles of foam at the corners of the mouth.

Mr. Steuer, by implication, let it be known that he could not welcome on the jury anybody whose idea of a happy Saturday afternoon would be one spent marching round and round Union Square with a banker's head on a pike.

To me, there is nothing sly in Mr. Steuer's expression. He is quiet, deferential, perhaps insinuating, in his manner. He entered the court each morning with his handsome client, and while Mr. Mitchell looked very grave, the lawyer was always smiling. Yet he took the trial with extreme seriousness, and recognized it as one of great importance to himself, no less than to others.

Seen in profile, the lawyer often looks up in a modest, deprecatory manner which suggests that gentle creature, the South American tapir. The ease with which Mr. Steuer stole the show from his resplendent client was a triumph of brains over beauty. For although he is, in popular and journalistic reputation, at any rate, America's most conspicuous jury lawyer, he has none of the gorgeous qualities of the famous advocates. We remember them as giants, men with waves of curly hair, who kept one hand in the front of their coats as their voices resounded through the court.

This is quite unlike Max Steuer. Think of yourself walking down some street on the East Side—Second Avenue, perhaps. You hear a small voice say:

"Sell you a nize pair of pents for two dollars an' a quarter!"

The little man who makes this friendly offer is standing in front of his shop in his shirtsleeves, with a tape measure around his shoulders. His hair, where he still has it, is gray, and his slightly wrinkled face wears the beginnings of a twinkle. Think of this man and you may see, in your mind's eye, the famous lawyer who defended Mr. Mitchell—and so many other people in trouble.

What the pants-dealer has not got in his small skull, and what few people had in that courtroom, or in any other, is the extraordinary brain, the alert intelligence, which enables Mr. Steuer not only to carry a mass of details in his mind but to seize opportunity when it offers.

Max Steuer's opponent in the Mitchell case was a man who might pass as a younger and rival dealer across the street from the clothing shop. Rather more, however, Mr. Medalie, the United States District Attorney, looks like a high-school teacher in the same district. He is small and gray and quiet. This was no loud and raucous proceeding with a couple of overbearing Nordics shouting at each other. Instead, the two little attorneys hovered over the jury like worker bees soothing the queen bee, and fanning her with their wings.

Sometimes, Mr. Medalie (pronounced "Me-dahlia") would tip Mr. Steuer a glance, and the two little gray men would stealthily, and side by side, mount the steps to the Bench. Judge Goddard, tall, dignified, and black-robed, would show obvious gratification. He seemed glad to be let in on whatever was going on down there below him. He would lean forward, and the three bald heads would be put close together. One such consultation lasted, in utter silence, for twenty mortal minutes. Then the two lawyers softly went down the steps, sat in their chairs, and stared at the wall for five minutes. Then, I hope I may die if they didn't go, panther-wise, up to the Bench again and whisper for ten minutes more.

This bade fair to be Mr. Medalie's last great case as prosecutor for the Government. Hence, its importance to him. And luck had been rather against Mr. Steuer since he lost the Pantages case in California, and others. So he sat up nights to study how best to make the jury adopt Mr. Mitchell's views.

He had one horrid moment. It came while he questioned a red-headed talesman—a man of iron face. The talesman said he feared that he hardly had an open mind.

"Why not?" asked the lawyer.

"Well, Mr. Steuer, you see I've always understood that nobody sent for you unless he was in a pretty bad jam."

One of Mr. Steuer's descriptions of his client was not precisely apt. Mr. Mitchell, with his admirably tailored clothes, and his ruddy complexion, would look at home in a very expensively furnished office. His good looks and his healthy appearance—in that court full of pale faces —suggested winter golf in the South or in Bermuda. I should say that he was easily the most radiant person who ever came out of Chelsea, Massachusetts.

But Mr. Steuer, telling how his client had impoverished himself to repay his loan from the Morgans, thrice described Mr. Mitchell as "thread-bare!"

Mr. Medalie also had his troubles with the jury. If Mr. Steuer wished to see no anarchists in the box, Mr. Medalie was sure it was no place for folk who burned too brightly as social lights. So he made all those garage owners from 185th Street, chicken farmers from Rye, and restaurant proprietors from the Bronx assure him, on their oaths, that they were *not* members of the Piping Rock Club or close pals of Mr. J. P. Morgan.

When Mr. Medalie told the completed jury about the complaints which the United States was making against Charles E. Mitchell, he seemed no more excited than a chemistry teacher in a high school telling his class that there had been too much skylarking in the corridors and that someone had broken three more test-tubes.

There was that sale of 18,300 shares of National City Bank to Mrs. Mitchell. Through it, Mr. Mitchell had recorded a loss of $2,800,000, and thus paid no income tax. Mr. Medalie said that this sale was a "wash," a "fraud," and a "sham." He bleated, as he said this last word: "sh-a-a-am."

And there was the pleasant little tip which Mr. Mitchell had received from the National City Company: the sum of $666,666.67. He had quite failed to record this in his income-tax return.

All the rest of that day, and for days thereafter, the court rustled and hissed with the words "Six hundred and sixty-six thousand, six hundred and sixty-six dollars and sixty-seven cents."

When Mr. Steuer came to bat, everyone was tired of hearing these figures. The night before, I had been listening to Mr. Aborn's blessed company in "Pinafore," and it seemed to me that Mr. Steuer could easily have moved the jury by song. Let him reach under the counsel table, bring out his guitar, and break into the Captain's solo:

> *Fair moon, to thee I sing,*
> *Bright regent of the heavens;*
> *Say, why is everything*
> *Either at sixes or at sevens?*

But there was no such luck. Mr. Steuer again went into long silences, silences from which arose, occasionally, the murmur:

"So he sat down and wrote a letter to Ryan."

Now and then, he was audible. For instance, he could be heard when he said that all of Mr. Mitchell's actions were legal and permissible, and many of them were in the highest degree patriotic. The private sales of stocks, for example, were arranged to prevent panic at a time when a public sale would have had woeful results.

Since the bank holiday, said Mr. Steuer, the mob was

hunting for a victim. Government had to provide one. Minnows would not do; they had to have a big fish.

"So they picked upon Charley Mitchell."

After Mr. Steuer's speech, the show dragged. Great, big, heavy men, who spoke only in monosyllables, came upon the witness stand. They carried, under their arms, great, big, heavy books which they admitted were office records of Mr. Morgan's company. The faces of the jury glowed. The Ark of the Covenant was revealed unto them.

And day after day, Mr. Steuer walked softly up and down in his narrow space, questioning and disputing. He opposed the introduction of much of the evidence. He brought out the fact that business transactions between Mr. and Mrs. Mitchell were a matter of long custom, and a source of profit to her. Except that they began and ended with letters starting with the words "Dear Elizabeth," they were like deals with the usual customer.

Often, it was a toss-up whether the District Attorney would prove more soothing than his opponent. But, taking it all in all, and considering the loud bellowing which sometimes splits your ears in court, you couldn't help being pretty grateful to Max Steuer. In the presence of a calm like his, it would be mean to look into it too closely, to see if it is a holy calm.

THE FIRST
GREAT DISAPPEARER

"Yes, 'twas Elizabeth—
Yes, 'twas their girl;
Pale was her cheek, and her
Hair out of curl.
'Mother!' the loving one,
Blushing, exclaimed,
'Let not your innocent
Lizzy be blamed. . . .'"

THE sentence of the Court is that you, Mary Squires, be hanged by the neck until you are dead. And that you, Susannah Wells, as a common thief, be branded on the hand, with the letter T."

The officers of the Court thereupon seized them both, and the sheriff's men being ready with their irons, the sentence of branding was then and there carried out on Susannah Wells. And the mob, watching this torture, howled with delight.

There was to be a short delay before hanging Mary Squires. Her crime was that she had stolen "one pair of stays, value ten shillings" from a girl named Elizabeth Canning. The offense of Susannah Wells was that she had allowed the Squires woman to remain in her house—that is, she had harbored and protected a thief.

All of this for the rather fantastic offense of stealing a girl's corsets.

Luckily for Mary Squires there was a wise and humane man in the office of Lord Mayor of London. I think that, even in those cruel days—the year was 1753—men of this type were more often to be found than some people would have us think. The Lord Mayor was not satisfied with the trial of the two women. He was too late to save Susannah Wells from branding with the red-hot iron, but he might save Mary Squires from the gallows.

He began to investigate Elizabeth Canning, upon whose testimony the two older women had been convicted.

She was a red-cheeked girl of eighteen. For about a year she was probably the most famous person in the world. Everybody talked about her and her strange mystery. They did more than talk. They quarreled and fought in the streets. To her friends and admirers she was a lovely heroine—good, pure and courageous. And to the others, she was a minx who had tried to cover up her scandalous escapades with lies, and thus caused one innocent woman to be punished cruelly, and another almost to be hanged.

Her friends eventually came to be called Canningites. The people on the other side were known as Egyptians. And when Canningites met Egyptians, there was apt to be a free fight. The Lord Mayor, for offending the Canningites, was nearly dragged out of his coach and lynched.

In America, today, there are probably hundreds of people who are direct descendants of Elizabeth Canning. They seem never to have heard of her. After the days of her fame were over, she was sent to America, where she married and had a number of children. Their mother's maiden name was soon forgotten, and it is through these children of a different name from Canning, that her descendants can prove their relationship to a girl who once was the center of great excitement; who interested every-one in England from the King down.

For many years, lawyers, writers, and people who love to solve mysteries, have studied the puzzle which surrounds four weeks in the life of Elizabeth Canning. Even those who disbelieve her story do not know what she was up to during those weeks. More people have wondered about it than have ever tried to answer the riddle of the disappearance of Judge Crater or Charley Ross.

Elizabeth's story was the first famous one of its kind. All of us have heard, and we still hear, of girls who un-expectedly vanish from home for a few days or a few weeks. The girl is usually seized by two men (some-times they wear masks) and hustled into a "big, gray motor-car." She is taken away and kept in a cellar or an attic, and is often abused or starved.

There is no talk of ransom in these yarns, and the cause for the abduction is rather mysterious, although the girl often hints that these wicked men were trying—unsuccessfully, of course—to induce her to stray from the paths of virtue.

The truth of these tales, as we frequently conclude, is that the girl has been on a wild party, and that she did not have to be dragged into the car. Or, perhaps, there had been a wild party, some time before, and she has been absent to hide the embarrassing result.

Elizabeth Canning, and her three or four young broth-ers and sisters, were the children of a widow. At eight-een, Elizabeth was a small girl, only five feet in height. As the oldest daughter of a poor woman she had been working since she was sixteen. On New Year's Day, 1753, she was in employment as a house servant with a family named Lyon. They lived in the same part of London—Aldermanbury—as Elizabeth's mother; probably only a few streets away.

No one, neither her neighbors, her former employers, or her present ones, the Lyons, had anything to say about her character and conduct except what was good. She was quiet, modest and well-behaved; the most obscure little maid in London, and except for the strange events of this New Year's Day, destined to a life of obscurity.

January first was a holiday for her, and the way she planned to spend it suggests that she was not accustomed to wild parties, and that she had no very attentive lovers or suitors. She went to see her uncle and aunt, Mr. and Mrs. Colley, who lived still farther toward the east end of London. They lived, in fact, in Whitechapel, the region made famous, many years later, by the crimes of Jack the Ripper. In Elizabeth Canning's time, it was a more open region, with some lonely roads and lanes.

When she left Mr. Lyons' house, she had with her some money, her "Christmas box": wages and tips which had been given her. There was one gold piece, some silver, and a few coppers. At her own home, she gave each of her young brothers and sisters a penny. One of her little brothers had been saucy to her, and she gave him nothing, although later she repented of this, and bought him a small mince pie. This she carried with her all day—expecting to give it to him when she returned at night.

She was dressed in her holiday clothes when she set out on foot for her uncle's house. She wore a purple gown, and a white chip hat, with green ribbons. The day at the Colleys seems to have been spent mostly in sociable family feasting. There was a cold dinner, some time in the afternoon, and a hot supper in the evening. Elizabeth probably helped her aunt with these meals, and

gossiped with her as they worked together. Once or
twice they looked in at Mr. Colley's workshop, to watch
him at his occupation. It was an interesting one, since
he was a glass-blower.

At nine o'clock, she started home, and the Colleys
walked part of the way with her. They went far enough,
as they thought, to see that she was perfectly safe: her
mother's house was not a mile distant. Still, there are
places in that part of London now, which are rather deserted at night, and in Elizabeth's time the streets were
dark.

When her uncle and aunt said good-night, her way
was along Houndsditch, toward the place where now
stands the Liverpool Street Station. She set out in this
direction—and vanished into a black cloud of mystery.

What actually happened to her; who met her, whether
he was a stranger or an acquaintance of hers; where he
took her, or whether she willingly went with him;
whether there was one man or more; whether the meeting was by chance, or whether she was keeping a date—
we do not know. After endless probing and investigating, and after one hundred and eighty years, we can only
guess at the puzzle.

Somebody, afterwards, remembered that on that night
he heard a woman scream, "in a hackney coach" (the
"big gray motor-car!") in a street near the place where
her relatives had left her. Perhaps he did, and perhaps
it was Elizabeth Canning. On the other hand, perhaps
his memory was faulty; he may have heard the scream
from the hackney coach on some other night.

At any event, the girl was missing, and her family
were soon hunting for her. As early as nine o'clock that
evening, Mr. Lyon was inquiring at her mother's house.
It seemed that Elizabeth was not supposed to have stayed

so late as she did. The Colleys had given her a cold dinner of "left-overs," and to make up for this, had urged her to stay for supper, which was a hot meal of roast beef.

Mrs. Canning, of course, was in misery at the disappearance of her daughter. With friends and neighbors she kept up the hunt; some one went back to the Colleys', and routed them out at midnight. In the following days, the hospitals and jails were searched, and advertisements were put in the newspapers. The disappearance of a respectable girl was a rare, if not an unknown event, and it caused great excitement. There were then no regular police in London, and, of course, no detective service at Scotland Yard or elsewhere.

Elizabeth Canning had walked into one end of a dark street, and left utterly no trace. Nothing but the doubtful story of the scream from the hackney coach.

Exactly four weeks later, at ten o'clock at night, Mrs. Canning was busy in her house, getting the children to bed. The door opened, and a woman came in. She was bent nearly double, and seemed to be clad in old rags. It was a number of minutes before they recognized Elizabeth.

Her face was dirty and bruised; her ear bleeding from a cut. All of her holiday dress was gone; the purple gown, the neat neckerchief, and the white hat with green ribbons. She had on an old shirt and a petticoat; over these a dirty dressing-gown. In place of a hat, her head was bound up with a piece of old handkerchief, bloodstained from the wound on her ear.

Mrs. Canning thought this might be her daughter's ghost, come from the grave. Either with that idea, or because of the girl's shocking appearance, her mother went into a fit. Neighbors and friends came in, and the kitchen was soon filled with excited, curious, indignant and sympathetic folk—not one of them able to deal with the situation.

What the girl needed first was some food. She said:

"I'm almost starved to death. I've lived on bread and water since New Year's Day, and since last Friday I've not even had any bread."

Then she should have had a nurse's attentions: be cleaned up and put to bed. Most of all, she should have been kept away from all this crowd of well-meaning but ignorant gossips, who crowded around her with their jabber of conversation:

"Why you poor darling! Who has treated you this way?"

"Well, I never! Such villains as there are in this world!"

"Who abused you this way, Lizzie, darling? They ought to be hanged for it! Tell us their names, and we'll have them in jail in no time."

Some responsible person, in the presence of one or two witnesses, ought to have questioned her a little that night, and again in the morning. Then, they might have found out what really had happened to her.

But everything was confusion, indignation and disorder, and the result is that we do not know exactly what Elizabeth Canning's first story was. We have it in disjointed versions from various recollections. We know that she told a story, two or three times afterwards, and under oath, and that it differed each time, and became harder and harder to believe.

On that first night, as far as can be discovered, while her little brothers and sisters gathered round her and stared, and while the neighbors cursed in their rage, or cried out in sympathy, Elizabeth sat near the fire in her mother's kitchen, and in a weak and faltering voice, said something like this:

"On New Year's Night, after uncle and aunt left me, I went on through Houndsditch, and over Moorfields, past Bethlehem Hospital. Here, two big, strong men, both in great-coats, caught up with me, seized me, and took away my money—the half guinea, and my silver shillings. Then they tore off my dress, my apron and hat, and one of them stuffed my clothes in his great-coat pocket.

"When they tore off my clothes, I screamed, and they gagged me and tied my hands behind my back. Then one of the men said:

" 'Damn you, you ——, we'll do for you, by and by!'

"He hit me with his fist on the forehead, as he said this, and I lost my senses and knew nothing more. It was six hours, as I think, before I came to myself again, and knew what was going on."

All her listeners groaned, and begged the poor girl to go on, and tell them just what these dreadful men did next.

"When I came to," Elizabeth continued, "they were dragging me along a road—a wide road—out of the city somewhere. There was water by the side of the road. One of the men said:

" 'You ——, why don't you walk faster?' "

The blank probably stands for the word "bitch."

"And about half an hour later, we came to a house, and they pushed me into the kitchen, where there were three women. They seized hold of me, and asked me if I would go their way. They said I should have fine clothes, if I would."

Elizabeth did not have to ask them what they meant by "go their way"; she seems to have known at once that it was the way of the sinful.

"I said 'No, I would not,' and so one of the women took a knife and I thought she was going to kill me. But she cut the laces off my stays with the knife, and took them off, and then they all struck me, and called me bad names and pushed me up some stairs into a hayloft. It was all dark, but there was a little bread there, and an old pitcher of water. They locked me in and left me there.

"I stayed there four weeks. I lived on the mince pie I bought for my brother, and on the bread and water. They never came near me again; never brought me any more to eat; and I never saw any of them again. Once, some one came, I think, and looked through a chink in the wall at me. Once, I tried the door, but it was locked.

"At last, this afternoon, about four o'clock, I pulled away a board that was in front of a window, and got out through the hole. I slid down over a penthouse, to the ground below. I found this old dressing-gown and hand-kerchief lying in the room, and I put them on before I jumped out the window. I caught my ear on a nail at the window as I jumped out, and that is why it is cut, and why all this blood is on the handkerchief.

"Then I walked along the road, and found my way back to my mother's."

There is no doubt that the girl was "all in." She was worn out—according to her account she had walked eleven miles that day—and she was—according to her story—half starved before she started. The mince pie which had helped sustain her was not a big, generous sort of thing, but a little penny or ha'penny affair—what is sometimes called a tart—a gift for a little boy, which he could easily eat on top of his dinner, and then look around for something more. Yet on this, and three or four pieces of bread, she had lived for a month.

Now the people who heard this story were so full of

pity for the wretched girl, and so moved by fury toward the folk who had imprisoned her, that no one seems to have thought for an instant that it was a queer tale. To speak now of only two of its odd features, it is unusual for a person to walk for six hours after being knocked unconscious. And, since no one bothered Elizabeth during her captivity, it was strange that she did not escape sooner.

On the night of her return, nobody considered these things. They crowded round, and wept over her; and lamented these wicked "modern times," when such villainy was abroad. They got a medical man to tend her ailments; and they congratulated Mrs. Canning that her daughter would endure suffering, rather than throw in her lot with the wicked.

Where had she been? And who were these fiendish women, who robbed her of her corsets and tried to rob her of her honor?

Either that night or very soon, Elizabeth said that she thought she had been on the Hertford Road, because she had looked out through a crack in the boards and recognized the driver of the Hertford Coach driving his coach by the house. Since she had walked back over the same road, part of the way by daylight, one might think that she would have been a little surer of what road it was. But Elizabeth was not at all clear about things, and the neighbors said:

"Poor lamb! How could she take notice of anything?"

But as soon as she mentioned the Hertford Road, there came an exclamation from a young man named Robert Scarratt, who had begun to take the greatest interest in the case. Said he:

"I'll bet a guinea to a farthing that you were at Mother Wells's!"

This was a disreputable house at Enfield, on the Hertford Road. Up to that time, it is fairly certain that no one, neither Elizabeth nor anyone else, had mentioned the name of Wells. But as soon as she heard it, she said she believed that she *had* heard the name Wells or Wills mentioned, while she was there.

In spite of Elizabeth's weakness and sufferings, she was able, next day but one, to go before an Alderman and ask for a warrant of arrest for "Mother" Wells. The Alderman questioned her closely, and so vague and unsatisfactory was her story that he hesitated to issue the warrant. He advised her to be careful.

"Be sure of what you say," he warned; "say nothing but what you can swear to."

But she was surrounded by her friends and family, who were determined that she should have "justice." So she persisted, and the warrant was issued. The Alderman, aside, remarked that he did not believe her story.

Either at this hearing, or at another, the dressing-gown was produced as a piece of evidence. Elizabeth claimed it, *as her mother's*, and tried to take it with her. She was reminded that she found it in her place of captivity. She blushed, stammered, and said no more.

Next day a cavalcade set out for Enfield. There were Elizabeth and her mother, with two more women, in a chaise; officers of the law, on foot and horseback; some of Elizabeth's more influential friends in a coach—altogether, a posse. They were out to "get" some one.

They arrived at "Mother" Wells's house a few at a time. The men in the coach and the mounted officers got there long before the rest, and their first examination of the place made some of them very uneasy. As one of the officers said:

"We have got into the wrong box!"

There was a hayloft, as in all such houses, but it was no such room as Elizabeth had described. There was no way of locking the door; the shape of the room was not as she said; the contents of the room were different; to see the coaches on the road you did not have to peer through a crack, as you could look at them through a window; while the other window had not been boarded up.

The officers found a strange collection of people in the house: a grotesque lot of mortals, some of them oddly named. All were destined to become notorious throughout England.

There was the keeper of the place, Susannah Wells, herself. There was an old gypsy woman, Mary Squires, who was sitting bent over the fire, smoking a pipe, her body swathed in a big cloak, and her head covered by an immense black bonnet. Her son and daughter, George and Lucy Squires, were also there. So was a man named Natus, with his wife. The parents of this man had conceived the notion of naming him Fortune, so it was as Fortune Natus that he was soon being discussed at every coffee house in London. In addition to these, there was a girl with the exquisitely inappropriate name of Virtue Hall.

Elizabeth Canning was asked to identify those who had robbed and imprisoned her. She was brought into the room where they were all gathered. Passing by Mrs. Wells, without noticing her, she pointed to the pipe-smoker by the fire, and said:

"That old woman in the corner was the woman who robbed me."

At this, the old gypsy rose, threw back her cloak and bonnet, and disclosed the most frightful and extraor-

dinary features any one had ever imagined. It was a face
to make children run away, screaming. Mary Squires was
very old, her figure tall and stooping. Her face was fear-
fully marked by scrofula; her nose very large.

"Such a nose as hers," someone said, "was never before
on mortal countenance."

But all these things were nothing compared with her
prodigious under-lip—it was said to be "as big almost as
a little child's arm."

This creature confronted Elizabeth Canning. She well
knew the danger in which she stood. Robbery was a
hanging offense, and people always believed the worst of
gypsies.

"Me rob you!" she cried. "I never saw you in my life
before. For God Almighty's sake do not swear my life
away! Pray, madam, look at this face; if you have once
seen it before, you must have remembered it, for God, I
think, never made such another. Pray, madam, when do
you say I robbed you?"

Of course we cannot be sure how correctly this is reported, but if the gypsy spoke in this fashion, most of
us will be inclined to think that her appeal sounds unmis-
takably like truth.

To her question as to the date of the robbery, Elizabeth answered that it was New Year's Day. The gypsy
replied:

"I was a hundred and twenty miles from this place
then."

George Squires, her son, said they were all at Abbots-
bury on January 1st. Fortune Natus and his wife, Judith,
said that they had been sleeping nightly in the hayloft
for the past ten or twelve weeks. Elizabeth persisted in
her accusations and pointed out Virtue Hall and Lucy

Squires as the two women who were present when she was robbed. Virtue Hall laughed in her face, and said:

"God forgive you, madam! I never saw you in this house in my life."

Now, people accused of crime usually deny it; and they can often deny with apparent sincerity, and much calling upon the sacred name of God. But there is one thing which is unaccountable in Elizabeth's identification of the old gypsy. It was impossible for anyone to see this woman and not be profoundly affected by her terrible face. Yet Elizabeth Canning had not mentioned it. She merely said there were three women in the room, and that one of them cut off her stays!

Doubts arose in the minds of a number of men who were there. And from this time, the people of England began to be divided in two camps: Canningites, the believers in Elizabeth; and Egyptians, who thought that Mary Squires told the truth. This term was used because gypsies were called Egyptians.

At first, however, the Canningites carried everything before them. They started with the idea that Elizabeth was a persecuted saint. Being a saint, she could tell nothing but the truth. If she had said nothing about a number of things in the room where she had been confined; if she had not mentioned, for instance, a lot of hay that was there, it was because her mind was confused, poor dear. If she said, at first, that there were only four or five pieces of bread in the room, and if, later these became twenty-four pieces—to make the story of her survival rather more reasonable—why, nobody noticed it.

So the gypsies, and everyone else in that old house, were dragged off to jail. Within a few days, Elizabeth came before Henry Fielding, the novelist, who was a

Justice of the Peace. He became one of the most energetic Canningites, and a firm believer in her innocence
and sufferings. This is explained on the ground that he
was a most tender-hearted man, quickly responsive to any
story of cruelty to a helpless woman. In our time, Fielding's great successor, Thomas Hardy, was similarly disposed.

The trial of the two old women for theft, as we have
seen, resulted in their conviction. Public opinion—which
sometimes means the cries of the mob—was dead against
them. Hardly anyone dared speak in favor of the gypsy.
And to make their fate more certain, Virtue Hall, who
was frightened for her own life, went back on her first
statement; turned King's evidence; and testified that
Elizabeth's story of what happened in the house was true.
Later, Virtue changed her story again, and went back to
her original statement.

Mary Squires, the gypsy, tried to prove an alibi; that
she was in Dorsetshire, more than a hundred miles away,
on January 1st. But the jury did not believe the few witnesses she was able to bring, and the death sentence was
pronounced.

Except for the efforts of the Lord Mayor, Sir Crispe
Gascoyne, the gypsy would have swung at Tyburn Tree.
He saw through the holes in Elizabeth's story and he
found no reason to doubt Squires' alibi. His petition
to the King resulted, first in a postponement of the hanging, and finally in a full pardon.

The Canningites boiled with rage. Not to hang the
gypsy was an insult to the virtuous maid to whose cause
they were subscribing money. It amounted to a suggestion that, while Elizabeth may have fallen among thieves
during the latter part of her absence, she was telling a

string of lies as to the events of most of the month. And, especially, that she was never at Mrs. Wells's house in Enfield at all!

For the next year, Elizabeth Canning and the gypsy were merely pawns in a game; the figures around whom raged a bitter fight. Interest in her case spread to Europe, and Voltaire wrote about it. As the young bloods in the London clubs drank toasts to "Bet" Canning, and raised money for her defense, so the other side, the Egyptians, collected money, and hired investigators to look into the truth of the tale of the gypsy's wanderings.

Late in the Spring of the following year, fifteen months after the night when Elizabeth had been set upon by the two big, bad men, who stole her dress but spared her mince pie, she was arrested and put on trial for perjury.

In the history of English criminal law, it was one of the strangest of trials. It lasted for seven days—a thing almost unknown at the time. The crowd of spectators filled the room and the air was stifling. The old gypsy, who had probably been kept in jail all this time, as a material witness, was brought in, seated in a chair, sick and faint. She swooned two or three times, and had to be carried out and revived. Elizabeth, now the prisoner, looked well and trim; her manner was modest and dignified.

Before the Court paraded an almost endless procession of witnesses. To prove Elizabeth a perjurer, it was necessary to show an alibi for the gypsy; and thirty-six witnesses, from various parts of the country, swore to Squires' presence in different country villages in the south of England. Innkeepers, tinkers, barmaids, fiddlers, and all the odd folk of rural life in the eighteenth century, traced the slow progress of the gypsy family from Dorset

to Enfield. According to this, they did not arrive at Enfield until the middle of January.

The jury heard a great number of stories about country dances, where the schoolmaster got "fuddled"; about
people sleeping in hedgerows and barns; and about the
love affair of Lucy Squires—who, in spite of her hideous
mother, seems to have been a pretty girl, around whom
the young men swarmed, contesting for her kisses at
Christmas parties.

Then, to give the jury as hard a problem as possible,
Elizabeth's lawyers produced twenty-six witnesses who
swore that the gypsy was at Mrs. Wells' on New Year's
Day.

The lawyer prosecuting Elizabeth showed that under
her window, in the loft where she said she was imprisoned, was a pond, where farmers watered their horses,
and where, when it was frozen, boys came to slide and
skate. Yet it never occurred to the poor prisoner to shout
to them for help!

In the end, after some hesitation and doubt, the jury
found Elizabeth Canning guilty of perjury. And the
judges, also after some disagreement among themselves,
sentenced her to transportation for seven years to "His
Majesty's plantations in America."

The controversy has divided literary men: Henry
Fielding, as we have seen, was a Canningite. So was An-
drew Lang. But Austin Dobson and Arthur Machen are
Egyptians. The legal writers, I think, are strongly Egyp-
tian.

If her story of her abduction and imprisonment was not
true what did happen to her? I think that the most reasonable suggestion is that she was carried away by some
one, perhaps by force. Perhaps no great amount of force
was necessary. That she went away to have a baby, or

"to get free of disorders common to the gay and young" is supported by no evidence. Indeed, what evidence there is contradicts these suggestions.

Having been carried away, it would not be surprising if, for two or three weeks, she led a life which she did not care to tell about. At the end of this time she may have fallen out with the people with whom she was living, or have been deserted, robbed and betrayed by them. It is unlikely that she was suffering and starving *all* the time for four weeks, although she did have a bad time for a few days. Her accusations against "Mother" Wells and the gypsy were put into her mouth by her over-active friends, and she found herself tangled in a net of perjury before she could back out.

Young Robert Scarratt was thought to have had more knowledge of her adventures than he admitted. And Mrs. Canning, perhaps unjustly, has been suspected of being in the plot—whatever it was.

Aside from the reasons for disbelieving her which have already been mentioned, there are still further improbabilities in her tale. Why should she be carried away by the men who robbed her? Even if she were taken to "Mother" Wells', and if she refused to "go their way," why did they keep her there? Her presence was dangerous to them. How did she know how to ration herself for a four weeks' imprisonment in the hayloft?

Moreover, she said that when she escaped from the window she let herself down by a penthouse. But there was no penthouse. How was she able to live so long on so little food? How did her feeble condition permit her to walk so far on her way home? Why did she not ask for food, water, and help on those eleven weary miles on a winter's night?

No, I fear that Elizabeth did not come back to her mother from so distant a place as Enfield; but that she was one of those pretty little liars, who are so often found among girls between the ages of twelve and twenty. Many a man has gone to prison, or even swung in a noose, because of the tales told by girls like Elizabeth Canning.

ELIZABETH CANNING IN AMERICA.—The writers who have discussed Elizabeth are chiefly English, and, after her conviction and sentence, they dismiss her, with little further information.

Wethersfield, Connecticut, where she lived and died, has forgotten her. A friend of mine who lives there, and is interested in local history, tells me that he had never even heard of her. Wethersfield's attitude may be indifference, or high-minded distaste for a malefactor, but it is clear that her memory has been allowed to perish, and her burial place is probably unknown.

This is not strange. Genealogists and local historians are morbidly reticent about immigrants who came to America under a cloud. Genealogists devote themselves to tickling family pride; while local historians are, first of all, local patriots. Most of our biographical dictionaries (with the honorable exception of the Dictionary of American Biography) were compiled as dictionaries of worthies; the editor excluding from his pages all those whom he would not care to entertain at dinner.

Nevertheless, by taking a hurried glance at a few of the more obvious sources of information (the Annual Register, 1761; *Gentleman's Magazine*, Aug., 1773; Dictionary of National Biography; *Law Quarterly Review*, Oct., 1897; Padget: "Paradoxes and Puzzles"; Henry R. Stiles: "History of Ancient Wethersfield"; *The Connecticut Courant*, June 15, 1773; John Harvey Treat:

"The Treat Family"; New England Historical and Genealogical Register) I have salvaged some trifling bits of news about the lovely perjurer.

Her sentence was for seven years; if she returned inside that time, death, "without benefit of clergy." (That does not mean that you may not have a minister to pray with you.) There is a rumor that she was again in England, in 1761, long enough to receive a legacy of £300. This seems unlikely, and has been denied.

The Government did not hurry her departure, nor treat her with great severity. She sailed, not in a convict ship, but in a ship selected by herself (probably the *Myrtilla*) from Deal, in August, 1754. The port of landing was Philadelphia, and on board the ship were Colonel the Reverend Elisha Williams and lady. They befriended Elizabeth, took her with them to Wethersfield, Connecticut (where many years later, by the hand of the hangman, perished Gerald Chapman, the gentleman bandit) and they gave her a home and, probably, employment.

On November 24, 1756, she helped establish a home of her own, by marrying John Treat. He is sometimes described as a Quaker; but American writers call him a "scatter-brain young fellow of good family." His great-uncle was Governor Robert Treat, so Elizabeth became a member of an honored family, whose name is still distinguished. Between them the young married pair had £1500 (the bride's portion must have come from her reverend benefactor) but this was soon dissipated and their home was sold. John Treat served the State in the Indian campaign of 1757-58.

John and Elizabeth did not live in much prosperity but she is said to have been respected by her neighbors. They had three sons and a daughter. Her eldest son, Joseph

Canning Treat, was a soldier in the American Revolution. On growing up, he dropped the Canning from his name, and I do not discover that any member of the family has ever again picked it up. Although London once echoed to the name of Canning, and it was cheered in the clubs, the Treat family have turned upon it their chilliest shoulders.

In June, 1773, when she was aged but thirty-eight or thirty-nine, Elizabeth Canning Treat died at Wethersfield. Even then, twenty years after her mysterious New Year's adventure, her death was of sufficient interest to be recorded in the London news-sheets and magazines. And almost twenty years after her death, a Member of Congress from South Carolina, visiting Wethersfield, had her house and one of her sons pointed out to him as objects of interest.

Only one other American relic of Elizabeth has come to my knowledge. It is fiction; a pamphlet called *Virtue Triumphant, or, Elizabeth Canning in America* (Boston, 1757). In it she is hailed as "true English-hearted Elizabeth, like the glorious queen after whom she was called. . . ."

In this tale, Miss Canning meets, at some unidentified place in America, a family named Wakefield. Again she is subjected to persecution, for although Mrs. Wakefield is kind to her, and listens to her story, Mr. Wakefield not only gives her "a smacking kiss" but attempts other familiarities, which naturally arouse her opposition. The eighteenth-century pamphleteer, like the twentieth-century writer for the tabloids, had to have his little leer.

The story continues by taking the heroine for a trip to Quebec. Then Mrs. Wakefield dies, and Elizabeth's pilgrimage is happily ended by her marriage to the lecherous Mr. Wakefield.

At the time of this publication, Elizabeth was already Mrs. John Treat, but the Boston pamphleteer, in the manner of all writers of third-rate fiction, doubtless believed that his standing as a "creative artist" would suffer unless he played hob with the facts.

MAJOR YELVERTON was embarrassed, one day, when he received a message from a lady. Letters from ladies were no news to the Major, but there was a peremptory ring about this one which fussed him. She was a terrifying lady—to an officer in the Royal Artillery —her name was Victoria, and she added that she was "by the Grace of God, of the United Kingdom of Great Britain and Ireland, Queen, Defender of the Faith, and so forth."

She gave him her greeting, but went on, in a nasty, dictatorial manner, to say that Major Yelverton owed a man named Thelwall £259 (plus seventeen shillings, thrippence) for the board and keep of Mrs. Yelverton. The Queen went into details about these moneys, specifying a horse at £25; cash, £50; and other items, down to six weeks' washing at six shillings a week. She intimated to the Major that unless he paid Mr. Thelwall, unpleasant things would begin to happen.

The Major replied, and respectfully informed the Queen that somebody had been kidding her. The lady, to whom Mr. Thelwall had been supplying horses and cash and washing, was not and never had been Mrs. Yelverton. Her real name was Miss Theresa Longworth, and she was a bold, brazen person, of a kind he hardly cared to men-

tion to the Queen at all. The actual Mrs. Yelverton had
formerly been named Miss Emily Ashworth, and she was
now at home, where she ought to be, taking care of their
two infants—both of them perfectly lawful little Yelver-
tons.

The Major was pretty serious: he had already spent a
few days in jail, charged with marrying Emily without
getting rid of Theresa. But he knew well enough that
Mr. Thelwall and the Queen were being dragged into
this row by the very lovely, extremely determined, and
thoroughly furious Miss Longworth. He, the Major, was
now stationed in Ireland, and in that country it was possible to get him on the witness stand, when the indignant
lady went to the mat on the subject of his philanderings.

Theresa had been pursued and courted by the rascally
Major all over Europe; there had been petting-parties by
land and sea; there had been two marriage ceremonies,
and any amount of traipsing about together in hotels; together with enough love-letters to sink a ship. Who?
cried Theresa, to the Lord Chief Justice of Ireland and a
special Dublin jury—who was married, if she were not?

The gallantry of the Dublin men knew no bounds.
Although the Major had been born in Ireland and
Theresa in England, the crowd raised the roof cheering
for her. Who could look at her, at her blonde hair, which,
said the reporters, was "of that rich and glowing golden
hue, in which Titian delighted to portray his ideal beau-
ties"—who could see this, and not be on her side? Not the
Dublin reporters!

As to the Major, one needed only to glance at him to
perceive that he was a Parlor Snake. Reporters were
shocked to observe the coolness with which he gave his
evidence, and "the revolting cynicism of his avowals
which caused a thrill of horror to run through the Court."

When Theresa testified, her "sweet and musical voice, and exquisite propriety of diction" enhanced her attractions and convinced her listeners. She told the jury:

"My parents are dead. One of my sisters is Mme. Lefebvre; she lives in Boulogne. I was educated in a French convent, and brought up as a strict Roman Catholic. In 1852, when I was twenty, I had been visiting my sister in Boulogne. One evening, in the summer, I took the steamboat for London. My sister came to the pier to see me off, and it was arranged that I should travel with two ladies who were on board. They stayed on deck all night with me; it was a warm night and the sea was calm. The ship was full of passengers and we preferred to stay on deck.

"Before we sailed, my sister threw a shawl to me from the shore, and it was caught by a gentleman, who was with these two ladies. He put it round my shoulders, and was otherwise polite and attentive. This gentleman was Major—he was then Captain—Yelverton. He fetched his plaid from below, and we put it over our knees, as he sat opposite me in a chair. We arrived in London at daylight. The two ladies said good-by; Major Yelverton got a cab for me, and then he went away—I do not know where. I went to visit the Marchioness de la Belline, at whose house my other sister was staying. Next day, Major Yelverton called, and my sister and I received him. He had asked to call; I did not invite him."

But when the Major gave his version of that night, the trip up the Channel became a bit more clubby and sociable. In his story, the two chaperons do not appear at all; the plaid, he hinted, enfolded Theresa and himself; and their conversation dwelt upon the happy chance of their meeting, and upon sunset and evening star and similar topics.

After all, you know, Yelverton was Captain the Honorable, the son of a peer, and he would one day be Viscount Avonmore. His erect, military figure (figger, to him) was something to see. As for his Dundreary whiskers, young ladies of 1852 considered them maddening; the Queen herself had acknowledged the fascination of a slighter pair.

The Major's account ended with a difference. When, at last, a breeze of morning moved, and the Planet of Love was on high, they saw with regret the smoke of London town. They did *not* part at the wharf. He accepted Theresa's invitation; accompanied her to her friend's house; went in and stayed two hours. A room was offered him, where he might change his traveling clothes. This he did. Nothing else happened, but the incident, if true, implied a sort of *camaraderie*.

After the call of next day, as both parties agree, there came an interlude in the friendship. They parted for more than three years. Theresa was in Italy; Captain Yelverton stationed at Malta. The fires of love were fanned by a correspondence—a shoal of love-letters so vast, so tender, and so puzzling that, in later years, it took many barristers to disentangle their meaning. Some of these lawyers set up carriages and sent their sons to the universities on the proceeds.

Theresa, when she dipped her quill in the violet ink, looked toward the moon, and addressed her beloved, set a standard to which no girl to-day can aspire. Her harsh native tongue was inadequate, and she had frequent recourse to the languages of passion: French and Italian. Nor was the Major, that man of action, much less literate.

They passed from "My dear Miss Longworth" and "Ever your sincere friend, Wm. C. Yelverton" to "My dear Theresa." Then suddenly, at his request for less formality, he was addressed as "Carissimo Carlo mio," while he responded "Cara Theresa mia." Finally, the Major achieved "My dearest little Tooi-tooi" as a satisfactory salutation to his sweetheart. He varied this with "Tooi-tooi carissima." He described a dream in which Theresa appeared to him, and ended:

"You're a dearest darling darling small tooi-tooi, &c., &c., &c., . . . and 'da capo.' Addio. Sempre a te.

Carlo"

To reduce the cruel distance between Italy and Malta, and to bring the lovers together, the Powers of Europe took up the gage of battle. The Crimean War broke out, and Yelverton proceeded to Constantinople. So did Theresa, assisting the French nuns as a nurse. To the Galata Hospital came the Major, and finding Tooi-tooi utterly fascinating in her uniform, besought her to marry him. She declined to leave her suffering soldiers. He went away, but came back, lovesick and miserable. The war ended, but Theresa lingered in the Orient, visiting her friends, General and Lady Straubenzie. Thither came the melancholy Major, and he was received by everyone as Theresa's plighted lover.

Wandering, one day, by her side, he disclosed the tale of an aching heart: he had no income but his pay, he was in a financial pickle, and he had promised his family to marry no lady who could not pay his debts. About £3000 would do it, said he, with the love-light in his eyes.

Theresa replied tenderly that the engagement must be broken; she was entitled only to the interest on her money. Next day, the Major returned with a new idea: they would secretly be wed at the Greek Church at Balaclava. But, to the devout Theresa, there were no true priests but the Catholic, and no true Catholics but the Roman. She declined again.

Now, Major Yelverton, as he stood in the Dublin Court, was in a frightful jam. He might admit that some time, in his pursuit of Theresa, he had been animated by the feelings of a true lover, an officer and a gentleman. If he did so, it would lead to the conclusion that his purposes were sort of half-way decent, and therefore that, perhaps, he really had ventured into matrimony. This would naturally lead him straight to jail, as the bigamous husband of Miss Ashworth. Or else he had to paint himself as a scoundrelly seducer, into whose head never entered the tiniest bit of honorable intention. And then, his trouble would be to escape being dissected by the infuriated populace of Dublin.

"Do you mean to say, Sir," inquired Mr. Sullivan, Q. C., sinking his voice to a scandalized whisper, "do you actually mean to say that it was your intention to make this lady your—your ——"

Mr. Sullivan glanced apologetically at the Lord Chief Justice, then looked down at the floor and hid his face with a bunch of papers:

"Your—*mistress!*"

"I do, Sir," replied the abominable Yelverton.

Two or three lawyers shrieked aloud, and had to be revived with smelling salts, and when the Major returned to his hotel that night, two squads of constables were needed, to protect him from a committee of gentlemen who had sworn to pluck out each hair from his whiskers, one by one, and then throw him in the river.

But he went on to worse things. He swore that the whole Crimean adventure was a relentless pursuit, of which he was the bedeviled victim. Theresa, said he, was always throwing herself at him, and as a result, "great familiarities" took place. The Lord Chief Justice faintly remarked that this was distasteful, revolting and hideous, but that they *must* have particulars.

When Theresa left Constantinople on a steamboat, the Major was there. Another nocturne at sea—and the Major began to describe it. Barristers and jurors leaped to their feet to remind my Lord that there were ladies in Court. The Chief Justice uttered a warning and a few ladies withdrew. He then said that if others chose to remain, he "could not help them." They would be contaminated beyond repair. After a few more appeals, the Court was, little by little, cleared of ladies.

The Major then admitted sitting on deck, with his arm around Theresa's waist; apparently he tried to snap her garter, but the scene was interrupted by some sailors who came on deck, while the reporting of it was checked by the swooning away of every newspaperman in Court. All the historians resort, at this point, to asterisks.

The lovers returned to England, and when the Major was ordered to Leith, Theresa turned up, with her friend Miss MacFarlane, at the near-by city of Edinburgh. He attended her every day; they rode together, and went to social functions as an affianced pair. The Major's first thought of a Greek marriage was now followed by the suggestion of a Scottish one. Any kind of wedding, so long as it was a little bit phony, seemed acceptable to him.

"One day," said Theresa, "he took the prayer book from the table, and I went to his side, and he read the marriage ceremony, and said 'That makes you my wife by the laws of Scotland.' I opened the door of the room in which Miss MacFarlane was sitting, and said to her: 'We've married each other.'"

After this, the Major, having assumed as few as possible of the responsibilities of a husband, claimed all the privileges. Theresa refused, and demanded a marriage according to the rites of her own Church. When the Major persisted that she now live with him, she discreetly fled from Scotland.

The Honorable the Major's story of the Edinburgh episode was that there was no prayer book, and no reading of the service. Instead, he persevered in his hellish designs, and accomplished them one day, "on the sofa in Mrs. Gamble's sitting room." The auditors, in Court, burst into boos and hisses, and the Dublin gentlemen announced their intention of drinking the Major's blood, hot, in the market place.

Some weeks after the flight from Scotland, so the lady testified, the Major invited her to join him in Ireland for a marriage before a Roman Catholic priest. They were never stay-at-homes, but were always eager to see what a new country might do for them. Yelverton went on leave, and the two met at Waterford in Ireland. There was a search for a priest, and for two weeks Theresa and the Major traveled around Ireland.

As Mr. Roughead, the only modern historian of the case, delicately puts it:

"They engaged, in the various hotels which they visited, a sitting room, a bedroom, and dressing-room which contained a bed, so there is no architectural reason for rejecting the lady's statement that until the religious ceremony was performed they occupied separate rooms. On the other hand, the moral probabilities are in favor of the Major's contrary assertion; and the pair were naturally regarded by the hotel witnesses as married persons."

On August 15, 1857, in the chapel at Rostrevor, Theresa and the Major knelt together at the altar and the ceremony was performed. There was some question as to the Major's religion, but Father Mooney was satisfied as to that. The Major's version of this did not differ greatly from Theresa's. He admitted that they knelt before the priest, who read "a portion of a marriage service."

They traveled together and parted, and did this more than once in the next year. They were in France together for three months, registering everywhere as Mr. and Mrs. Yelverton. Theresa's passport was in that name.

Next summer, leaving Theresa in France, the Major went to Edinburgh. Here he found the £3000 which his family honor required. It was inextricably attached to the person of Miss Emily Ashworth. He married her, and, it is good to record, was promptly clapped into jail for bigamy. His defense, at the trial in Dublin, was that the Scottish marriage never happened; and that the Irish one was illegal, since he was not a Roman Catholic.

The jury found the defense to be a miserable subterfuge; both marriages, they said, were valid. The crowd took Theresa's horses out of her carriage and drew her, in triumph, to her hotel. Everyone, including the gentlemen's vengeance committee, got so illuminated, that Yelverton, the serpent, wriggled out of town with his life.

He squirmed over to Edinburgh, and laid his case before a Scottish judge. This old gentleman was not allowed to see Theresa's golden hair, and so he gave a decision against her. There was another appeal, and three more judges divided 2 to 1 in her favor. The Major now raised the money (from Emily, I suppose) to take the case to the House of Lords, and their Committee voted 3 to 2 for Yelverton. Thus, by the margin of one judge, Emily and not Theresa was finally established as Mrs. Yelverton, and later as Viscountess Avonmore.

The Army had already thrown out the noble lord, and England, generally, seemed to hope he would choke.

When, in 1883, he died at Biarritz, he was an obscure person.

Theresa traveled far and wide, lectured and wrote books. Novels were written about her romantic life. She came to New York, and had a talk with Horace Greeley in the old Hotel Albemarle. He and his *Tribune* warmly supported her cause, and denounced the Major. Theresa's lectures in America were not successful, but she wrote a book about us, and also a novel, with the scene placed in the Yosemite Valley. My devotion to her memory has caused me to try to read it.

To the end, she remained strikingly beautiful, spirited in mind and body, but saddened and lonely. She died in South Africa, before the Major.

It had been her fate to expend her energy fighting to prove that she was the wife of a man whom the late Brander Matthews once described to me as "a singularly perfect specimen of the skunk."

SCENERY BY
CURRIER & IVES

COLONEL WALTON DWIGHT was the kind of colonel who is always called "doughty." Importance surrounded him like a golden haze; in his presence a turkey gobbler would seem to be suffering from an inferiority complex.

The Colonel appeared in Binghamton, New York, at the close of the Civil War. He rose six feet three inches, from the ground, and he weighed 225 pounds. His beard, at that time, was long and blond and wavy. He was robust in health and hearty in manner.

The military title was no pretense: his career in the War had been distinguished; it included four great battles and fourteen minor engagements. At last, severely wounded at Gettysburg, he retired from the army, married the rich Miss Deusenberry, and looked about him for the triumphs of business and politics.

I always see Colonel Dwight, at this period, as the central figure and hero of a Currier and Ives print. Let it be *Winter Sport*, and there he is, driving a fast pair of long-tailed horses along a snow-covered road. His fur coat and cap are regal in their magnificence; they indicate the opulence of the 1870's.

If the picture is *American Home Life in the Country*, there he is again, with his jigsaw house, the artificial pond (with swans), the croquet lawn, and the big, bursting barn. The Colonel, not much smaller than the barn, is complacently surveying his property from horseback. He has not one bronze stag on the lawn, but two; a complicated swing; a hammock between two purple beeches; and a fountain with a pair of metal children under an umbrella, and a silver ball rising and descending in the stream of water.

In and about Binghamton, the earth shook beneath his tread. His clients and his lictors referred to him as a "splendid fellow"; and his own description of himself was as a man accustomed "to bore with a big auger."

When he was but twenty-eight he wished to raise $300,000 to buy timber lands in Canada. He approached those whom an irreverent writer calls "the cautious fossils" of the Broome County Bank, and such was his magic that they let him have the money. He became a dealer in manufactured lumber, a mine operator in Pennsylvania a landlord in Chicago, and the owner of Canadian forests.

For other activities, the Colonel built a section of the city, called Dwightsville (no longer so called, I think) and put up a grand hotel, the Dwight House, with fifty cottages. He was Mayor of Binghamton about 1871.

Now, there were certain privileges in ruling over the city at that period. One of them was that it might have brought him into contact with the Herr Dr. Rulloff, who had temporarily abandoned the study of philology in New York to engage in a little burglary and murder in Binghamton. Yet the learned historian of this region is coy, almost to the point of studied reticence, in his admission that Colonel Dwight once wore the robes of the Lord Mayor's office.

The reason for this must be found in some events of

later years, particularly on the last night of all: the much-discussed Death Bed of Colonel Dwight.

The time was a midnight of November, when, as the Shropshire Lad has noted, "Dead Man's Fair is nigh." The Lad goes on, in a manner almost reminiscent of the astonishing mystery of Colonel Dwight, to observe:

"The living are the living, And dead the dead will stay, And I will sort with comrades That face the beam of day."

It was to solve the problem, which were the dead, and which the living, and where on earth, or under it, was Colonel Dwight, that agitated dozens of lawyers and doctors for many years. There are at least four theories as to what happened after dark on November 15, 1878. Let us take them in order, the plain and prosaic ones first, rising to the odd and romantic.

It was all very sad and simple, said the friends and retainers and heirs of the Colonel. That officer and gentleman, having with forethought insured his life, passed away from the effects of gastric fever, at the untimely age of forty-one. And, with certain honorable exceptions, the insurance companies chose to enact the rôles of an obscene flock of vultures, and to repudiate their just debts to the bereaved family.

Not so; not so, at all, returned a great swarm of insurance companies—about twenty of them. They kept up their contention, by legal methods, until, at last, the whole case was exposed in Court, at Norwich, in 1883.

And still, when gray-bearded insurance officials gather round a winter's fire, the tale is told, of how the Germania Company fought the good fight, in the brave days of old.

They raked up some curious facts. It is denied by nobody that the Colonel's vast financial operations went to smash, not long after his term as mayor. He spent all his own fortune, whatever that was; all of his wife's, which was considerable; and accumulated a grand total deficit of $400,000. Father-in-law Deusenberry, with a fine gesture, offered him a check for quarter of a million; and the Colonel, equally magnificent, declined it.

In the summer, less than six months before the event which some persons described, with the sarcastic aid of quotation marks, as the Colonel's "death," he became very active. He had been discharged from bankruptcy, and any payments of money on insurance policies, for instance, would fall to his heirs, and not to his creditors.

With the grandeur of him who always wielded the big auger, he applied to every insurance company in the country but one. Why he discriminated against this company, which was in California, I cannot discover. Twenty-one companies accepted the risk and the sum on the Colonel's life was not less than $390,000 and is sometimes given as $420,000.

His other actions were alarming. He repeatedly swam the Susquehanna River in cold weather, at peril of pneumonia; and he engaged, during October, in a long and fatiguing hunt in the woods and hills around Windsor, N. Y. He also took large doses of morphia and gelsemium. These things laid the foundation for belief that he had been trying, heroically but illegally, to destroy himself and thereby enrich his heirs.

His celebrated deathbed was spread for him in a room in one of the Binghamton hotels—not the Dwight House. Here on the last day of his life he was able to be up and dressed, to receive friends, execute legal papers, and, most strangely, to sacrifice that source of pride and glory, his hair and beard. A barber came and shore them quite away.

A gentleman named Hull was the only person present when the soul of the great Colonel passed from earth. This was an unfortunate fact, and the name was doubly unfortunate, since another Hull of Binghamton had recently been exploiting a colossal fake, purporting to be a human body, and known as the Cardiff Giant.

The chief contention of the insurance men, led in the test case by the Germania Company, and speaking through physicians who performed the autopsy, was that the body produced for their inspection had come to death from strangulation—that is, through hanging. This suggests that the Colonel, with or without the connivance of Mr. Hull, arose at some time during the evening, and hanged himself to his bedpost. Descriptions of the bedpost have been furnished, to show that it was adequate for the purpose.

The Colonel's last will and testament needs much more explaining than his heirs seemed to offer. Its public bequests were many and lavish. A thousand dollars for an annual dinner for newspapermen, and $7,500 for the public library shall never be condemned in my presence. Nor have I fault to find with $10,000 for an annual Christmas dinner for the poor, or $3,000 for the firemen. But $5,000 for the Coroner who was to view the body, and $10,000 for the Surrogate who was to pass upon the will—these would plant suspicion in the mind of a saint.

It should be said that either one, or two, companies, including the Equitable of New York, after investigation, paid the full amount of their policies—$50,000. This money must have been useful in the long-drawn-out litigation which followed. In the end, the Germania won its test case, on appeal, but the decision did not concern the main point of interest.

The Colonel's estate lost, because of false statements

which he had made in his applications. The other suits
were finally compromised on payment of about $2,000
each. Meager moral victories, these, for the estate, with
many of the Binghamtonites dissenting from the word
"moral."

Now for the more picturesque theories. The first and
less romantic of the two was that Colonel Dwight slipped
out of the back door, on that doleful night, and that Mr.
Hull, or somebody, fetched in a spurious Colonel, who
happened to be in the neighborhood, conveniently deceased. To discover a dead man capable of duplicating
the Colonel's glorious proportions would assuredly need
some doing. But the adherents of this theory point to the
mysterious shave procured by the chief conspirator that
morning, and suggest that he had been told that it was
necessary, since his understudy was not suitably bewhisk-
ered. The loss of the beard would also be convenient, as
a disguise during flight. This flight, they said, led to
Mexico or South America, and there were strong men
who offered, if suitably rewarded, to go down into these
countries, and fetch the Colonel back, *alive*.

The ultra-romantic seized upon the gelsemium as the
clue to the mystery. This drug, so they asserted, could
produce suspended animation and a semblance of death.
It had the properties of the liquid swallowed by Juliet
when she wished to seem to die, and the Colonel had used,
or attempted to use it, for the same purpose. The chief
trouble with the theory is the difficulty of imagining
Colonel Dwight as Juliet in the tomb of the Capulets.

The disappearance theory and the substitute body have
the greatest attraction for me. Ordinarily I am opposed
to painting the lily and bringing extra elements of romance into such cases. People sometimes comment with
chill disapproval on my failure to inject fiction into the

painfully veracious histories which I strive to record. It is contrary to my usual inclination, therefore, when I say that it seems to me likely that the Colonel chose to sort with comrades that faced the beam of day.

First, there is the will, which plainly indicates some kind of flim-flam. Second, there appeared at the trial a physician of high repute and long experience, Dr. John Swinburne, at one time Mayor of Albany. He said, under oath, and he could not be confuted, that the body which he saw at the autopsy was not, in his opinion, the body of Colonel Dwight.

For these reasons, and also because it offends my sensibilities to think of so splendid a creature going down into the grave at the age of forty-one, I prefer to fancy that the Colonel made a clean getaway, to Tia Juana—or whatever place, in 1878, was its equivalent. There I like to picture him living the much-praised life of Riley. And there he could be joined later, when his beard had grown again, by Mrs. Dwight, born Deusenberry.

PARSONS' PLEASURE

"Nevertheless, it appertaineth to the discipline of the Church that inquiry be made of evil ministers, and that they be accused by those that have knowledge. . . ."

I. THE ARCHDEACON'S PAJAMAS

"THERE remains," said the Lord Chancellor, "the very serious difficulty with the pajamas."

The scene was as impressive as any the mind of man may conceive; the Court as august, its robes, suits and trappings more splendid than any other on this planet. To the right and to the left of Lord Chancellor Birkenhead sat Lord Buckmaster, Lord Dunedin and Lord Shaw; while these peers were flanked by four lords spiritual: the Bishops of London, Gloucester, Rochester, and Ely. These Right Reverend prelates sat "as assessors."

And I trust that you know what that means, because if you do not, I am too ignorant to be able to inform you.

These great personages, forming the Judicial Committee of the Privy Council, representing the King's Most Excellent Majesty, holding in their hands the thunderbolts of the law, and the keys of heaven and of hell, had at last reached the crucial question of the Archdeacon's pajamas.

In the gloom of the great Gothic hall in which they

sat, its crimson and purple lights falling upon their gowns, their wigs and their lawn sleeves, they were forced to admit the perplexing nature of the problem why the Archdeacon of Stow (who was also Canon and Precentor of Lincoln Cathedral) should have suddenly abandoned his lifelong devotion to the old-fashioned nightshirt, in favor of these new-fangled garments.

Upon one point everyone agreed: all these nobles; all the array of counsel before them; and all the swarm of witnesses—bishops and rural deans, waitresses and chambermaids, poets, peasants and policemen, school teachers and horse traders.

This was that the Archdeacon of Stow, who was also Vicar of Kirkstead (in addition to his other titles already mentioned) had twice visited the Bull Hotel at the cathedral town of Peterborough. These visits happened in the spring of 1920.

Alone, said the Archdeacon.

Yes, alone, said a cloud of witnesses.

Bringing with him the simple nightshirt of his forefathers, and no other sleeping clothes, said the Archdeacon.

By no means alone, said the Bishop of Lincoln, and the Rector of Nether Seale, and a considerable body of hotel people, policemen and others.

Bringing with him not a nightshirt, but pajamas, marked with his name, and *also* bringing with him a nightgown much too trimmed and decorated for masculine use.

And also bringing with him an occupant for that gown. She had been seen, the hussy, dining and breakfasting with the Archdeacon, and visiting points of interest in the town.

She was a myth, a fancy, retorted the Archdeacon, and

his host of sympathizers; a myth, concocted by wicked and vengeful men.

And so the issue was joined; the battle was on. For except on the bare fact that the Archdeacon did twice put up at The Bull, the opposing factions agreed on nothing. The time of his arrivals and departures, the rooms he ate in, the wine he drank or didn't drink, the state of the weather, and the clothes he slept in, were all hotly disputed by these folk of Peterborough.

The Consistory Court of the Diocese of Lincoln had believed in the pajamas, and the other garment, and all the scandal which these implied. They had condemned the Archdeacon, and sought to cast him out from his numerous holy offices, and perhaps from the priesthood as well. But the Archdeacon, who never lacked the courage to fight, had appealed to this highest Court of all. So the Lord High Chancellor, and these others, were hearing again all that the snoopers—or the horrified and godly folk—had discovered.

In some instances, such a case might be dismissed as "sordid." But scarcely, in these ecclesiastical and exalted circles. There is, moreover, another very curious aspect to the appeal of the Archdeacon against his overlord, the Bishop of Lincoln. It was a conspicuous example of a trial which resulted in flat contradiction of testimony between people, most of whom had no apparent object in lying. It had also at least one instance of the method in which testimony against an accused man may be invented or perverted by a careless or overzealous witness.

The Archdeacon was sixty-one; he had a good reputation, and was everywhere in demand as a preacher. His wife and family, and many of his friends and associates in the Church testified in his behalf. His character witnesses included the Bishop of Lichfield, and one of the other Canons of Lincoln.

He came, so testified the innkeeper, to The Bull on a Sunday evening in Lent. He was accompanied by a lady in a dark blue dress.

The innkeeper's wife saw the lady, but her testimony and that of other employees varied from that of the innkeeper in certain details. The latter seems to have changed his testimony at some time, in order to make it square with the others.

The Archdeacon and the lady, to tell the tale as his enemies told it, dined together, in a grill-room, or in a private room (the hotel people disagreed) and shared a bottle of Pommard. On Monday, they breakfasted together (again a dispute about the room) and visited a "tapestry school" near the Cathedral. The lady who superintended this school saw them and recognized the Archdeacon.

Later, they visited Peterborough Cathedral. There was a snowstorm that day, and these sightseers got their clothes wet. The "bathing apparatus" at The Bull was out of order—that is, the arrangements for heating water —and no baths being available, the two visited another hotel, where they took hot baths and dried their clothes. The chambermaid remembered drying the clergyman's socks.

The police seemed to have marked them in the streets, though why an Archdeacon, in gaiters, apron and shovel hat should have aroused suspicion in a cathedral town is not clear. Anyhow, they inquired at the hotel, with the result that the innkeeper, or his wife, became disquieted, and found fault with the entry in the register. They wished the lady to sign, as well as her husband. The Archdeacon refused the request.

So the innkeeper's wife went upstairs and looked at the nightclothes. There was a pair of pajamas, marked with the Archdeacon's name, and there was also a night dress. They thought the name on the pajamas and that on the register did not agree.

Counsel for the Archdeacon, Sir Edward Carson, at this point asked:

"Instead of peering into an old clergyman's nightclothes, why did you not ask him what his name was, and say that you could not make it out in the register?"

Answer: "I don't know why."

There was much confusing evidence about the entries in the register, and about the amount of the bills paid. The prosecution claimed that the words "and wife" were at some time added to the clergyman's name, by his own hand. The defense asserted that the innkeeper unjustifiably added the words himself.

Again, two weeks later, the Archdeacon came to The Bull, and again, so his opponents said, the mysterious lady in dark blue was with him.

The Archdeacon's reply to all this was a complete denial of the lady in dark blue.

A serious bit of evidence had been given by a waitress. She testified that she saw the clergyman at dinner, with his partner in sin, and that he spoke sharply to the woman, with reference to the fact that she wore no wedding ring:

"Take your hand off the table! Do you want to get us thrown out of here?"

This, as testimony for the prosecution, was utterly destroyed by the poet, Edmund Blunden. Mr. Blunden, sufficiently eminent in Britain's Choir to have been mentioned for the Laureateship, at the latest vacancy, was dining, that night, at The Bull, together with Mrs. Blunden, and a friend named Porter. It was Mr. Blunden who addressed the remark to his wife, in jest. The Blundens both appeared at the hearing to testify to this, and Mrs. Blunden, who saw the Archdeacon at breakfast, was able to add that he was eating alone.

Similar things, doubtless, may easily happen in cases like this: an innocent remark transferred by an officious witness to other lips, is made to seem a proof of guilt.

The Archdeacon denied the bottle of Pommard, and another statement concerning champagne. He never drank champagne, and to say he did was an aspersion on his character.

To the defense of the Archdeacon there also came a curious group of men who would hardly be apt to perjure themselves in behalf of a clergyman accused of wicked frivolity. A horsy and sporting lot, they would be more likely to regard his plight with cynical glee.

Yet, one Lindley, a horse trader; Joseph Kay, a farmer, attending the horse show; John Appleby of Stafford; Joseph Thomas of Hereford; Thomas Baxter, a scout-master; John Lennard, an engineer; together with others, horse breeders or vets, all testified to seeing "the old parson," at various meals, or meeting him on the stairs and here and there in the hotel, and that he was, on all these occasions, alone.

The morals of the higher clergy were conserved, so far as possible, during the hearing. The admission, by the Bishop of Lincoln, that he was playing golf on a certain Saturday was received in the Court with "laughter." The Lord Bishop had this set straight in the record: it was *not* on the Saturday of Holy Week, but on the Saturday before Palm Sunday.

The pajama scandal was refuted by the Archdeacon's wife and housemaid. He had never worn them in his life, except once (in 1919) when, as a concession to the more abandoned manners of Europe, he used them during a trip to France.

What could be the explanation of all this? Was there another person, some gay dog, in the vestments of a parson, gallivanting about upon his unholy amusements, and did the good Archdeacon suffer from the likeness to himself?

He did not say so. Rather, his theory was that of a conspiracy, and he named the conspirators, two personages right out of the pages of Anthony Trollope: the Rector of Nether Seale, Ashby-de-la-Zouche, and the Vicar of Appleby Magna. These two had been his enemies for years. One of them was his brother-in-law—but that only made him more dangerous.

There was an old quarrel about a church, which the Archdeacon had reopened, despite the wishes of the Vicar of Appleby Magna—whose name was Moore. The Archdeacon wished to preach in this church, and recreate the spiritual life of the parish, but Mr. Moore, filled with Christian spirit, had the building encircled with barbed wire.

When the Archdeacon broke through the wire, the Vicar, making strange use of the language of Chicago gunmen, had exclaimed:

"All right, all right, *but I'll get you yet!*"

Now, the Vicar and the Rector, it was shown, had been moved by holy zeal for uncovering the Archdeacon's misdeeds, as soon as rumor reached them. They had promptly hired an ex-policeman to act as detective.

Yet the Lord Chancellor, and their Lordships, sniffed and pooh-poohed at the notion of such a vast conspiracy.

It was unbelievable, they said, and the Archdeacon's

witnesses must be mistaken. They upheld the lower Court, and threw out his appeal.

And the Archdeacon was left to the cold comfort of public meetings; the support of the paper, *John Bull*; and the exhibition of "cinema shows, portraying various incidents connected with the case."

II. PRONOUNCED "STEWKEY"

AMERICAN sojourners in London, in the spring of
1932, found thorns in their paths. The horror of the
Lindbergh kidnapping was at its height, and the best-
intentioned Englishmen could not refrain from asking
their Yankee friends questions which raised the bitter subject of our standards of behavior. It had not then been
revealed that the arch-criminal in the Lindbergh case was
an intruder from Europe.

At last—although it was wholly irrelevant—the scandal
of the Rector of Stiffkey (pronounced Stewkey) rose
above the English horizon, and the badgered American
took shameless refuge in a *tu quoque*. Henceforth, all
for which he had to apologize was the career of Al
Capone, the Prohibition mess, and our disgraceful blunders in eating our breakfast marmalade out of its proper
time.

To the horrified ears of the Chancellor of the Diocese
of Norwich, the history of the Rev. Harold Davidson,
Rector of Stiffkey, was laid bare. For weeks and
weeks, during a good part of the summer—almost to
the grouse and salmon season—the Chancellor sat at
Church House, Westminster, to judge the case of the
Bishop of Norwich *versus* Mr. Davidson. For even a
Bishop cannot remove a properly ordained clergyman—
strip him of his benefices—without long and painful
process—if the clergyman chooses to resist. And Mr.
Davidson was a prince of resisters.

The eminent King's Counsel, Mr. Roland Oliver, un-
folded to the Chancellor the complaints of the saddened
Bishop. Mr. Oliver fumbled his papers, adjusted his wig,

blushed once or twice—preliminary, trial blushes, to see
that all was in order—coughed, and began.

Stiffkey (still pronounced Stewkey) is near the North
Sea. The parish has 500 people—not enough to occupy
the time of an active-minded man, like Mr. Davidson.
And Mr. Davidson troubled his parish little. He had been
there for more than twenty years. Except on Sunday,
when he conducted the services, he was not seen in
Stiffkey.

Year in and year out, he took the London train on
Sunday evening, arriving in the city in the small hours.
He returned to his cure of souls on the following Saturday night. Who performed the marriages and buried the
dead, does not appear. But the usual week-day activities of
a rural rector occupied him not at all: Lady Bracknell's
tennis-tea for the benefit of the blanket fund was not
graced by his presence; the Mothers' Meeting had to
content themselves with a wandering curate, if one was
at hand; and the Boy Scouts lacked his ghostly counsel,
as well as his help at cricket and rugger.

Why was he in London six days every week? Well, he
was supposed to be looking for a "Mr. G." from whom
he had expectations. The whole alphabet was represented
in this case, with Miss X., Mrs. Y., Mr. A. and others.
Some of them appeared in person, but Mr. G. forever remained off-stage. His only real function was revealed,
late in the hearing, as the lender of a suit of pajamas.
The Rector, like the Archdeacon of Stow, had indig-
nantly denied owning or wearing pajamas. At last, in the
face of overwhelming evidence that he had been seen in
such a costume—silk ones, too—he remembered that Mr.
G. had lent them.

The Rector's other purpose in London, said Mr. Oliver,
with downcast eyes, was rescue work among young

women. Very pretty young women. Chiefly from the age of sixteen to twenty. He took them to theaters, cinemas, luncheons, teas, taxi-rides, and he paid for their lodgings. He called on them at all kinds of unearthly hours, and these calls took place, usually, in "bed-sitting rooms."

"A curious place," observed the K.C., in an acid tone, "a curious place to proselytize young women."

The Chancellor of the Diocese maintained the best traditions of the English bench. He was more innocent than a dove. Everything had to be explained to him.

Somebody was testifying about Nellie Churchill. (She was the model, whom the Rector, two or three times, had taken to Paris—with the laudable purpose of finding work for her.) The witness sarcastically remarked that Nellie "tried to speak with an Oxford accent," and the Chancellor blandly inquired:

"What is an Oxford accent?"

Mr. Davidson's sacerdotal labors carried him often into taverns and tea-shops, into A.B.C. and Lyons' Restaurants, so that one had to be conversant with this side of London life. Some one spoke of his custom of annoying the employees. Mr. Oliver's exact, though regrettable, phrase was that there was "soft handling and pawing." And this occurred among the "trippies."

The Chancellor doubtless knew his Barrie, and had heard of "Tweenies," but he had never taken judicial notice of "trippies."

"What," he asked, "what on earth are *trippies?*"

He was enlightened by courteous counsel. They were "girls between sixteen and eighteen, before they become waitresses."

It also appeared that the Rector, sitting on a park bench one day with Miss Barbara Harris, related the story of the Scot and his appendicitis. The Scot had asked a girl of his acquaintance if she would like to see the place where he had his appendix removed, and while the girl was hastily disavowing curiosity, he pointed to the Charing Cross Hospital, remarking:

"Yon's the place."

The Chancellor severely remarked:

"I never heard a joke with less joke in it."

Most of the time, however, the Chancellor treated the Rector with consideration. He listened to the long tale of his curious exploits, and gave polite attention to the Rector's defense. He heard, for instance, of the beginning of the years of acquaintance with Barbara Harris—the chief witness for the prosecution.

Miss Harris was standing, one day, near the Marble Arch, when the Rector, his collar reversed (he did not wear clerical dress in London) walked past her, two or three times, and finally approached with the grave inquiry:

"Excuse me, but are you Miss X., the film actress?"

It was Barbara's good fortune to resemble sometimes Miss Greta Garbo, and at other times Miss Lilian Harvey. Which incarnation was uppermost that day is not in the record, but, without directly answering the gentleman's question, she smiled at him, brightly, and accepted his invitation to tea. Thus began a long friendship which was at least indiscreet; and was bitterly regretted by both.

Toward the end of the trial, Miss Harris referred to the Rector's everlasting attempts to get her to write to the Bishop of Norwich in his behalf.

"He has almost driven me potty!"

In this testimony, Barbara was fully sustained by no less a person than the Lord Bishop of London. Appearing as a witness for the Rector, the Bishop testified that he had never heard anything against Mr. Davidson's moral character—ahem—at least, not before the present case. But his Lordship agreed with Miss Harris, as to being driven potty—he admitted that the Rector was "a nuisance, a very great nuisance, and a busybody."

If the Rector had not been so eccentric he might to-day have been undisturbed in his living; might still be preaching in Stiffkey on Sundays, and proselytizing the trippies in London, the rest of the week. But he had many peculiarities beside those enumerated in the formal charges. For one thing, he practically never slept. Whether in the country or in the city he was rushing about all day and all night, and often whooping under his friends' windows at three o'clock in the morning. I fear this will alienate from him the sympathy of many serious sleepers, whose Christian tolerance would have forgiven his more scarlet sins!

For my own part, I count it against him that he boasted of being a lifelong teetotaler, and that he warned Barbara Harris against detective stories "as likely to give a suspicious and unbalanced view of life."

He testified in his own behalf. He described his early career on the stage, and his struggle to enter the Church. He had always been known, he told his Bishop, as the Prostitutes' Padre, and it was his best title. Even in his Oxford days, one of his jesting friends used to speak of "Mr. Davidson and his harmless harem."

He had tried to found a club for dancing girls in Paris, and it would be well "if the icebergs of the Church would not draw their skirts away from these girls." They were folk of evil mind who thought evil of his trips to Paris with Nellie Churchill, and of his acquaintance with Barbara Harris and Miss Holt and Mrs. B. and Mrs. Y., to say nothing of a further group of ladies who filled the alphabet from A to Izzard.

Going into particulars, he denied that someone, behind the bar in a London pub, had greeted him with the remark:

"Hullo, you old thief! How are all the girls?"

That he was known, in one shop in St. James', as "The Mormon" was possible. It was a joke.

Found in a room—not alone—at 11 P.M. on one occasion, with the lights out, was easily explained. The lighting system had failed.

As for Sylvia Harris' testimony that he called Barbara the "Queen of My Heart," it was true. He often called people that. He called his landlady, Mrs. Walton, "Queen of My Heart." It came from a song "You Are Queen of My Heart To-night." He could sing a stave or two, if the Chancellor wished it.

The Chancellor hastily disclaimed any such wish.

As for Mr. Oliver's statement that, one day when Barbara and the Rector called on Mrs. B., that lady—a music-hall artist—received them in a *robe de nuit*, and performed what Mr. Oliver sourly called some "gymnastics or acrobatics," that was not true. Mrs. B. merely did some "tapping," and the Rector "illustrated with his toes."

A rather unusual amount of kissing, the Rector's counsel explained by alluding to the practices of the early Christians. His landlady, Mrs. Walton, testified that he often kissed her, but that in no wise disconcerted the family—he often kissed Mr. Walton, as well. Later—and for good measure—Mrs. Walton added:

"And the milkman, too."

The photograph, in which the Rector was shown adjusting a shawl about a lady (who might easily be chilly without it) was not hard to explain. Taking this picture was a trap into which he had been lured. Moreover, the sudden explosion of the flashlight caused him nearly to drop the shawl. The Chancellor gave this rather compromising picture his most scrupulous attention and called for a magnifying glass, to examine the picture and test the truth of the Rector's statements.

In the end, however, the Chancellor found all the charges sustained. All of them; including the conduct with "a woman named." There was also an event, not described, but referred to under a title which might have come from Sherlock Holmes' notebook: The Incident in the Chinese Restaurant in Bloomsbury.

The Rector knew not the meaning of defeat. When the verdict was pronounced against him, he picked up his silk hat and raced out of Court, where he was instantly surrounded by his sympathizers, men and women, including clergymen.

And at last reports, he had not given up the fight. In order to raise money for another appeal, he was exhibiting himself in the pleasure grounds at Blackpool, sitting in a barrel all day long. In the next barrel was a girl who was engaged in fasting. The Rector left his barrel for luncheon and tea, and occupied the rest of his time by writing his memoirs.

The London newspapers were greatly amused, that summer, by the American mania for "flagpole sitting." Barrel-sitting, however, was said to be "something quite different"—and I suppose that it is.

THE END

ACKNOWLEDGMENTS

These are the principal newspapers, books and articles which have been consulted.

Some of the books contributed a single valuable suggestion, or the description of one interesting incident. To others, my debt is heavy.

NEWSPAPERS

The Sun (New York), *The New York Tribune*, *The World* (New York), *The New York Times; The Boston Herald; The Los Angeles Times, The Los Angeles Examiner; The Times* (London).

The Illustrated London News.

BOOKS, ESSAYS, ETC.

Stratagems & Conspiracies to Defraud Life Insurance Companies. By John B. Lewis & Charles C. Bombaugh.

The Descendants of John Dwight of Dedham. By Benjamin W. Dwight.

The Yelverton Marriage Case: Thelwall v. Yelverton. (London. n.d.)

The Canning Wonder. By Arthur Machen.

The Great Alibi. By Hugh Childers.

Elizabeth Canning & the Gypsies. By Bernard Darwin.

The Druce Case. By Sir John Hall, Bart.

Burke's Peerage.

The Balham Mystery. (London, 1876)

Malice Domestic; or, The Balham Mystery. By William Roughead.

The Official Report of the Trial of Bertram G. Spencer.

The Trial of Daniel McFarland. By a Practical Law Reporter.

Crime, Abnormal Minds & the Law. By Ernest B. Hoag & Edward H. Williams.

Trials of Charles Peace. By W. Teignmouth Shore (Notable British Trials)

A Book of Remarkable Criminals. By H. B. Irving.

Trial of George Chapman. By H. L. Adam. (Notable British Trials)

Trial of S. H. Dougal. By F. Tennyson Jesse. (Notable British Trials)

The Green Bicycle Case. By H. R. Wakefield.

Trial of the Wainwrights. By H. B. Irving. (Notable British Trials)

Murder Mysteries of New York. By Frank M. O'Brien.

Trial of H. R. Armstrong. By Filson Young. (Notable British Trials)

The Monster of Düsseldorf. By Margaret Seaton Wagner.

The Robinson Locke Collection in The New York Public Library.

The Official Report of the Trial of S. J. Robinson.